War art: murals and ...ary life, ...version

War art: murals and graffiti – military life, power and subversion

By
Wayne D Cocroft, Danielle Devlin,
John Schofield and Roger J C Thomas

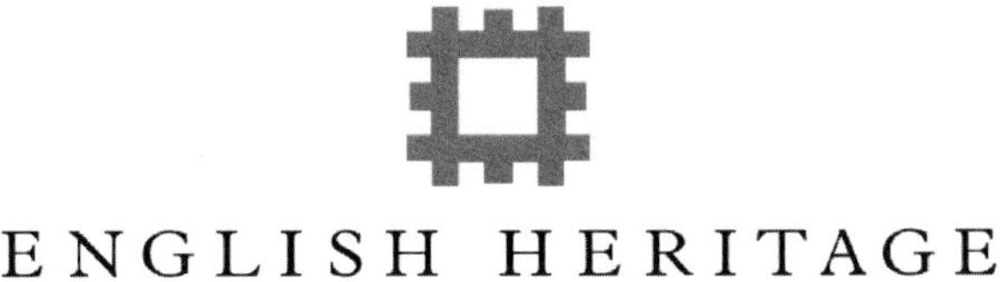

ENGLISH HERITAGE

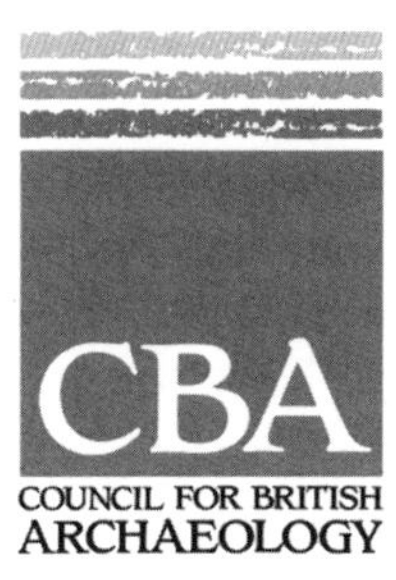

CBA

COUNCIL FOR BRITISH
ARCHAEOLOGY

CBA Research Report 147

2006

First published in 2006 by The Council for British Archaeology,
St Mary's House, Bootham, York, YO1 9WA

ISBN 1-902771-56-7

British Library Cataloguing-in-Publication Data

A catalogue record for this book is available from the British Library

Designed, typeset and printed by Alden Press, Oxford

Edited by Jane Thorniley-Walker, CBA

The publisher acknowledges with gratitude a grant from English Heritage towards the cost of publication

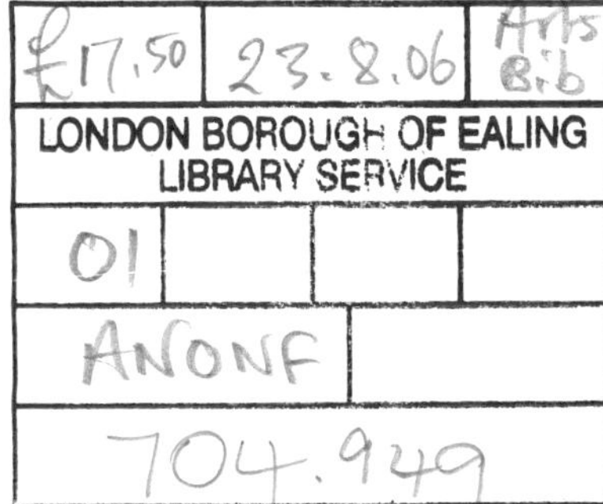

Front Cover
RAF Upper Heyford, Oxfordshire, detail of an F-111 aircraft from a mural by Kenneth B Gore (1978–79)
(© English Heritage AA051444)

Back cover – top to bottom
1 East Side Gallery, Mühlenstrasse, Berlin, in the foreground 'Tolerance' by Mary Mackey of Denver, Colorado, photographed in September 2000 shortly after the image was repainted by the artist
(© W D Cocroft)
2 RAF Upper Heyford, Oxfordshire, raven cartoon in a building used to service F-111 aircraft flight equipment (© Roger J C Thomas)
3 Nedlitz barracks, Potsdam, Germany, 'Victory' parade ground mural (© Angus Boulton)
4 RAF Fowlmere, Cambridgeshire, mural painted by Aircraftsman Robert Hofton in preparation for a Christmas 1940 party. At the time he was serving with 19 Squadron which during 1940 had distinguished itself during the withdrawal of the British Expeditionary Force from Dunkirk and during the Battle of Britain (© English Heritage AA051483)
5 Nevada Peace Camp, Nevada, USA, one of four masks placed within stone circle (© W D Cocroft)
6 Rangsdorf, Brandenburg, Germany, former Soviet helicopter maintenance works, recreation room, 'Warrior Airmen! Serve in your Red Army Airforce units with pride' (© Angus Boulton)

Contents

Acknowledgements

The authors are indebted to many individuals who have contributed to the words and images included in this book. As the main focus of the work is visual it makes sense to begin there. Numerous photographers are represented, and have kindly given their consent for images to be included in this collection. Individual credits are included in the captions. In alphabetical order the photographers are: Keith Angus; Angus Boulton; Ian Evans; Aldon Ferguson; Veronica Fiorato; Alistair Graham-Kerr; Anthony Harding; Jonathan McCormick; Basil Nash; Nicholas Saunders; Leo Schmidt and Raymond Towler. We are also grateful to South Gloucestershire Council, the Desert Research Institute (Las Vegas), the Imperial War Museum, and the Royal Commission on Ancient and Historical Monuments in Scotland for their permission to use selected images. Other images are reproduced courtesy of the National Monuments Record, English Heritage, many of which were taken by Steve Cole and we are grateful for his cheerful enthusiasm for the project and assistance in selecting the images for publication. We are also grateful to Derek Kendall who photographed locations in London and the south of England, to Alun Bull, and Mike Hesketh-Roberts. Some photographs by the authors are also included.

The text reached its final form with the considerable assistance of Robert Gowing of English Heritage, who participated in this project including drafting conservation guidelines that appeared in the English Heritage Guidance Note (2004). His advice is gratefully acknowledged, in particular for helping to shape this project in its early and formative stages.

Many of the sites recorded here are known to us only because people have told us about them. We would also therefore like to thank all those that have provided tip-offs over the years. Special mention should be made of Bernard Lowry and Alistair Graham-Kerr of the Fortress Study Group, Jean Thomas (Dale WI), and our colleague Elizabeth Whitbourn from London Region. We are also grateful to the many private owners who have granted us access to their buildings and organisations permitting us to record murals, in particular the North Oxfordshire Consortium at Upper Heyford (Jim Roberts, Don Todd, and Keith Watson), Wigmore Abbey (John Challis), Harperley PoW Camp 93 (James MacLeod), Pingley Farm PoW Camp 81 (Harry Thorpe), Mill Lane Farm, Hatfield Heath, St Johns School, Redhill (Marion Cassidy) and Sayers Croft, Ewhurst (Ray Hewitt and David Quoroll), both in Surrey. Our colleagues David Easton and Geoffrey Stell, Royal Commission on the Ancient and Historical Monuments of Scotland, have also alerted us to some outstanding examples of wartime murals in Scotland.

Our greatest debt however is the most difficult to acknowledge. Except in a very few cases the artists represented here are unknown, and probably have no idea their work is being published and given value by those of us that study this recent past. We acknowledge their contribution to our understanding of the past use of these military sites and landscapes, and dedicate this volume to their memory.

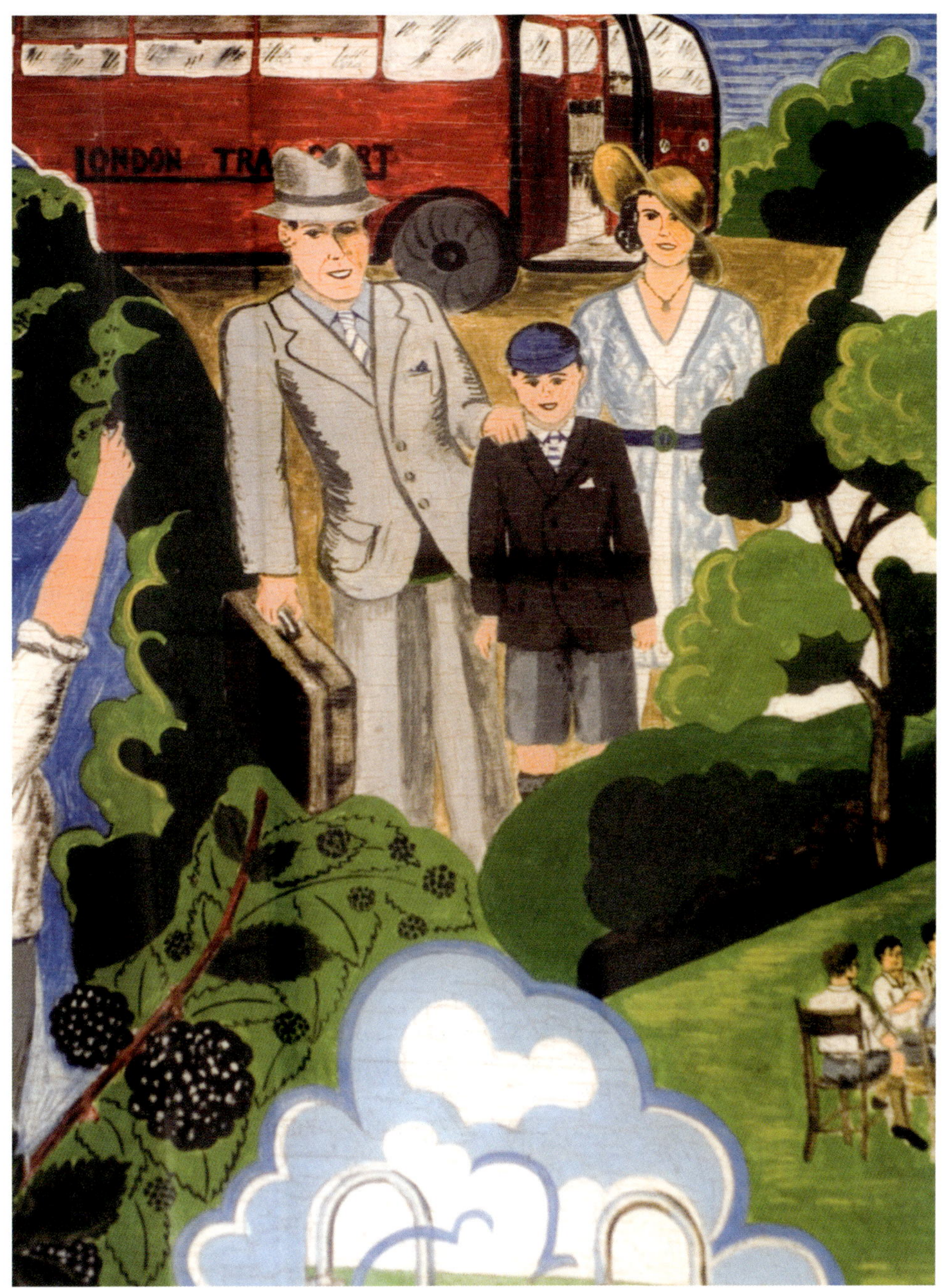

Sayers Croft, Ewhurst, Cranleigh: an evacuee leaving his parents

P A R T I

'The Art of War'

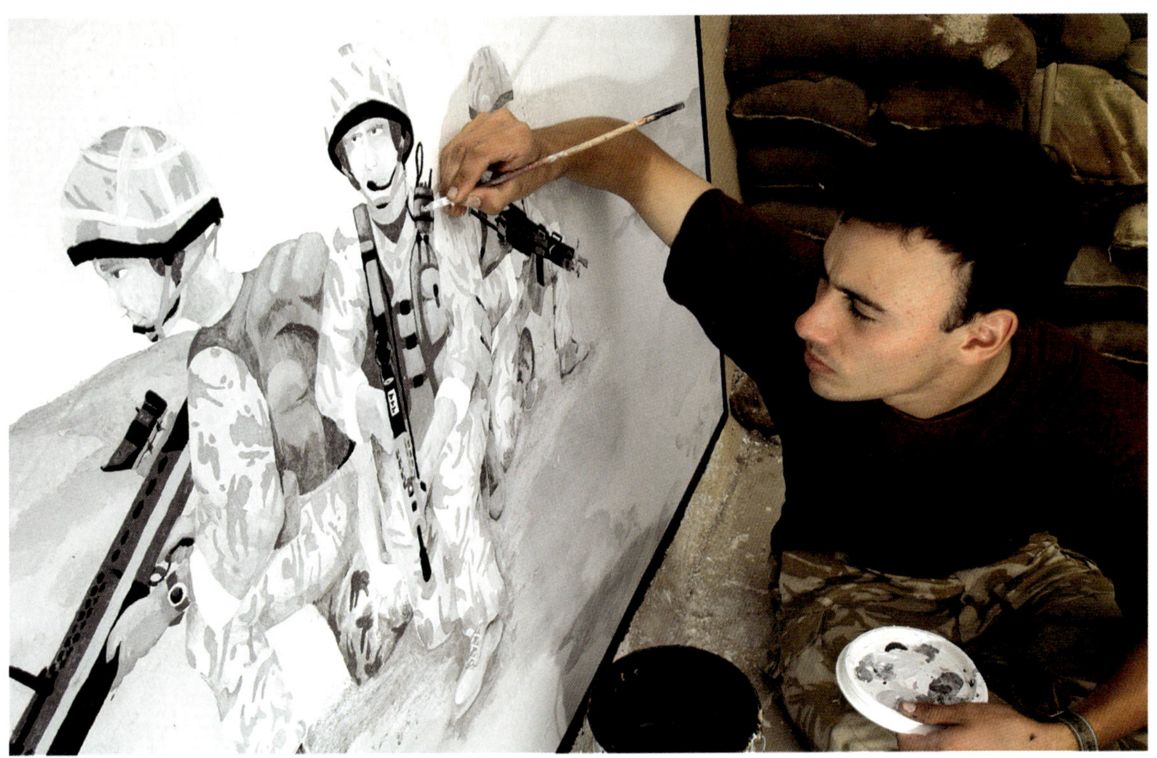

© 2006 Crown copyright; Mural in Basra, Iraq

INTRODUCTION

One characteristic of later nineteenth- and twentieth-century warfare is the significant impact these historic episodes and events have left on the landscape. In Britain, the First World War saw considerable construction on the home front, whilst during the Second World War there was not an area in the British Isles that wasn't touched in one way or another by the conflict. Even today many traces of Second World War activity survive, albeit more subtle than some might imagine; whether it is a fading sign pointing to long removed air raid shelters, or the glimpse of a solitary hut covered in undergrowth. With the passing

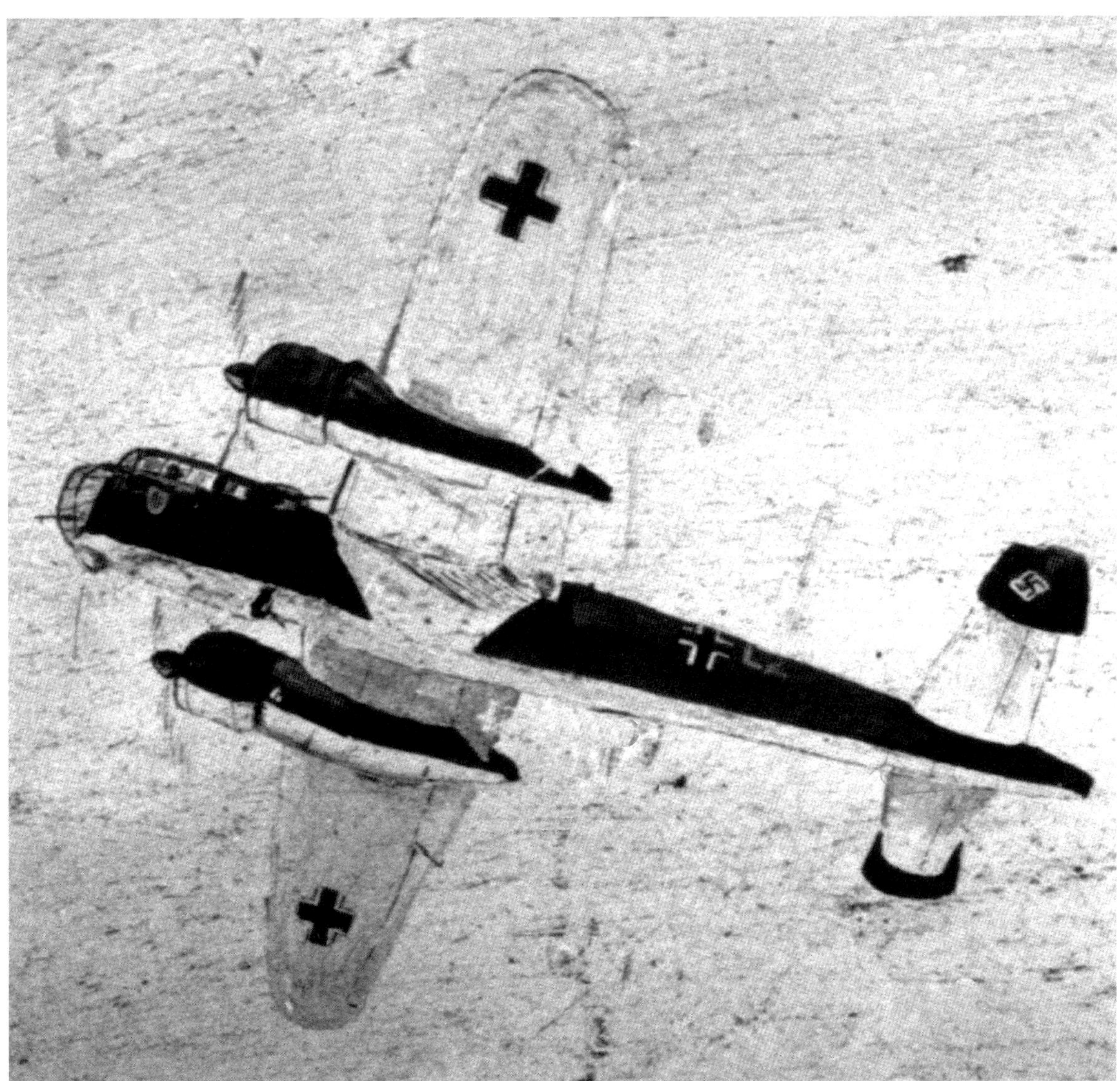

Halsham, East Riding, H6 Heavy Anti Aircraft battery, motor transport workshops, Dornier 217 (© R J C Thomas)

DEFINING WAR ART

War art is defined here as any deliberate expression that has been applied onto, or is integral to understanding, any built structure, site or area in the context of its military occupation or use. Alongside wall paintings, murals and graffiti, this definition deliberately includes artistic expression applied to any artificial surfaces such as roads, fence posts and free-standing signage, and also on natural surfaces. While the term 'war art' is traditionally confined to wall paintings, notices, or instructions applied officially or unofficially by servicemen, it has more recently been given a broader definition that can include: building decoration, camouflage, scribbles, scratches, drawings, paintings, stencilling, photographs, carvings, bas-relief, castings, rubbed brick-work, and graffiti. These can be on military buildings or beyond them, placed outside their security fences by those opposed to the military activity within. In other words, war art is very broadly defined, taking in all images and representations of power and subversion that relate directly to the militarised landscape.

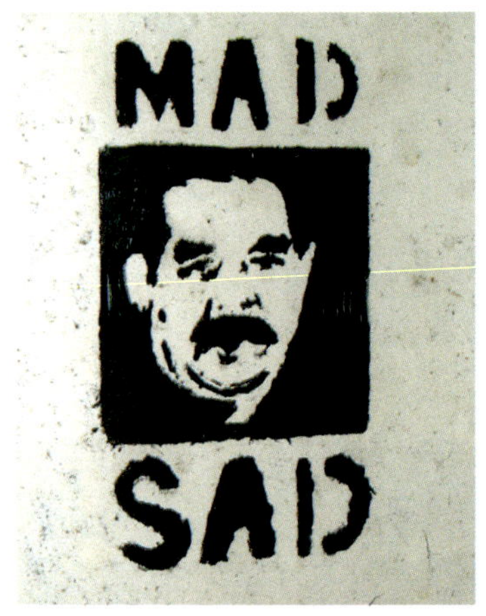

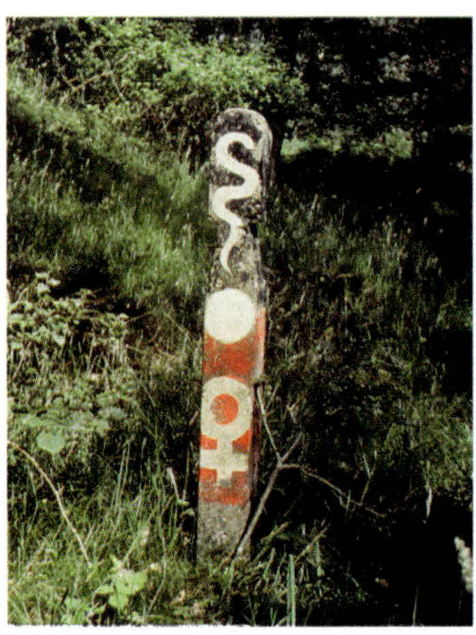

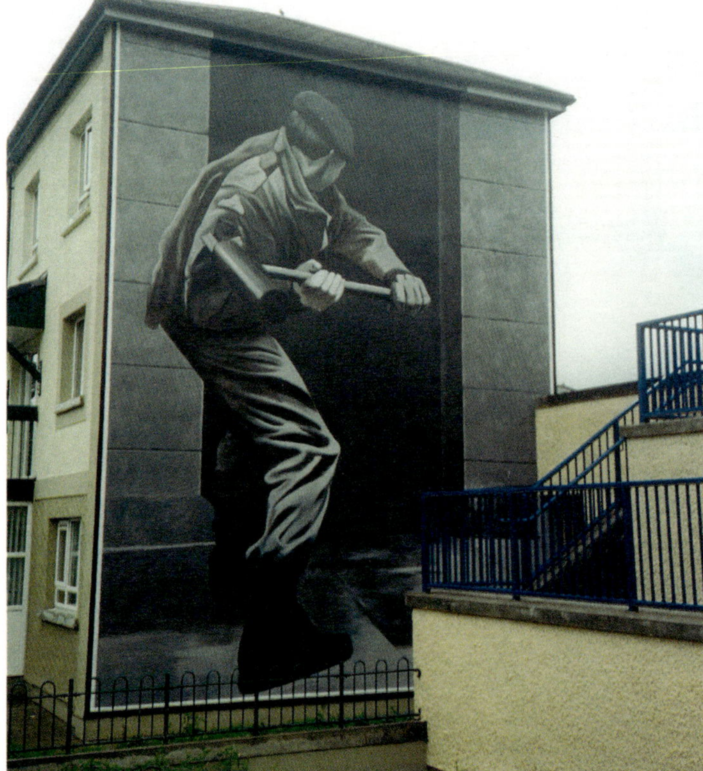

Top: **Royal Naval Armament Depot Trecwn, Pembrokeshire; Mad Sad stencil, Gulf War 1991 (© R J C Thomas)**
Bottom: **RAF Greenham Common, Berkshire; Painted post (© Veronica Fiorato)**
Right: **Operation Motorman, Derry (© Jonathan McCormick)**

INTRODUCTION

One characteristic of later nineteenth- and twentieth-century warfare is the significant impact these historic episodes and events have left on the landscape. In Britain, the First World War saw considerable construction on the home front, whilst during the Second World War there was not an area in the British Isles that wasn't touched in one way or another by the conflict. Even today many traces of Second World War activity survive, albeit more subtle than some might imagine; whether it is a fading sign pointing to long removed air raid shelters, or the glimpse of a solitary hut covered in undergrowth. With the passing

Halsham, East Riding, H6 Heavy Anti Aircraft battery, motor transport workshops, Dornier 217 (© R J C Thomas)

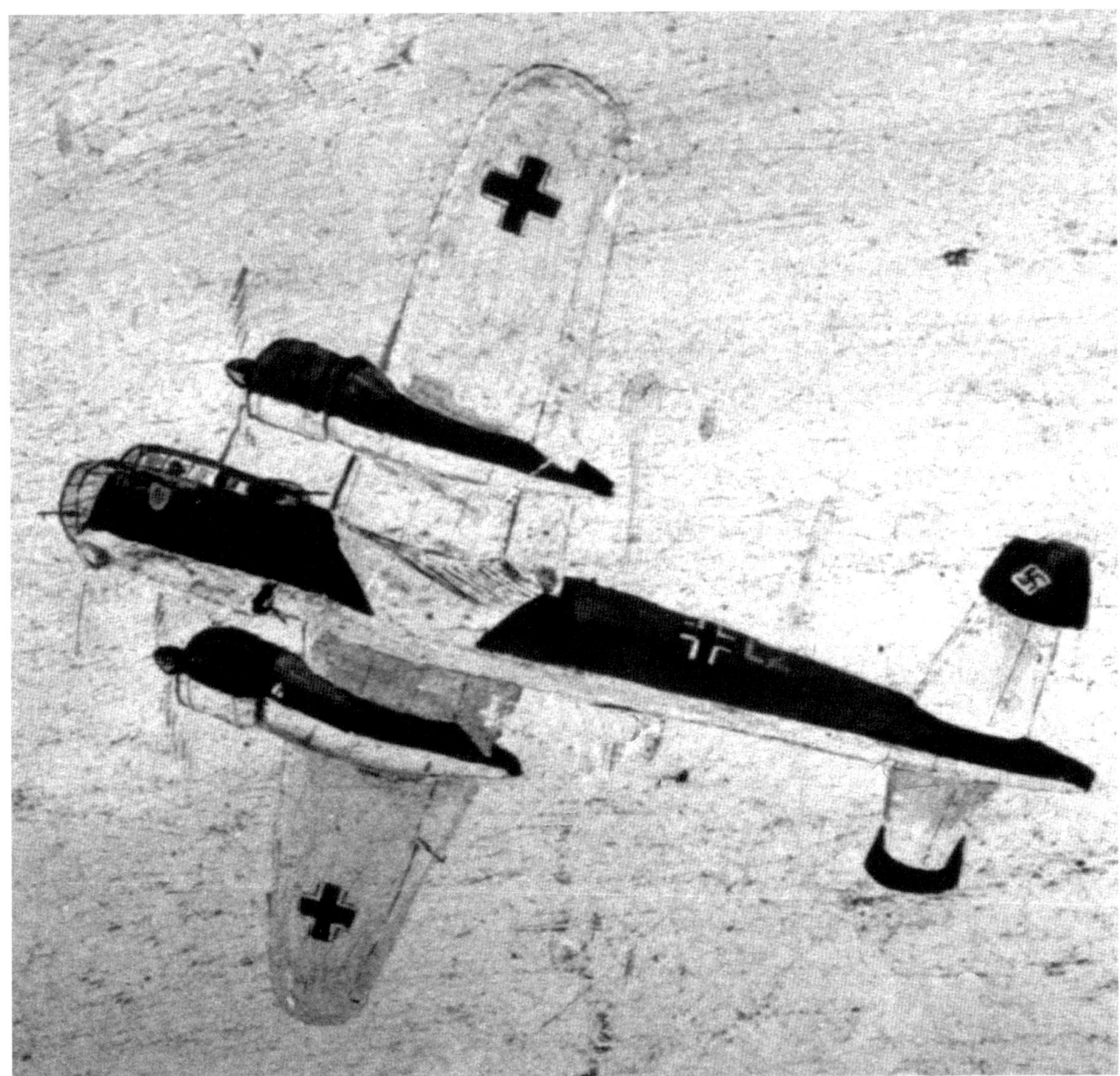

of each year, the stock of these older buildings and sites becomes progressively smaller, whether due to coastal erosion, dereliction, redevelopment, or changes in agricultural policy. These same factors also apply to military sites that were in operation as recently as the 1980s before becoming redundant with the ending of the Cold War.

At first glance, many of these often abandoned and semi-derelict buildings and sites offer little to suggest their original purpose, and the history of their occupation and use. But on closer inspection the surviving surfaces can reveal visual traces of the past, providing insight to the lives of their former occupants. The walls may be adorned with decoration, often a combination of sanctioned military imagery such as unit badges, sortie records, or official notices and instructions, as well as less official paintings and drawings, of women and aircraft, and personal messages. The name, rank, number, and the unit of an individual serviceman can often be found pencilled on the walls. Graffiti gives a more casual and personal expression, often including social comment and humour. It is these visual representations of conflict that this book describes, with examples drawn mainly from England, albeit within a wider geographical and political context.

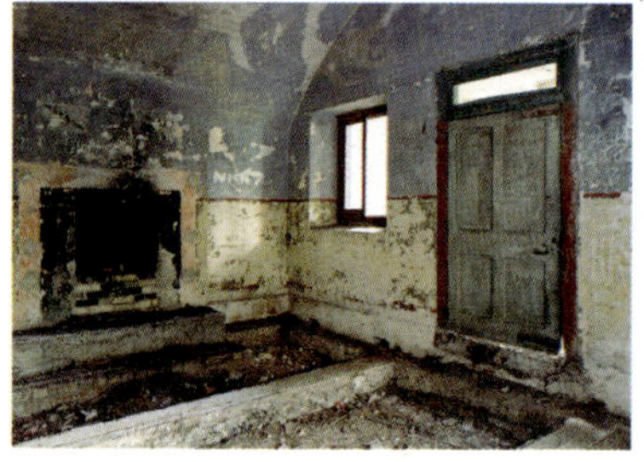
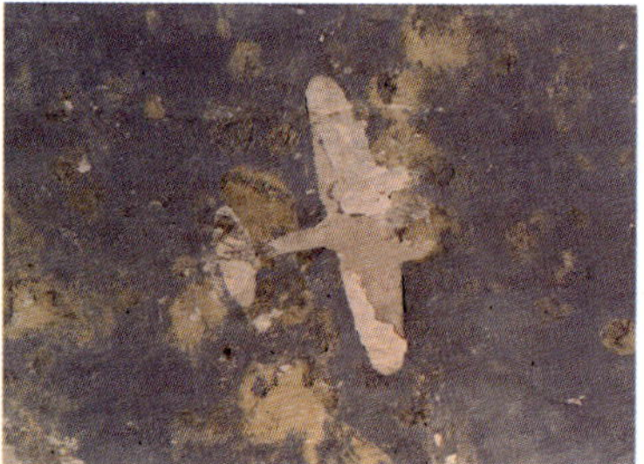
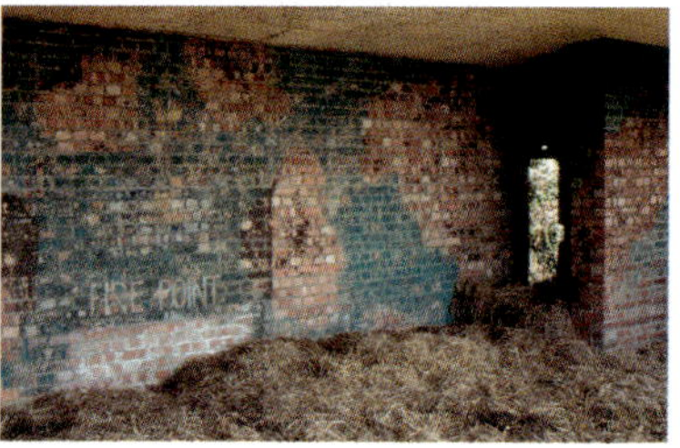

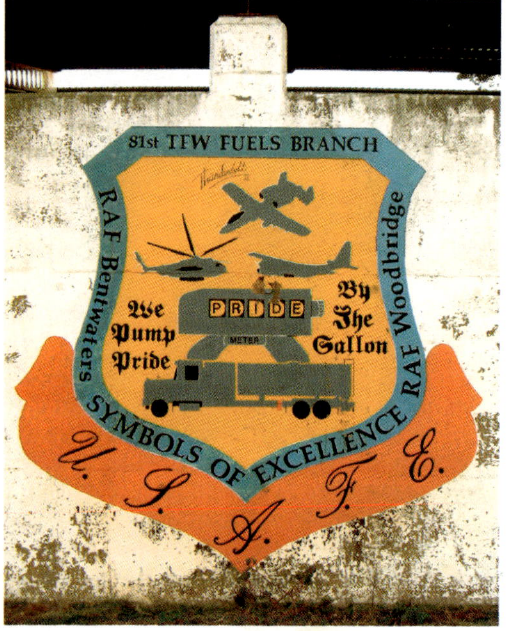

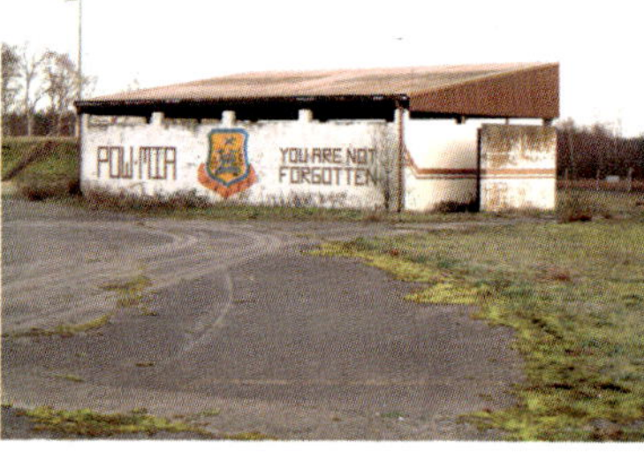

*Top: **Left** – Fort Borstal, Kent, nineteenth-century mobilisation centre reused as an anti-aircraft battery during the Second World War. Guardroom with painted ceiling (AA023970 © English Heritage); **Middle** – Fort Borstal: Detail of an aircraft (AA023973 © English Heritage); **Right** – Soldier's Rock Battery, St Ishmael's, Pembrokeshire, coastal artillery battery camouflaged gun house (© R J C Thomas); **Bottom:** RAF Woodbridge, Suffolk, 1552 fuel pump house, 81st Tactical Fighter Wing fuels branch; **Right** – POW MIA You are not forgotten (AA054186 © English Heritage); **Left** – 'We pump pride by the gallon' (AA054187 © English Heritage)*

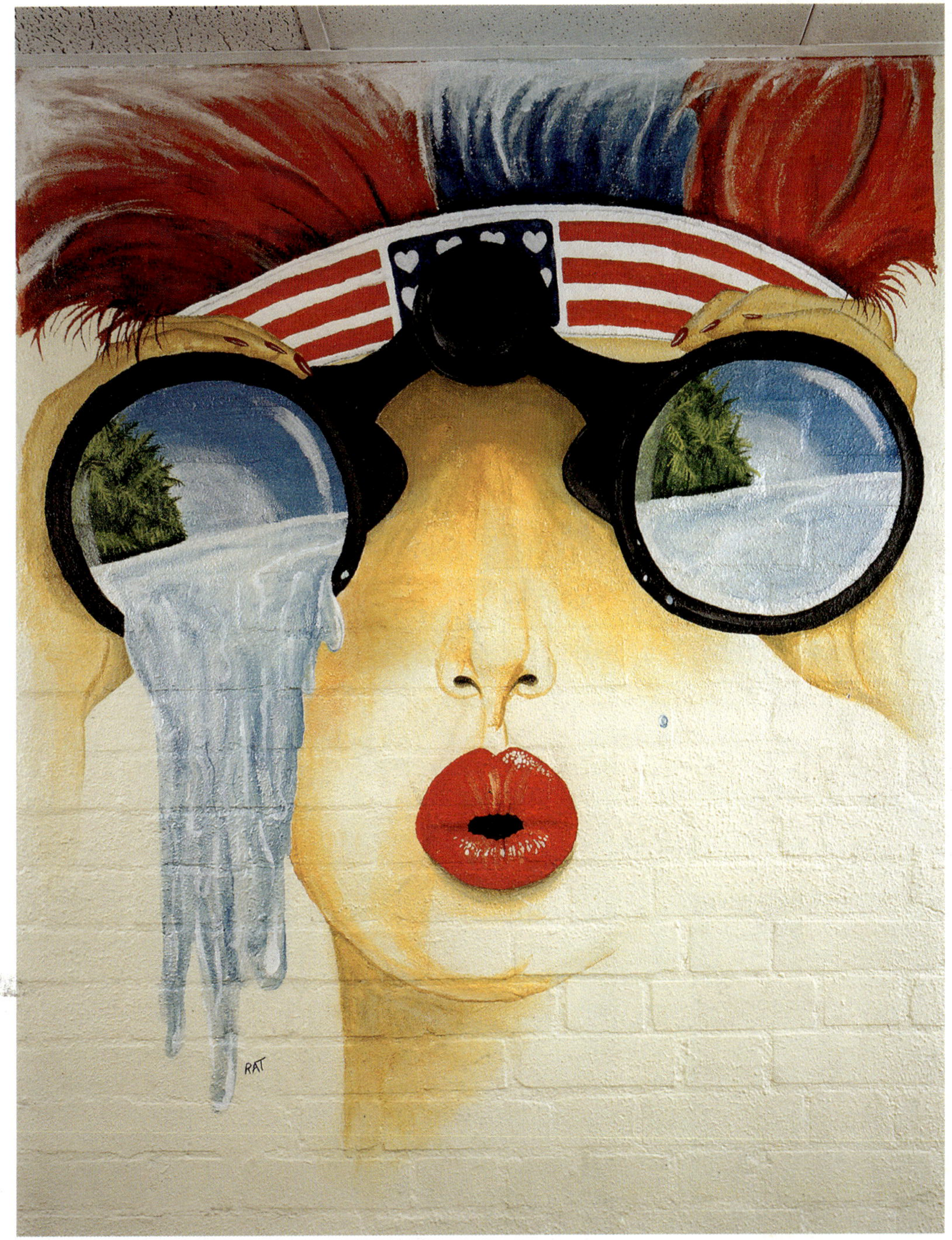

Upper Heyford, Oxfordshire, Dormitory 445; First floor corridor, Woman with binoculars, signed **R A T** (AA054130 © English Heritage)

DEFINING WAR ART

War art is defined here as any deliberate expression that has been applied onto, or is integral to understanding, any built structure, site or area in the context of its military occupation or use. Alongside wall paintings, murals and graffiti, this definition deliberately includes artistic expression applied to any artificial surfaces such as roads, fence posts and free-standing signage, and also on natural surfaces. While the term 'war art' is traditionally confined to wall paintings, notices, or instructions applied officially or unofficially by servicemen, it has more recently been given a broader definition that can include: building decoration, camouflage, scribbles, scratches, drawings, paintings, stencilling, photographs, carvings, bas-relief, castings, rubbed brick-work, and graffiti. These can be on military buildings or beyond them, placed outside their security fences by those opposed to the military activity within. In other words, war art is very broadly defined, taking in all images and representations of power and subversion that relate directly to the militarised landscape.

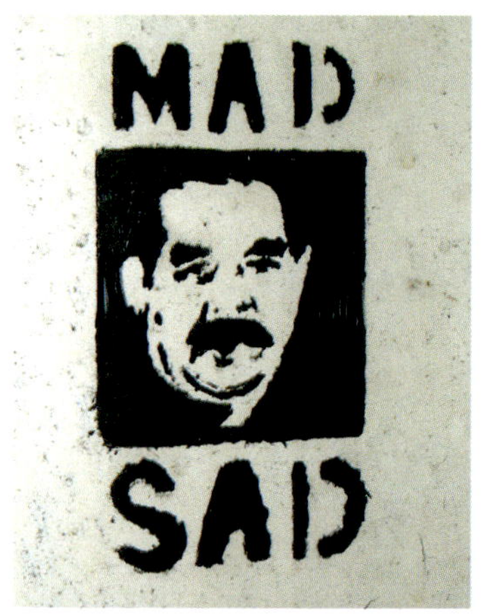

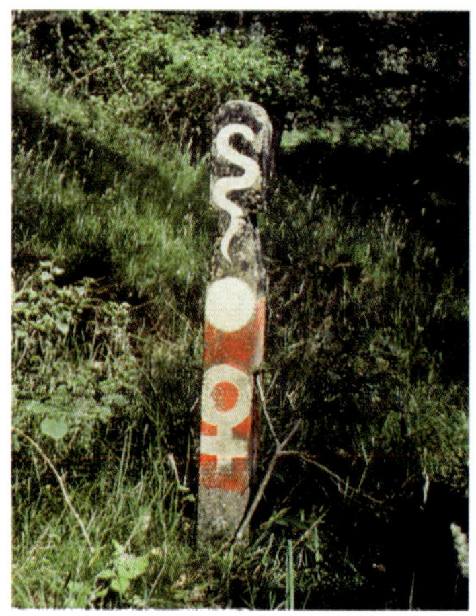

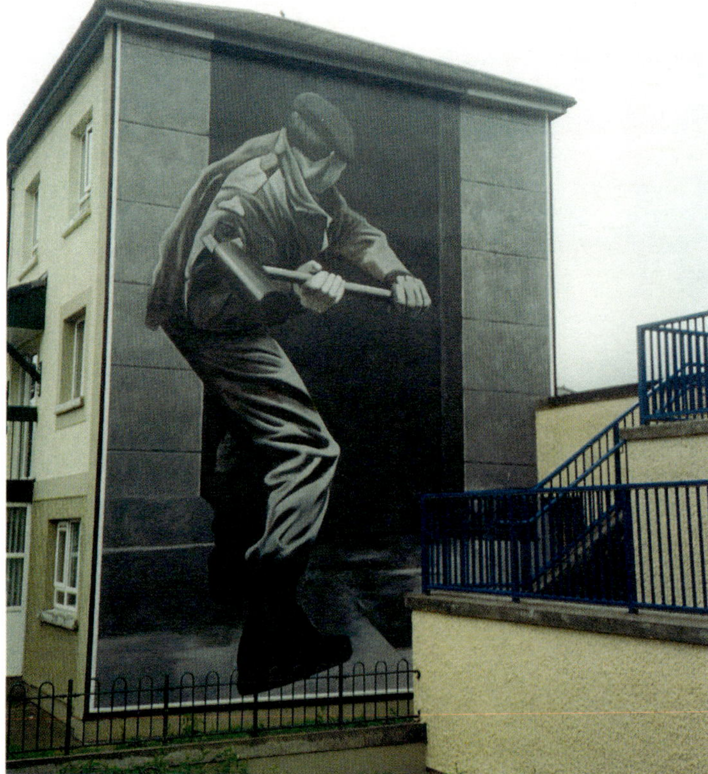

Top: Royal Naval Armament Depot Trecwn, Pembrokeshire; Mad Sad stencil, Gulf War 1991 (© R J C Thomas)
Bottom: RAF Greenham Common, Berkshire; Painted post (© Veronica Fiorato)
Right: Operation Motorman, Derry (© Jonathan McCormick)

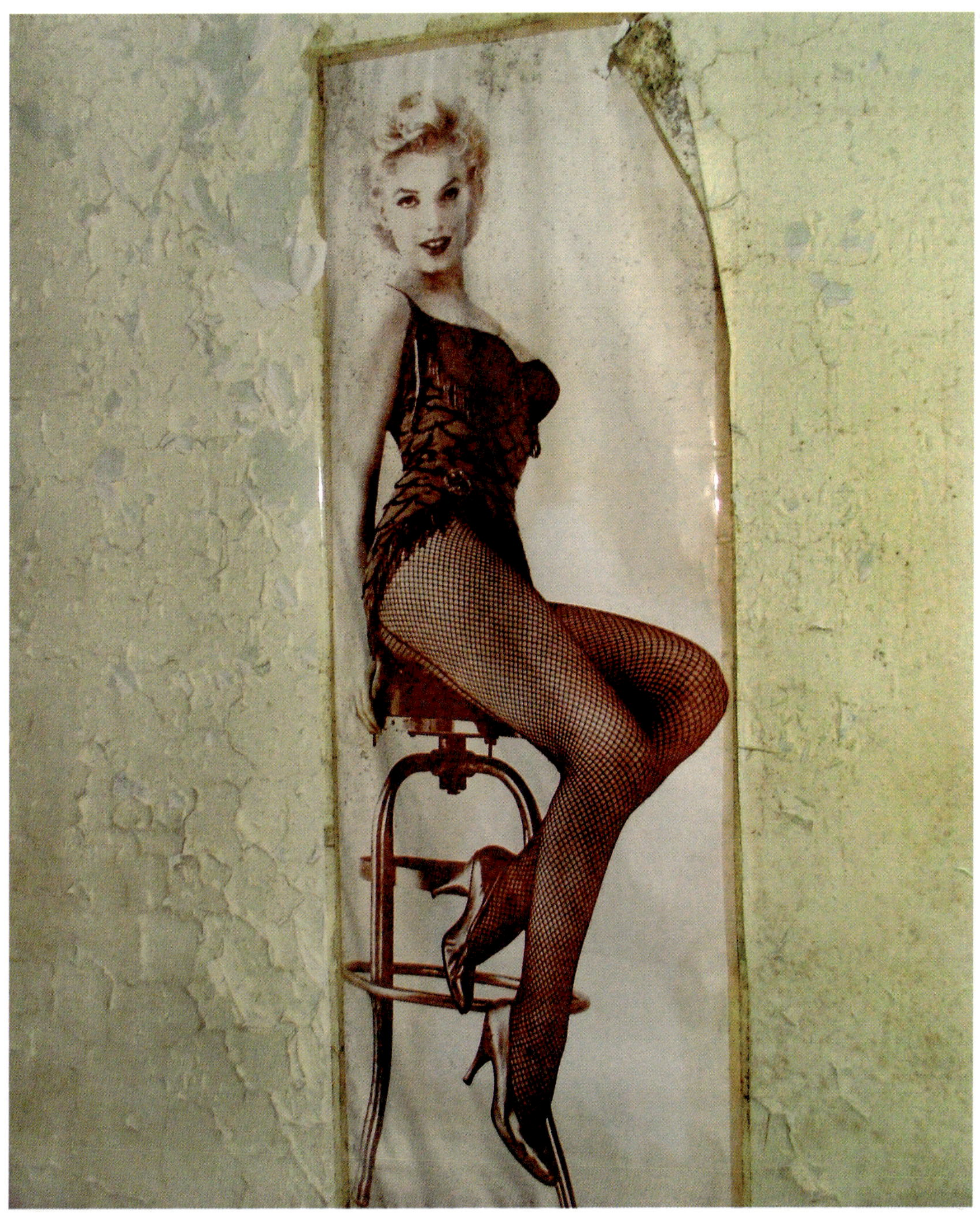

Middleton St George, County Durham. Marilyn Monroe poster in the base jazz club (© R J C Thomas)

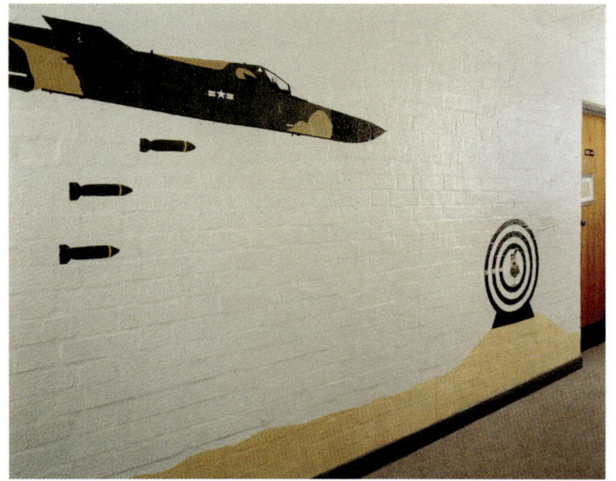 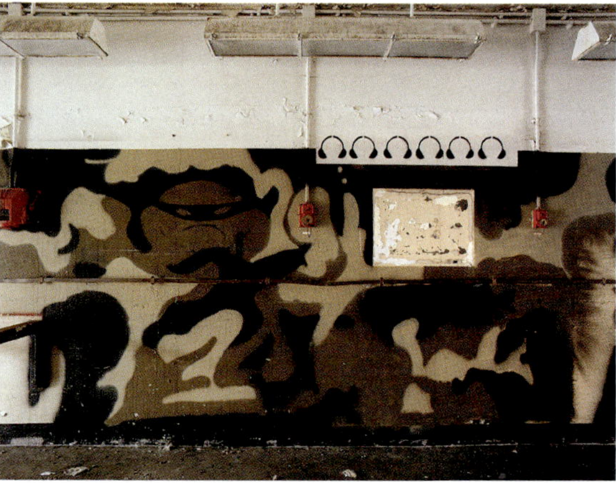

Left: RAF Upper Heyford, Oxfordshire, Dormitory 446; North side first floor corridor, early 1990s cartoon of a F-111 (AA051470); *Right:* RAF Woodbridge, Suffolk, Special Weapons Maintenance building 264; Camouflage wall – look carefully! (AA054179) (© English Heritage)

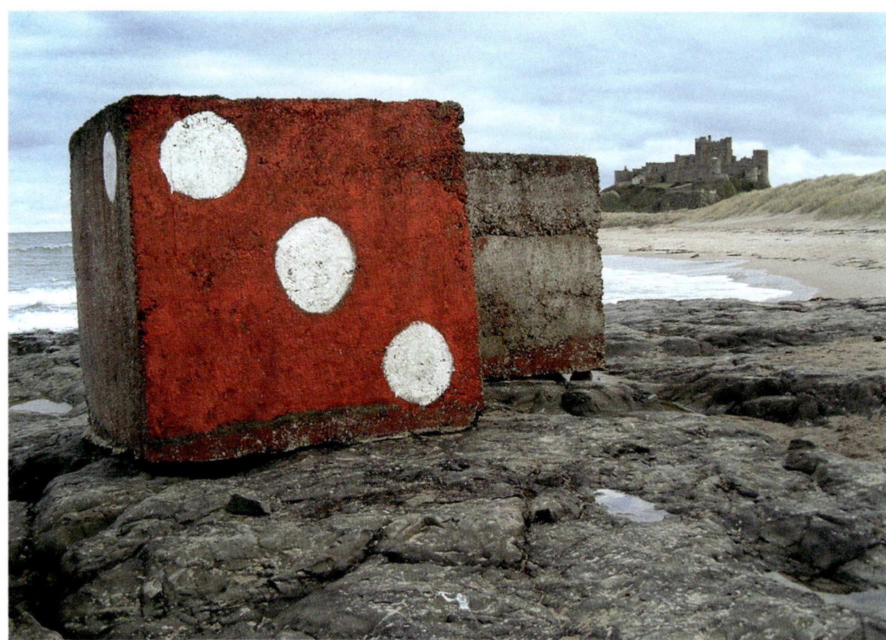

Bamburgh, Northumberland, Second World War anti-tank cube with dice (© R J C Thomas)

MATERIALS AND EXECUTION

Most of the war art illustrated in this book was produced for the instant with little thought that it might survive beyond the moment or perhaps a few months, and certainly with no idea that it would one day be an object of study. Before the end of the Second World War the only practical writing implement for soldiers in the field was the pencil, or coloured pencils for map work. Given wartime shortages the materials chosen to produce war art are diverse and often demonstrate remarkable ingenuity. As well as traditional materials including pencils, coloured pencils, inks, wax crayons, oil pastels, oil paints, and water colours, there was use of candle or cigarette lighter carbon, cellulose vehicle and aircraft paints, cellulose spray paints, boot polish and vegetable dyes.

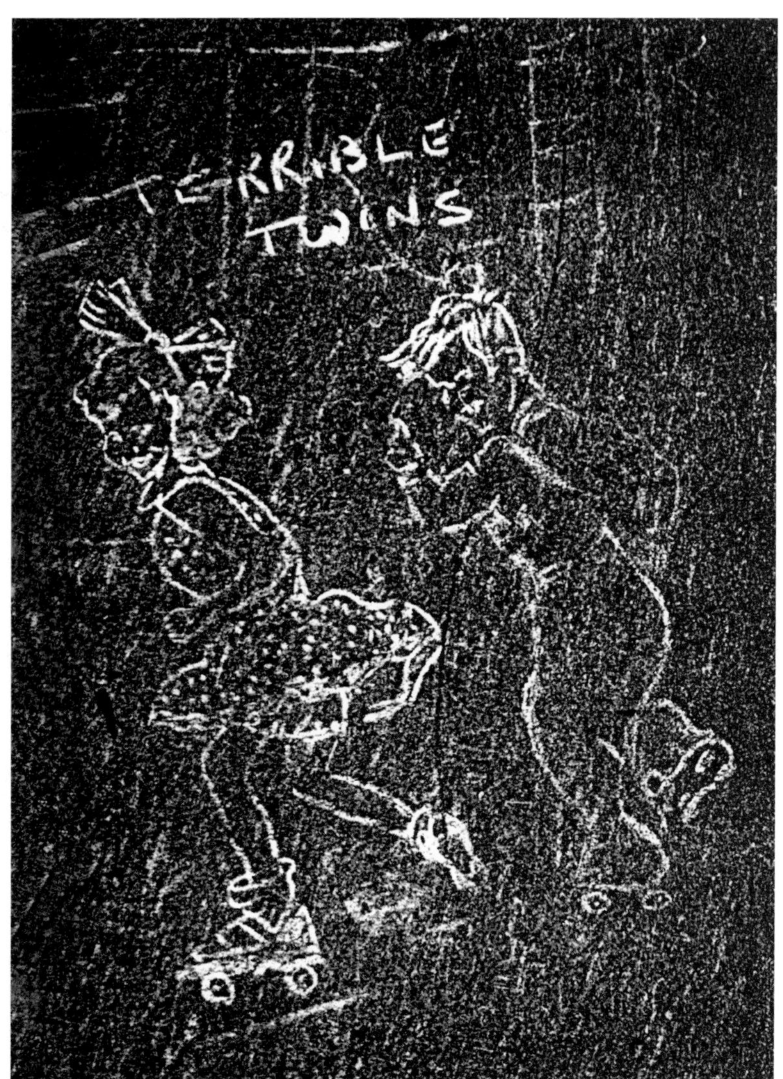

Royal Naval Armament Depot, Broughton Moor, Cumbria
'The terrible twins', chalk on black board, early 1950s
(© R J C Thomas)

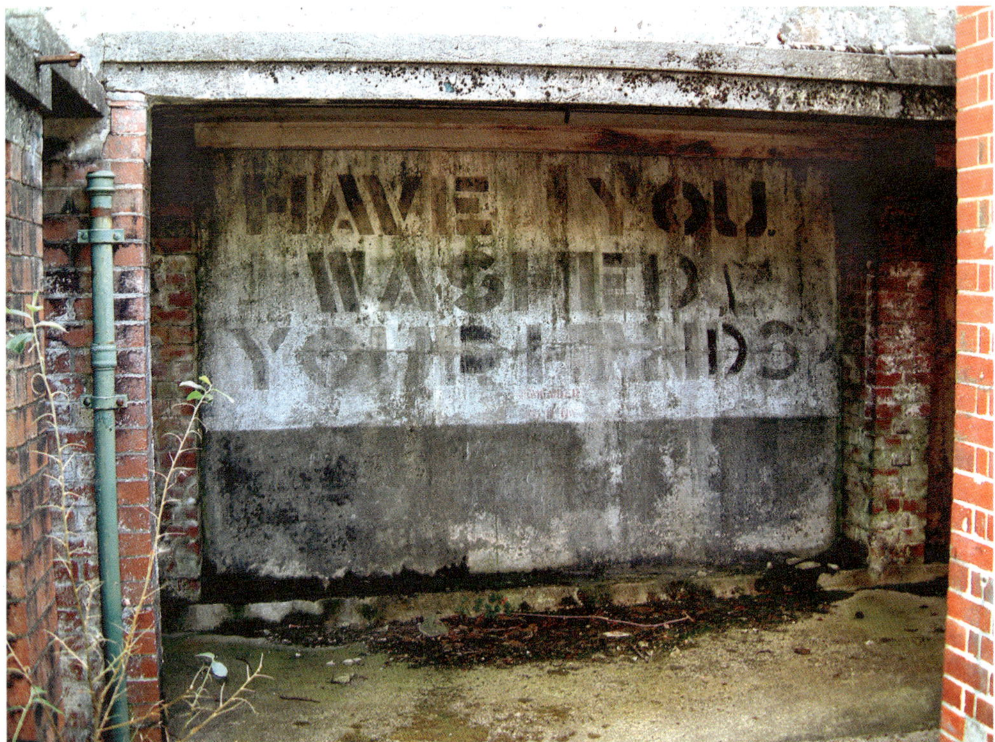

**Royal Naval Mine Depot
Newton Noyes,
Pembrokeshire
Entrance shifting area
(© R J C Thomas)**

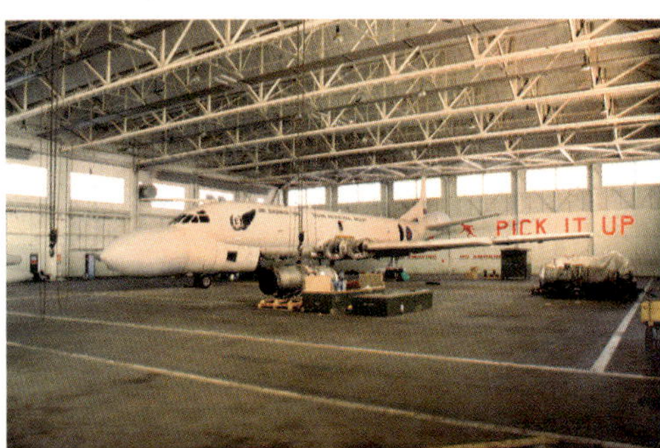

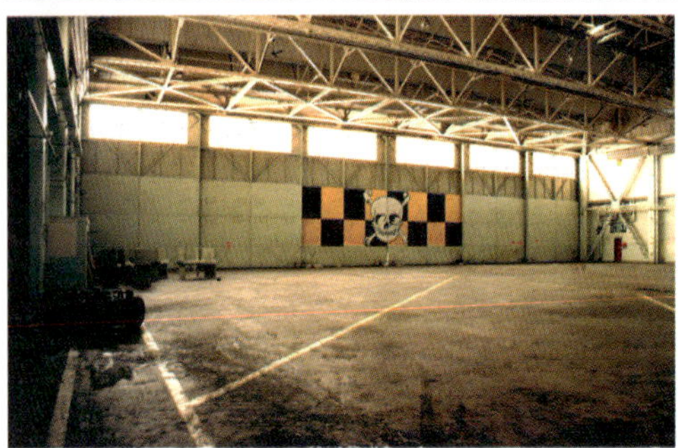

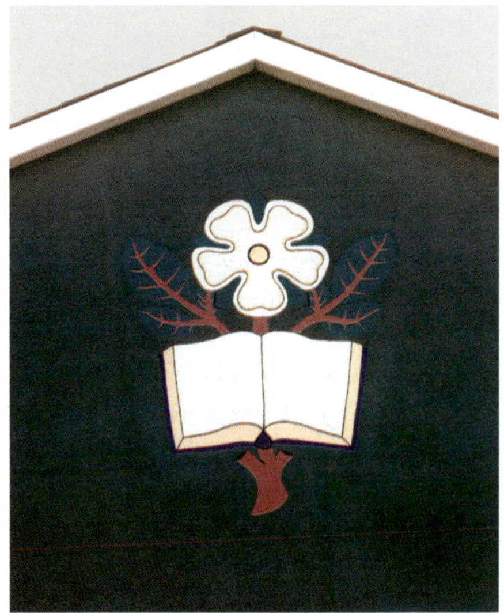

RAF Finningley, Doncaster
Top: Left – Hangar interior,
writing on the door warns
'FOD pick it up'
Bottom: Left – Hangar
interior 11 Squadron badge
Right: Yorkshire University Air
Squadron (© R J C Thomas)

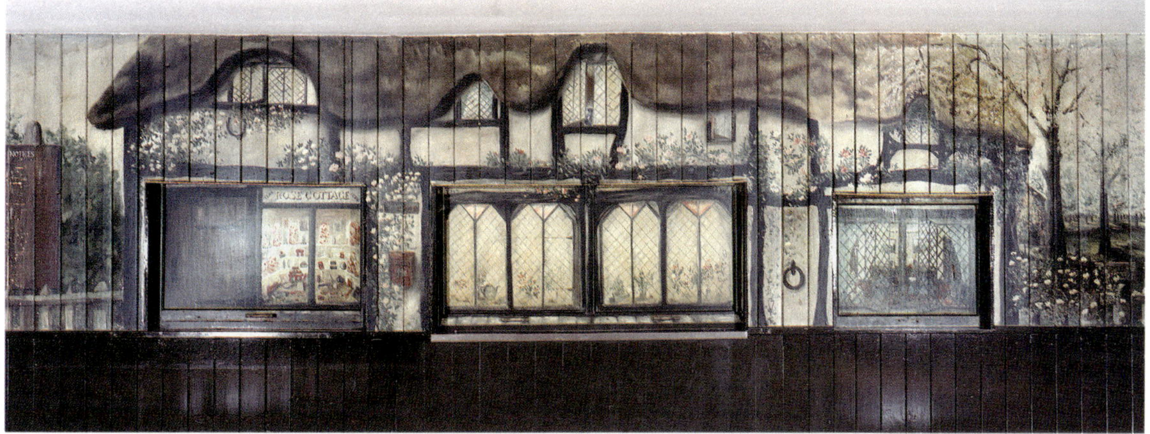

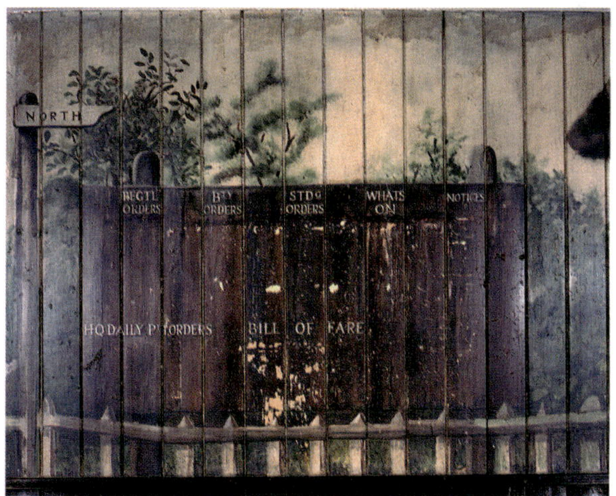

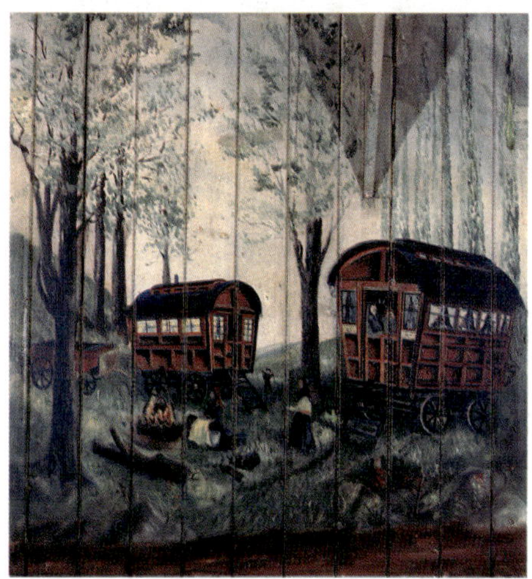

Ness Battery, Stromness, Orkney, canteen (© Crown copyright RCAHMS)
Top: **Cottage scene on wall with serving hatches (SC446615)**
Bottom: Left – **Notice board (SC 446613)**
Bottom: Right – **Caravans (SC446614)**

Given the high losses amongst allied aircrews, the often fragile murals from the wartime airfields have a particular poignancy as they adorned some of the last buildings many would have seen before setting off on their missions. The surfaces upon which they are applied are equally diverse: stone, fair-faced brick, mortared brick, cement render, pre-cast concrete panels, asbestos cement panels, hollow terracotta blocks, fibre-board, hardboard, plaster-board, and lath and plaster. War art is also applied to surfaces in the open: roads as well as fence posts and even natural surfaces where stone arrangements can resemble work by established landscape artists such as Richard Long. This combination of materials, techniques and locations reflects the wide range of decorative styles, a diversity that greatly affects their present condition and the chances of long-term preservation.

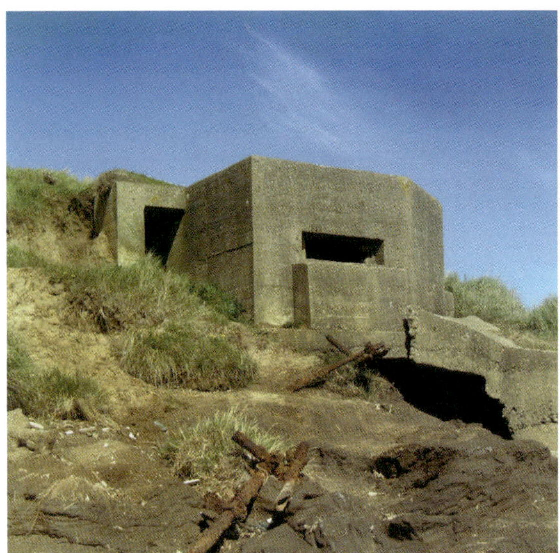

Auburn, near Bridlington, East Riding:
Left: Pillbox
Below: Inscription in cement 'Earwig villa'
(© R J C Thomas)

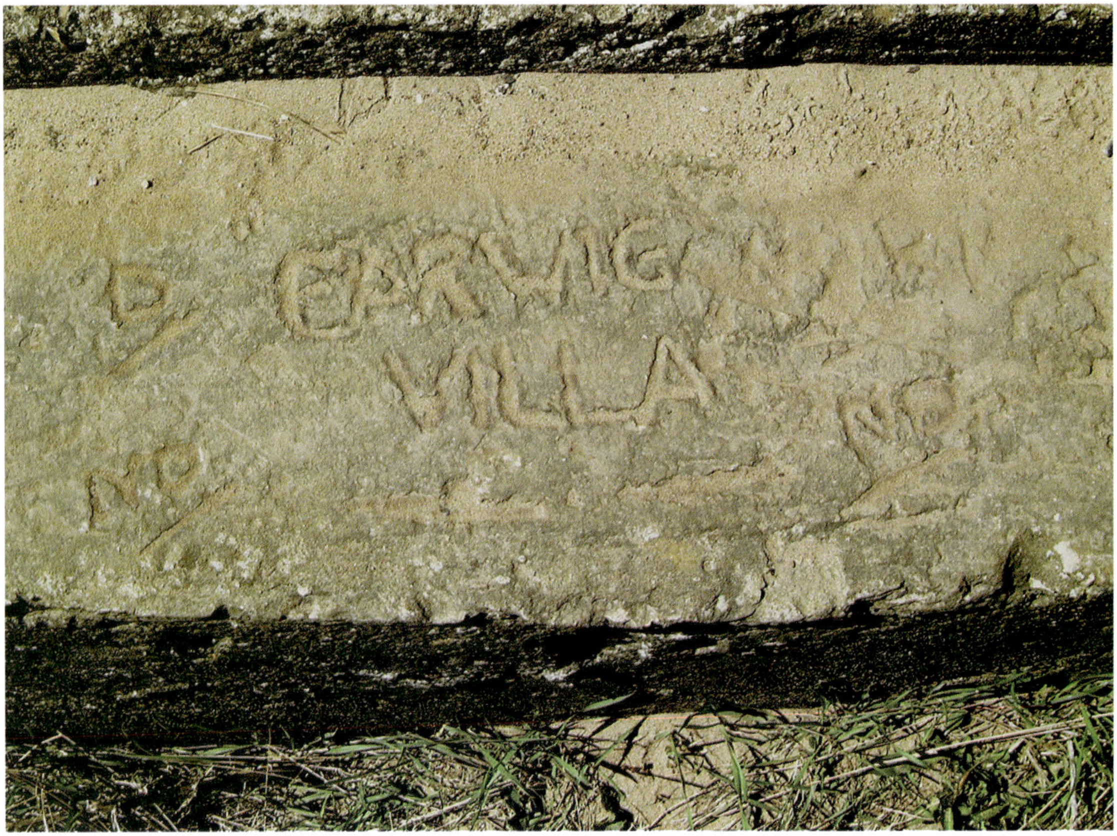

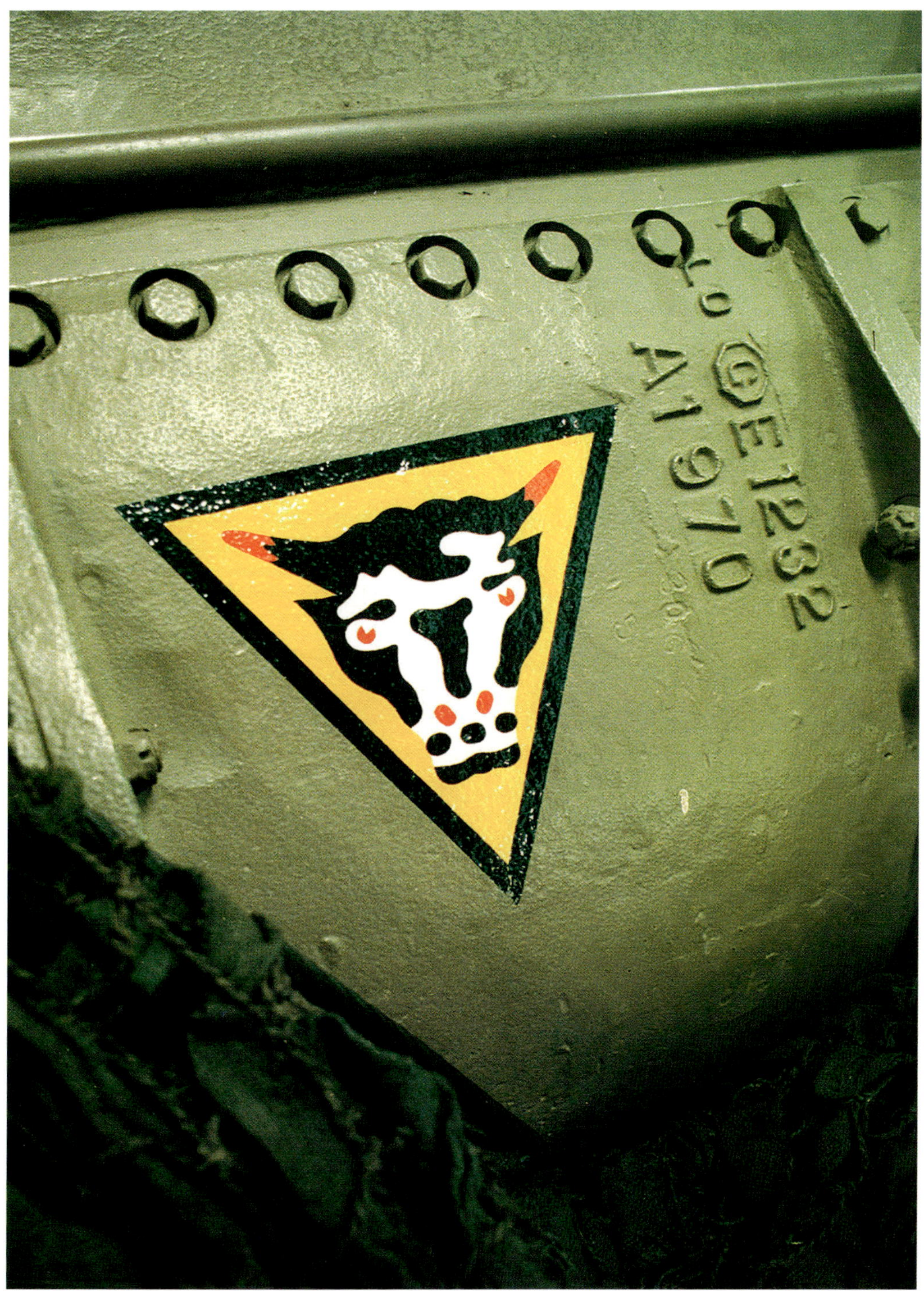

Emblem of the 79th Armoured Division (© R J C Thomas)

THE ARTISTS

Military service, like any career, has its peaks and troughs. Many prisoners of war were at an obvious low-point, but in relation to all military personnel, it is crucial to recognise that military life can be – and has often been – spent waiting for something to happen; passing time. It can be lonely, tedious and repetitive, and much war art reflects this fact. But the compulsion to artistic expression is not just induced by boredom and alienation; there are many other reasons to produce artwork, whether for private consumption or for the benefit of others.

One common theme for example is the need to establish communal identity, an *esprit de corps*, that exhibits pride and devotion to the group, whether as small as a platoon or as large as a squadron or regiment. Symbols and badges often take pride of place on vehicles, aircraft, office accommodation and mess walls. National identity can also be a motivation, as well as being an influence on the style and form of expression.

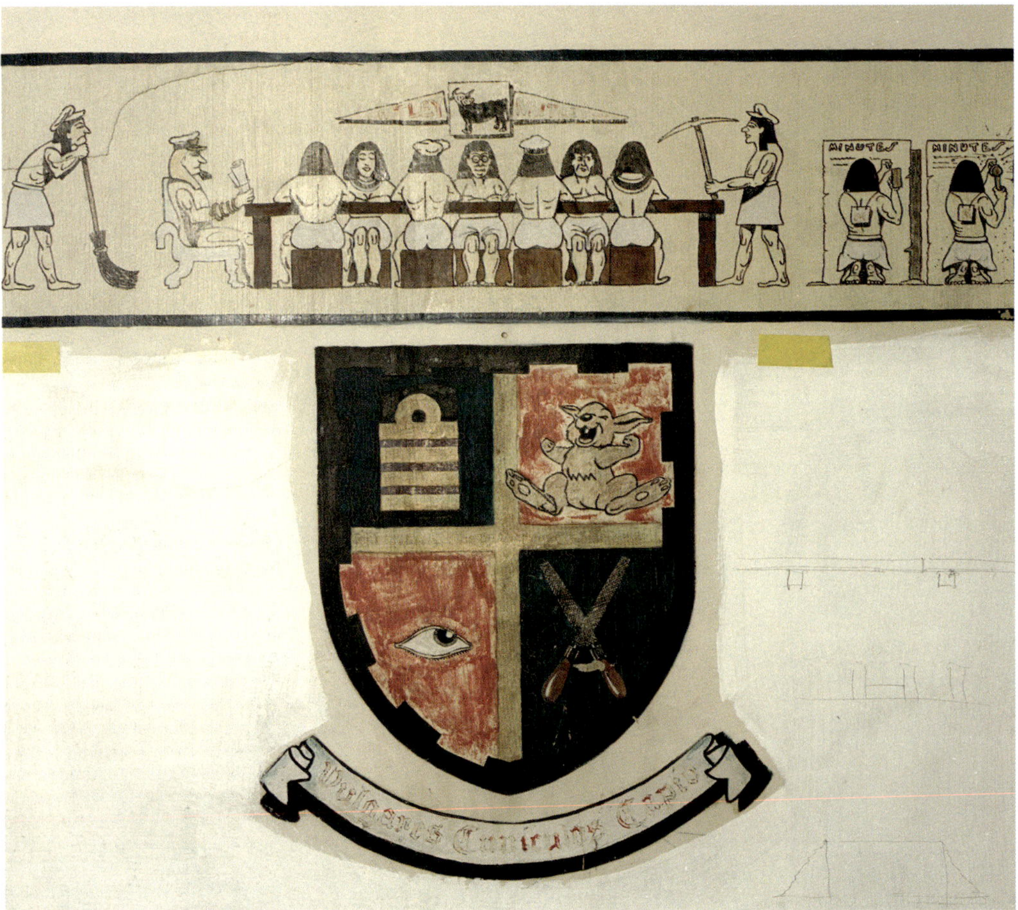

Donibristle Airfield, Fife, HMS Merlin, a repair depot for naval aircraft (SC924209 © Crown copyright RCAHMS)

PRISONERS OF WAR

In prisoner of war camps, there are particularly discernible trends that indicate an influence of popular styles and genera of art current at the time in the artist's country of origin. For example, war art painted in the Second World War by Italian prisoners included devotional subjects, gentle flattering portraits of women, and Disney characters. German prisoners of war however painted landscapes, and where women are represented they are strident and heroic, similar in fact to their depiction in Nazi propaganda posters. Here war art is produced by prisoners to create reminders of their homes and loved ones, the act of remembering being integral both to the production of artwork, and its continued presence thereafter. In other camps, art works depicting openly defiant Nazi inspired imagery is found, reflecting the strength of political views amongst the different grades of German prisoners. But the style of expression varies, being culturally constituted, albeit with personal touches.

In addition to the war art produced by prisoners of war, two main constituencies or groups of artists are worth briefly reviewing, as these feature strongly in the images represented in this book. They are Home Forces, and Foreign Forces stationed on home soil. As discussed below, there were significant differences in the style of artwork.

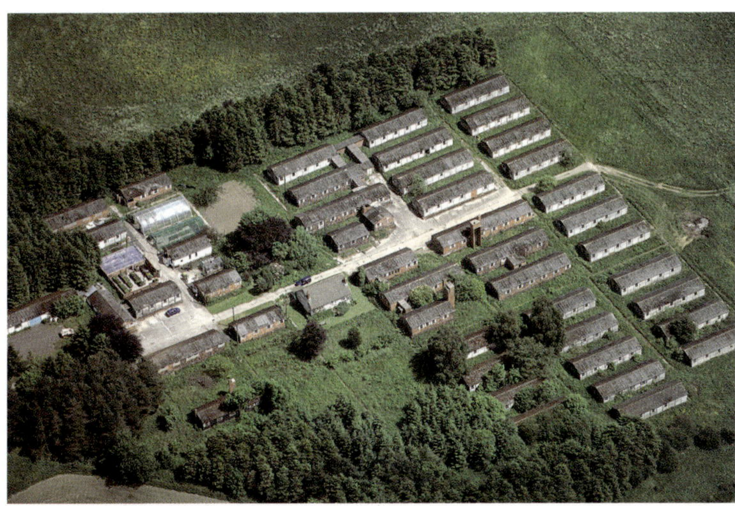

Harperley, Crook, County Durham.
The prisoner of war camp was established in 1942, initially as a camp for Italians, but from late 1944 it held German prisoners who remained until 1947, when it became a foreign labour camp.
Top: **Air photograph (NMR 17259/16)**
(© English Heritage)
Bottom: **Prisoners' Chapel, Harperley Camp**
(© English Heritage via James MacLeod)

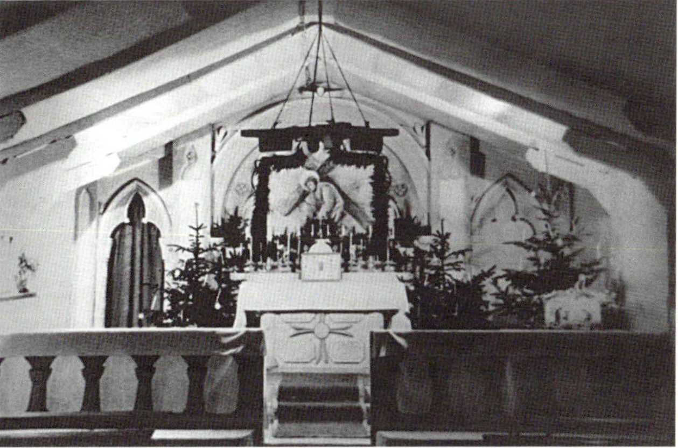

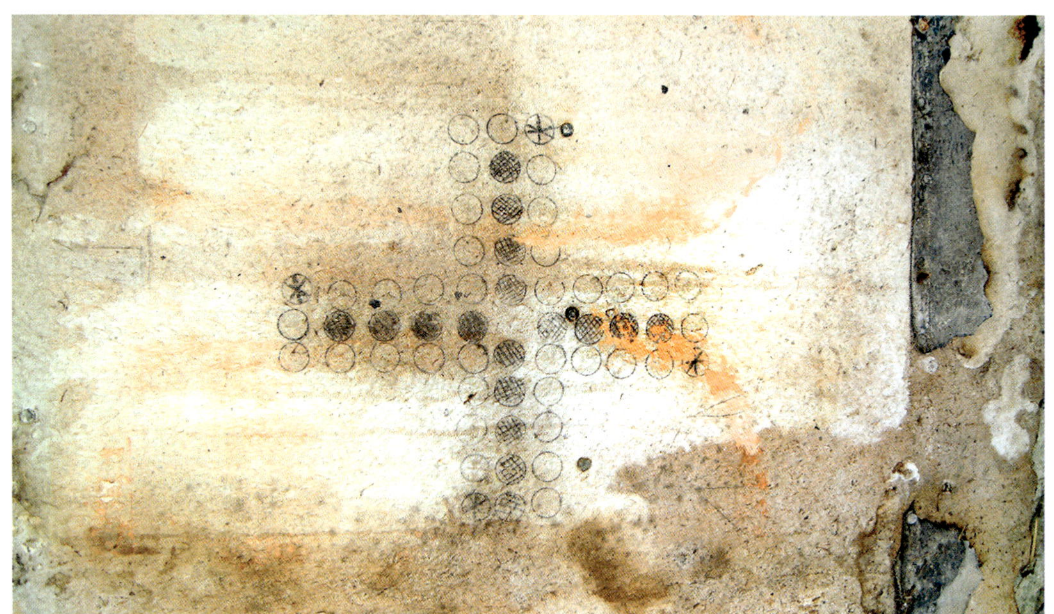

Harperley, Crook, County Durham. Pencil work revealed beneath a peeling paint wash was probably produced by Italian prisoners who built the camp.
Top: Ludo board, probably drawn on the board before it was fixed in place
Bottom: Pipe smoker
(© R J C Thomas)

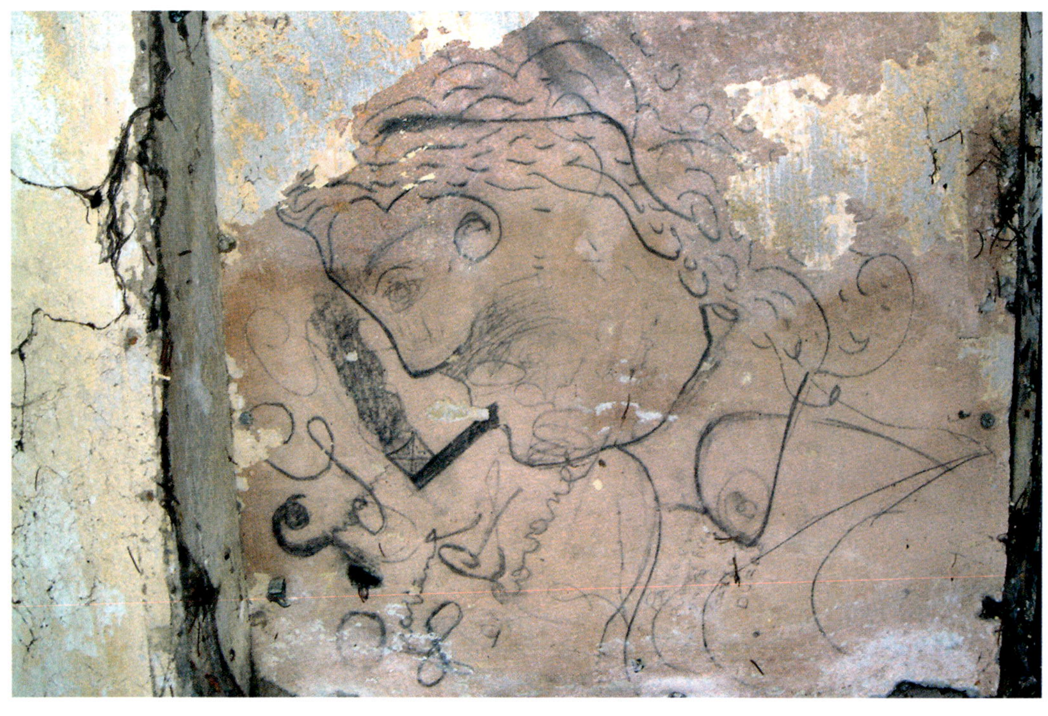

Harperley, Crook, County Durham. German artwork:
Top: Hut interior with artwork on the panels between the windows (AA035120)
Bottom: Left – Piper in a rural idyll (AA035109)
Bottom: Right – Alpine scene (AA035104) (© English Heritage)

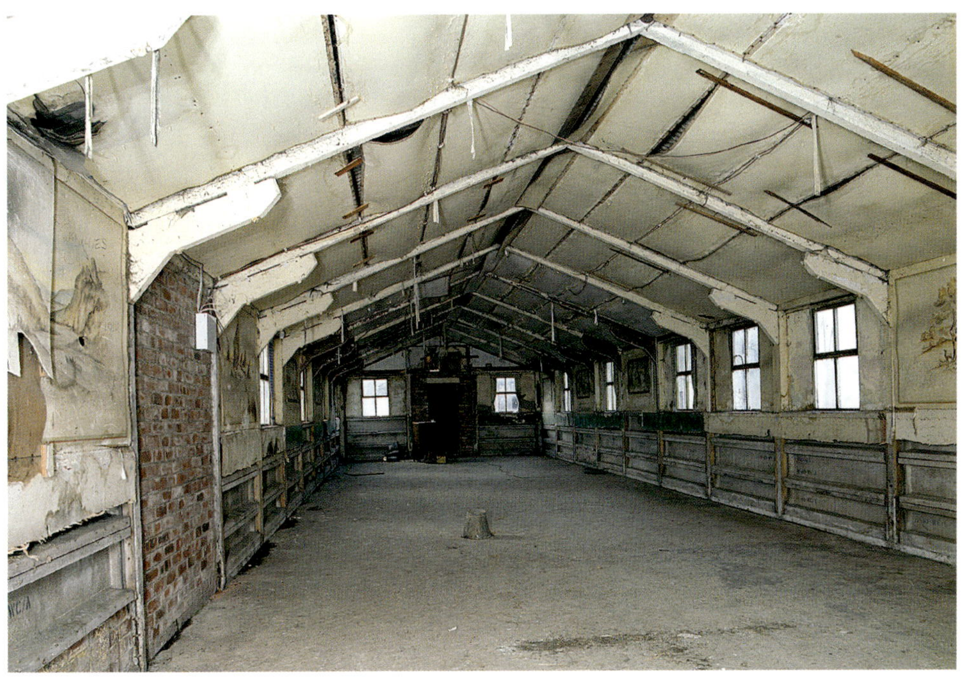

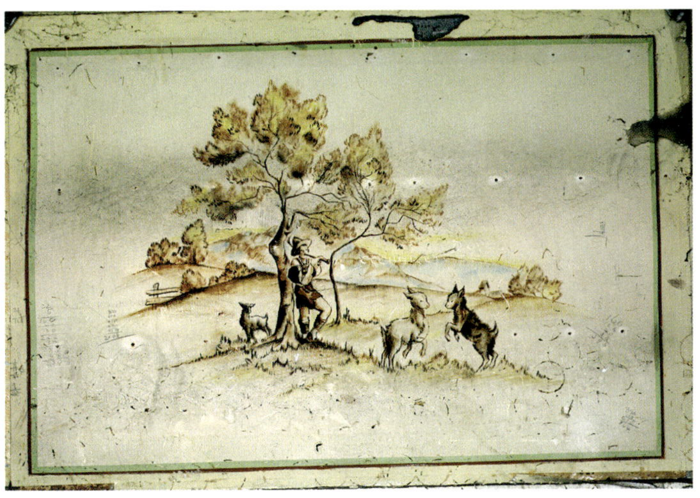

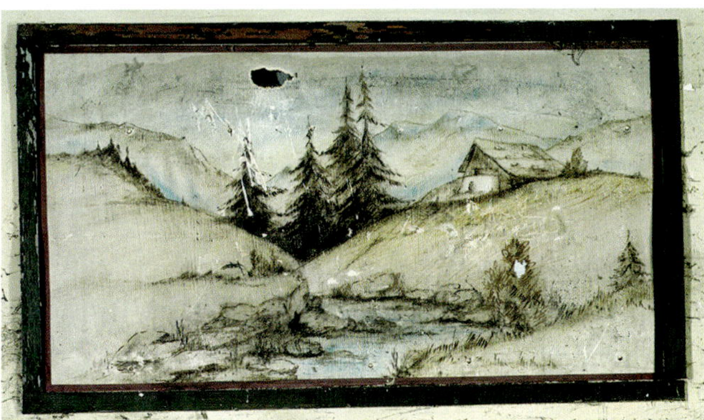

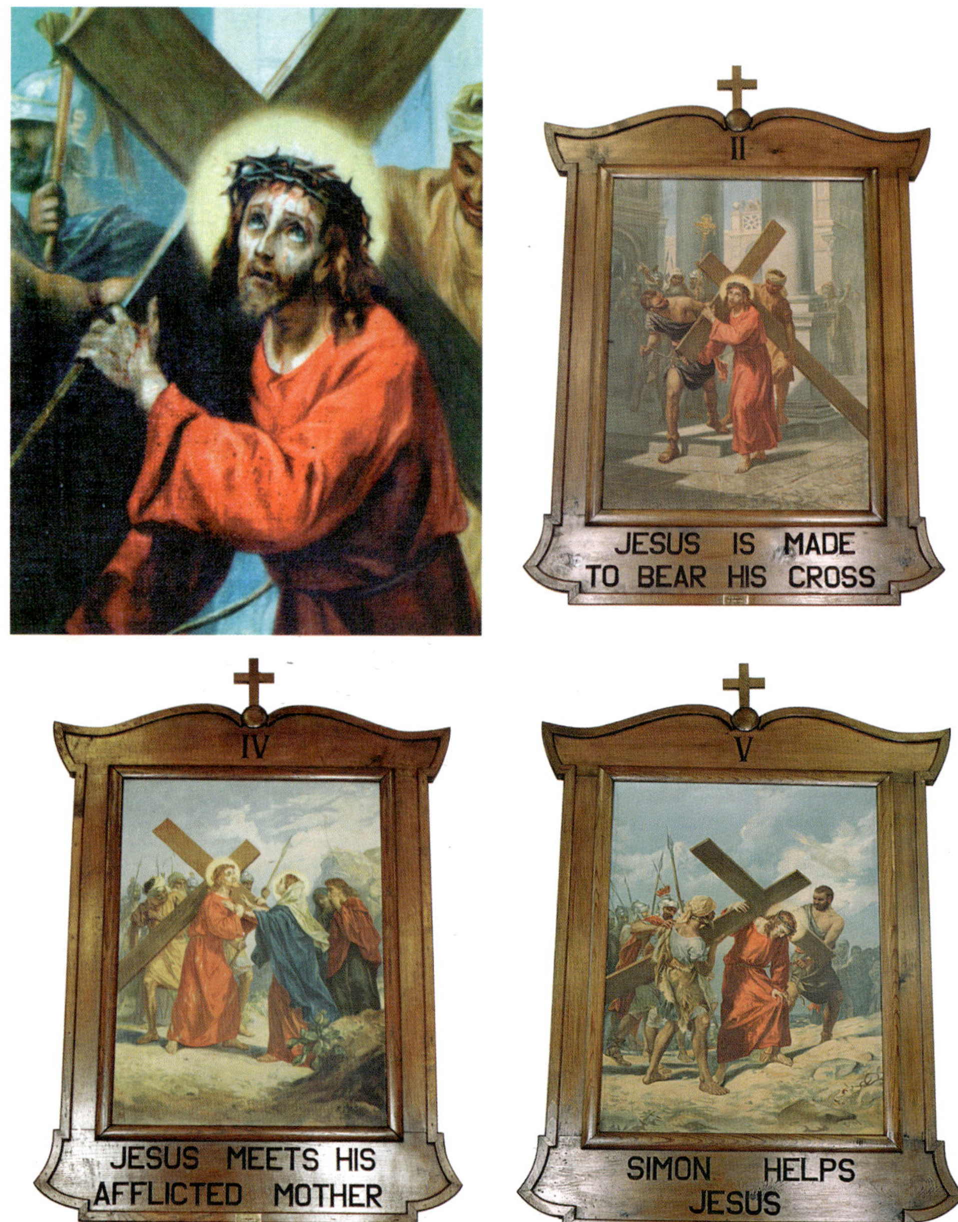

Stations of the Cross series, St Thomas of Canterbury Roman Catholic Church, Wolsingham, County Durham. Italian prisoner of war paintings (Framing completed by German prisoners of war at a later date).

Top: **II** Jesus is made to bear his cross: *Left* – detail (© R J C Thomas), *Right* – full framed version (**AA040756** © English Heritage)

Bottom: Left – **IV** Jesus meets his afflicted mother (**AA040758** © English Heritage); *Right* – **V** Simon helps Jesus (**AA040759** © English Heritage)

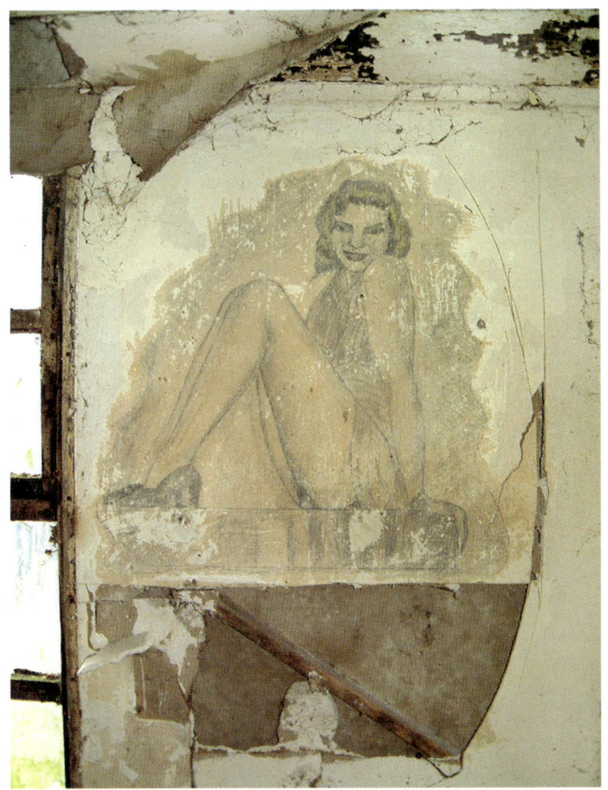

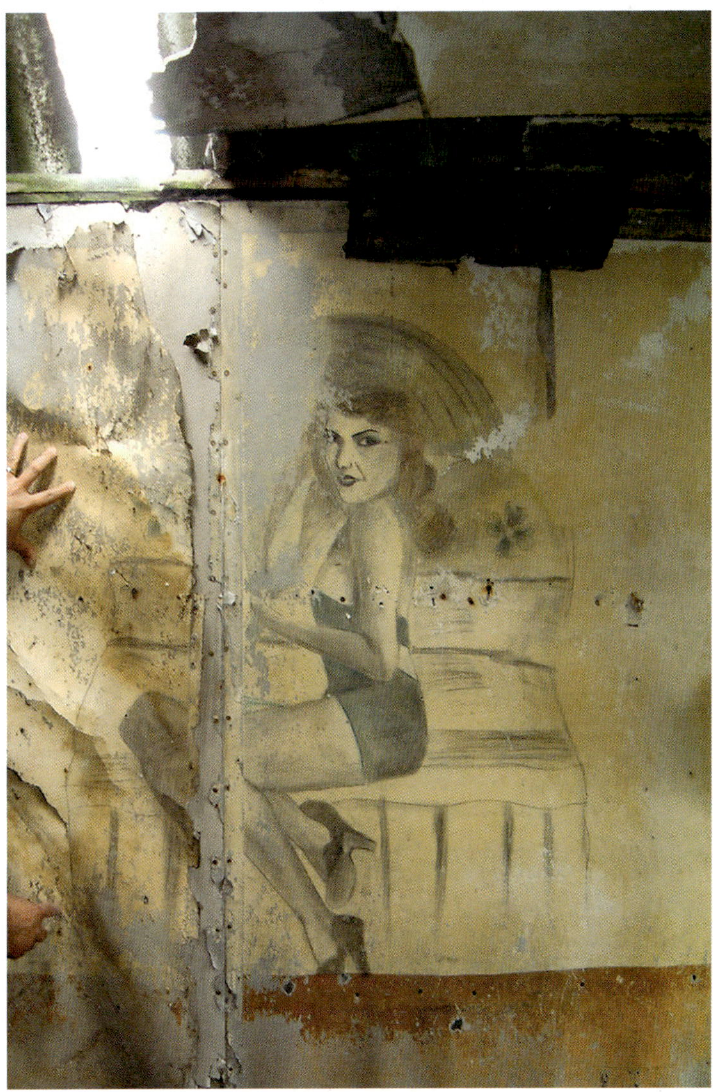

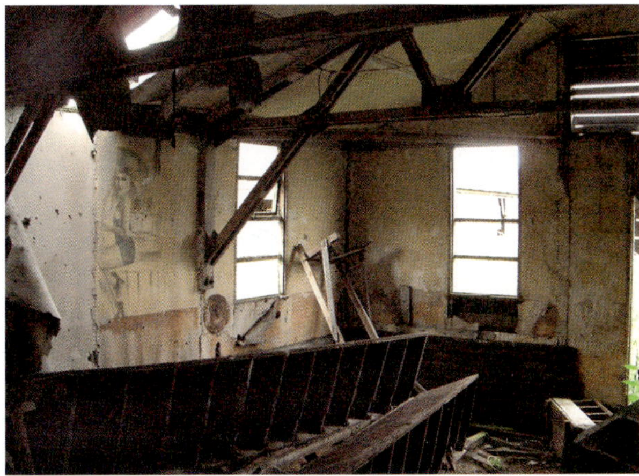

Pingley Farm, Brigg, Lincolnshire, Camp 81, prisoner of war camp, artwork probably produced by Italian prisoners
Left: Top – Woman on bed; *Right:* Woman in swimming costume
Left: Bottom – Hut 43 (© R J C Thomas)

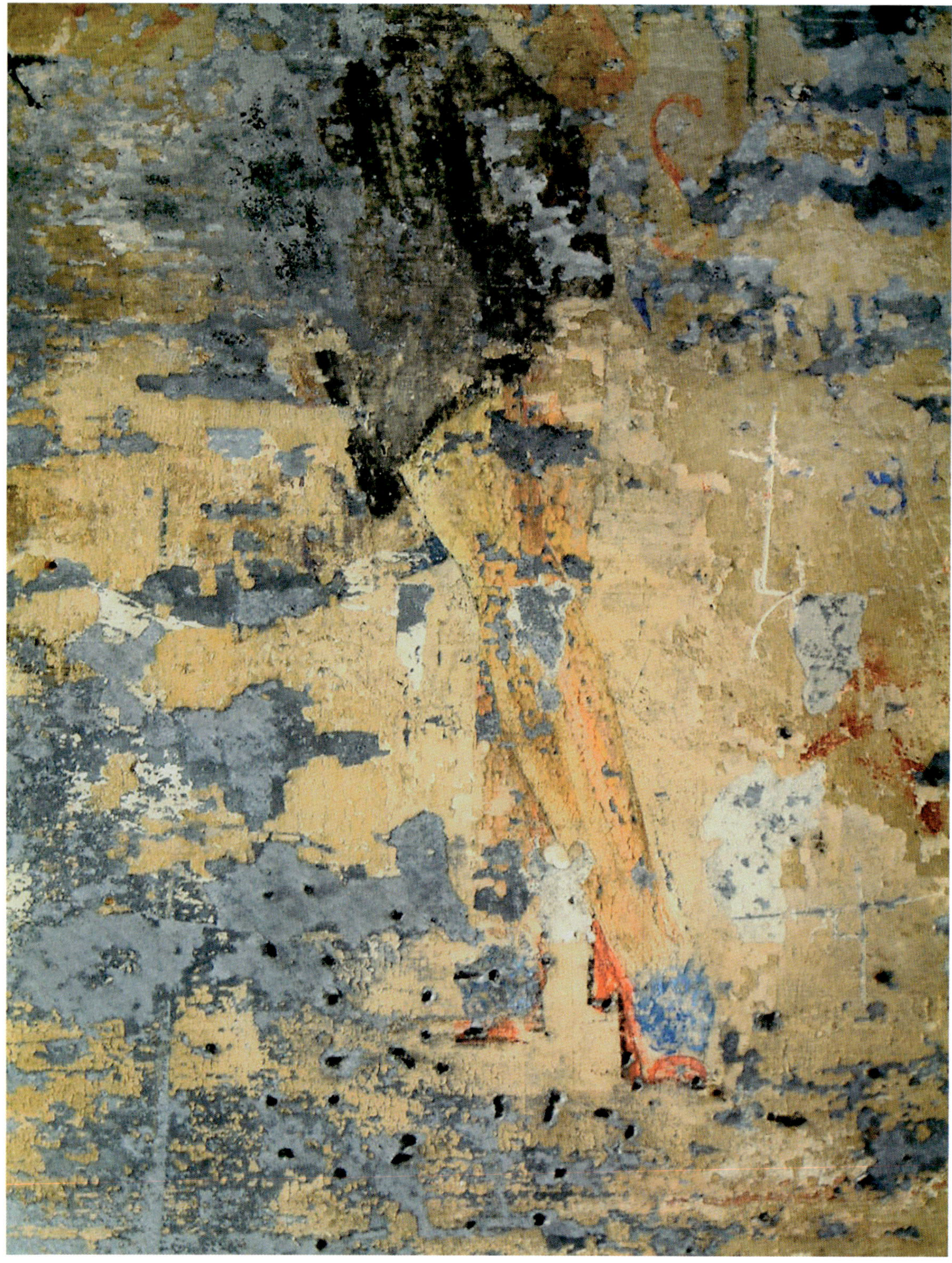

Hatfield Heath, Mill Lane Camp, Essex, prisoner of war camp, fragment of German wall art (© R J C Thomas)

HOME FORCES

British war art is predominantly semi-official and sometimes humorous. Although the artwork was officially frowned upon, the need to maintain and encourage morale within the armed forces often resulted in the time honoured practice of 'turning a blind eye', provided the artwork was not deemed too outrageous. Female figures do appear occasionally on sites occupied by Home Forces, chiefly in the form of the cartoon character 'Jane', but these are tastefully done: most pin-ups remained firmly on the inside of locker doors.

The largest proportion of British war art is found in communal areas like messes, NAAFI/canteen buildings or in huts used as theatres, and on operational sites where aesthetic and functional motivations are evident. Regimental crests and graduated panoramic views of the area of water commanded by the

HMS Goldcrest, Royal Naval Air Station Dale, Pembrokeshire
Top: Left – **Contemporary photograph of an officer's bed surrounded by aircraft cartoons painted by Anthony R Dashfield 1946–47**
Bottom: Left – **Angel in flying goggles (© R J C Thomas)**
Top: Right – **Fairey Firefly cartoon (© R J C Thomas)**
Bottom: Right – **Fairey Fireflys over Skomer (© Basil Nash)**

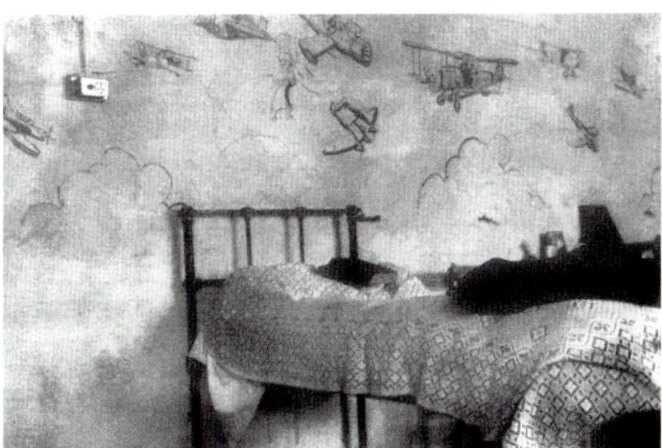

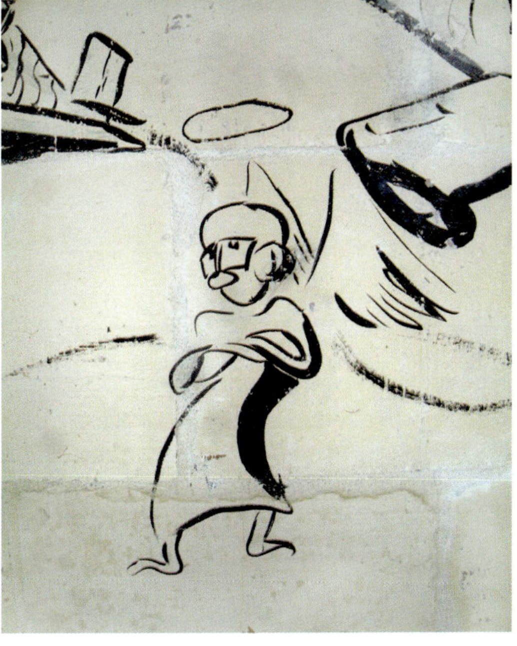

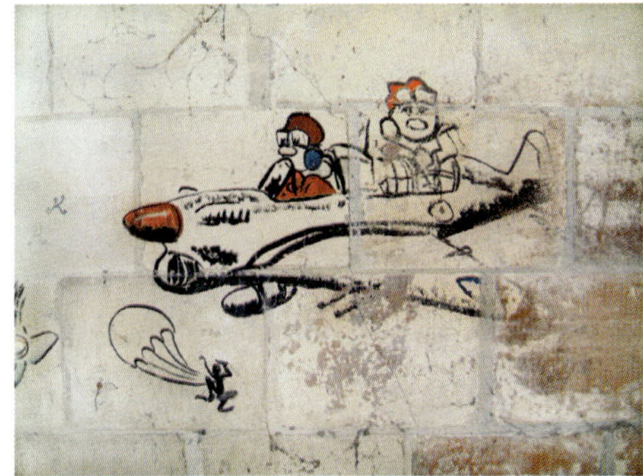

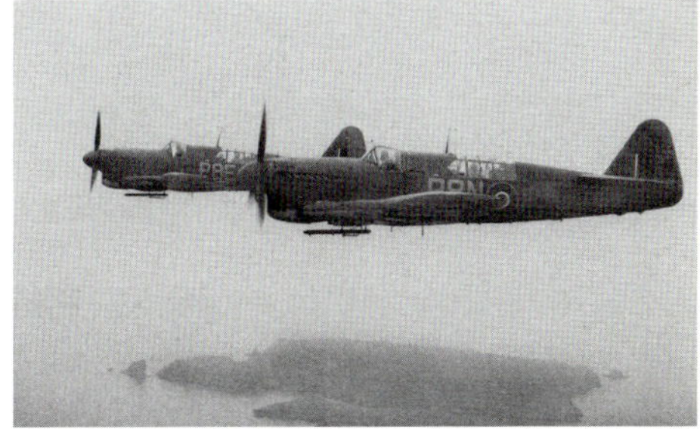

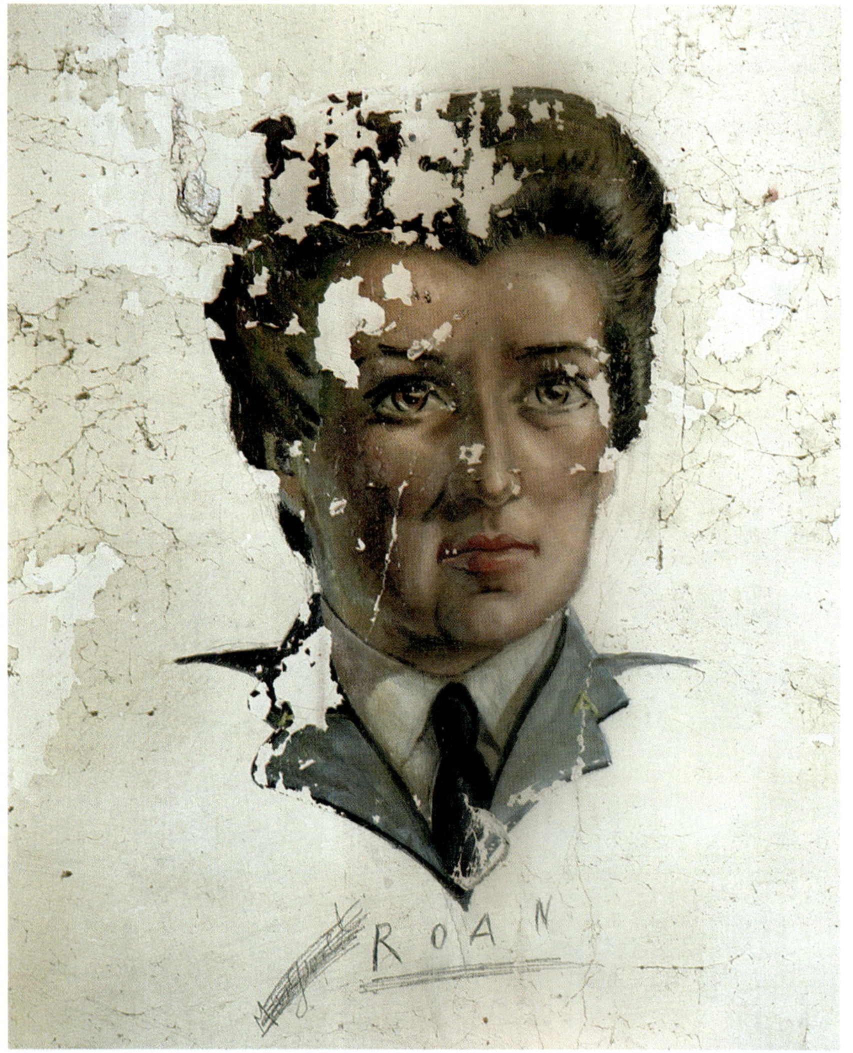

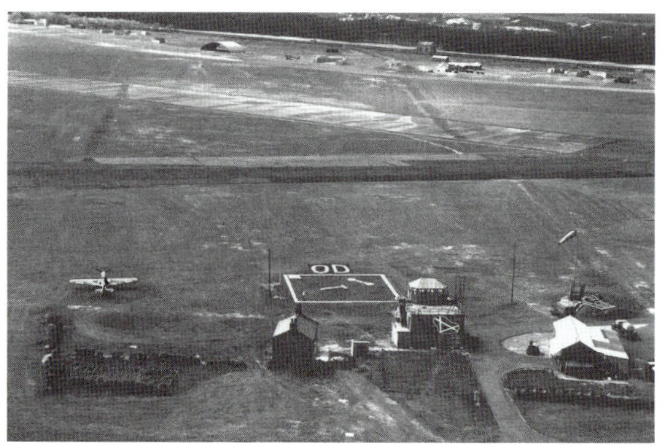

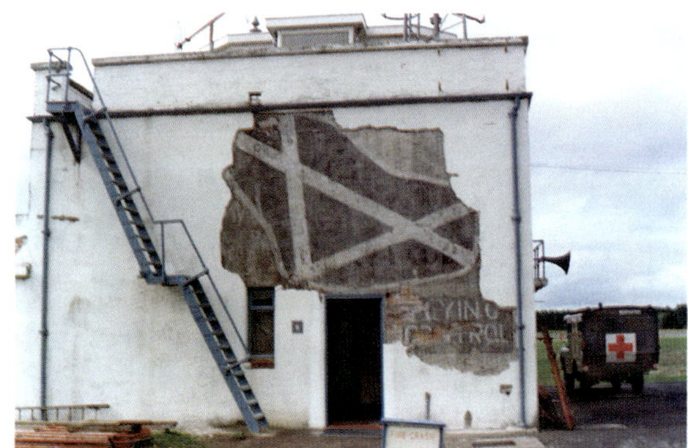

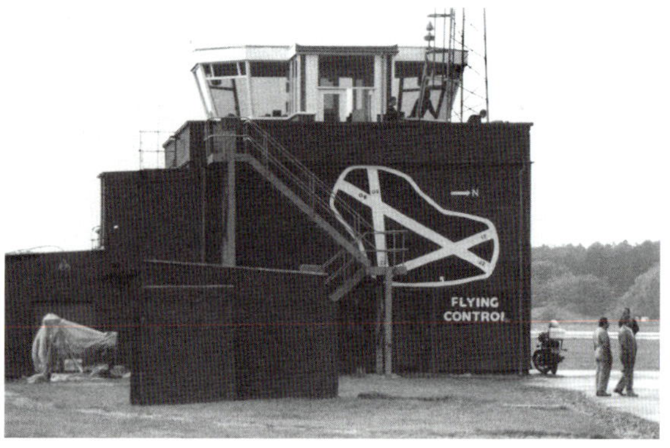

Castletown, Stangergill Bridge, Highland
Portrait of a member of the Women's Auxiliary Air Force on the wall
of a church used as the officer's mess for Castletown airfield
(SC 923035 © Crown copyright RCAHMS)

RAF Woodvale, Lancashire.
Top: Right – During the Second World War information for visiting
pilots was often displayed on the control tower (watch office) and in
this aerial photograph taken in 1945, the airfield layout plan can
clearly be seen painted on the rear wall of the watch office
(© Aldon Ferguson)
Bottom and middle: Right – The painted airfield plan is revealed in
1975 and – restored in 1987 (© Aldon Ferguson)

East Ware, Portland, Dorset, nineteenth-century detention barracks
Graffiti of various NATO ships' names and pennant numbers
(© R J C Thomas)

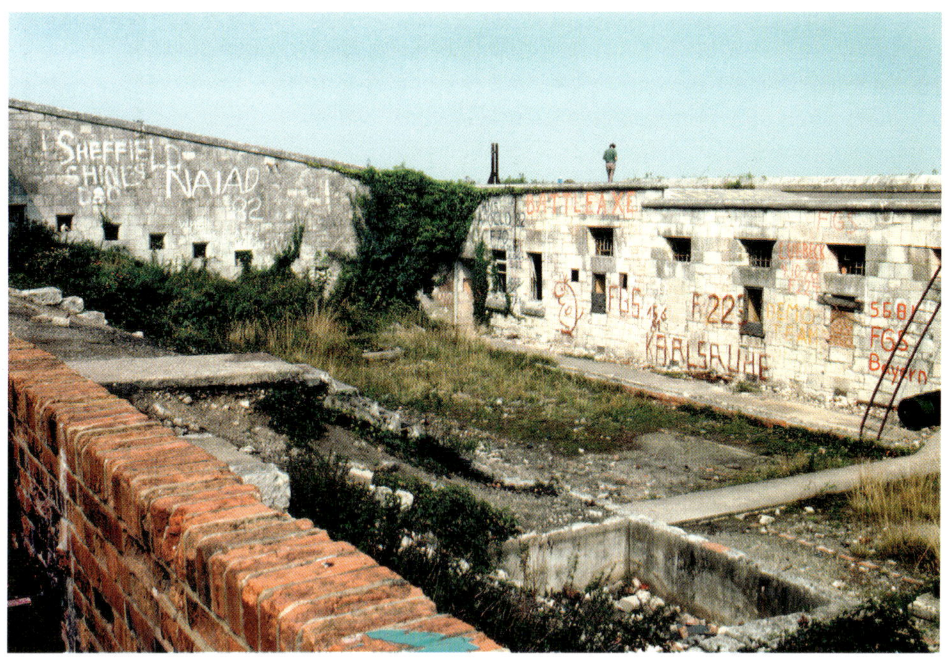

1980s German Bundesmarine ships' crests, Bremen and Fregatte 210 Emden
(© Alistair Graham-Kerr)

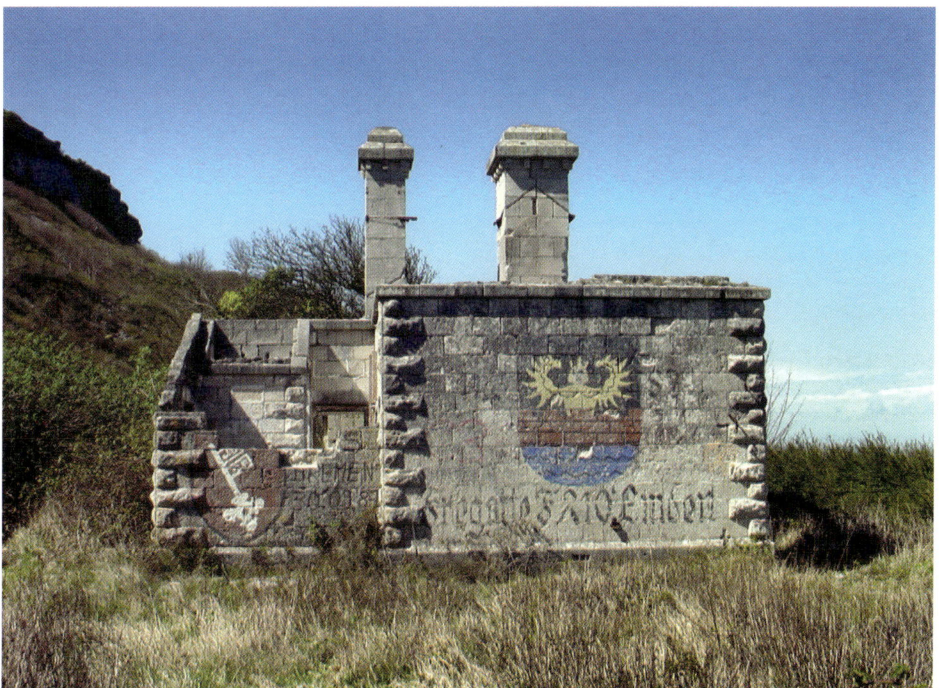

guns are reasonably common images found at former coast artillery sites; the crest to engender pride and the panoramic view to enable the rapid allocation of target bearings. Similar range and bearing markings can be found painted above the gun loops of anti-invasion pillboxes. At anti-aircraft batteries the pictures are most often of aircraft profiles, for training and recognition purposes, but occasionally they are more expressive representations of aircraft in flight.

British examples of war art are much rarer than those created by American servicemen. Less may have been created, but this is more likely due to the majority having been placed at sites that were built for the 'duration', rather than in the established barracks, airfields and depots, where discipline was often much more rigorously enforced – 'If it moves salute it, if it doesn't white-wash it', to cite a catch-phrase of the time.

FOREIGN FORCES

American war art was often colourful and brash featuring national symbols, unit badges, cartoons, aircraft and above all women. During the Second World War, from 1942 to 1945, The United States Army Air Force (USAAF) operated from numerous bomber and fighter airfields across East Anglia, the midlands and the southern counties. Images of scantily clad or nude women or cartoon characters often adorned the noses of aircraft as lucky tokens; the same 'nose art' also appeared both on the flying jackets of the crews and in their communal areas. At RAF Raydon (Suffolk) a large 'Aces Honour Roll' was painted onto one of the gable walls of the Briefing Room flanked by naked 'honour guards'.

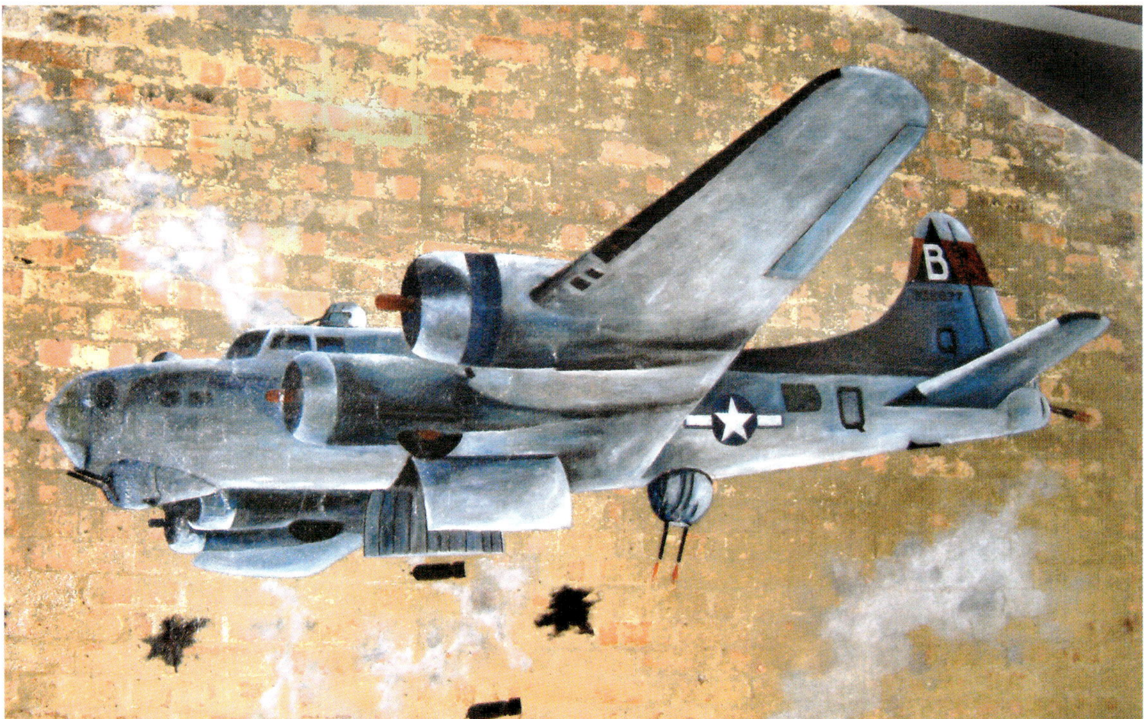

RAF Poddington, Rutland
B-17G Flying Fortress, removed to the Imperial War Museum, Duxford and repainted
(© R J C Thomas)

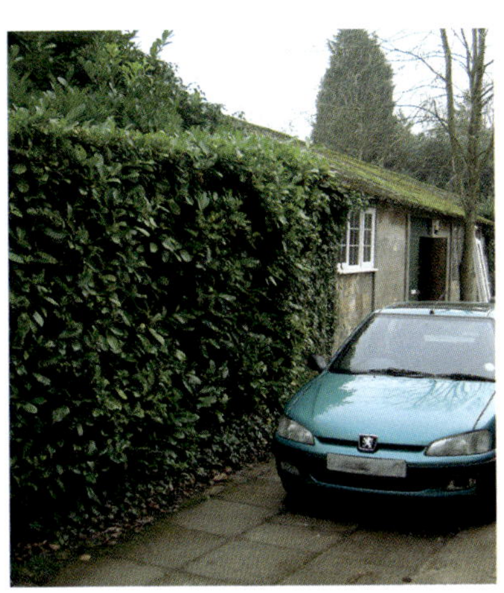

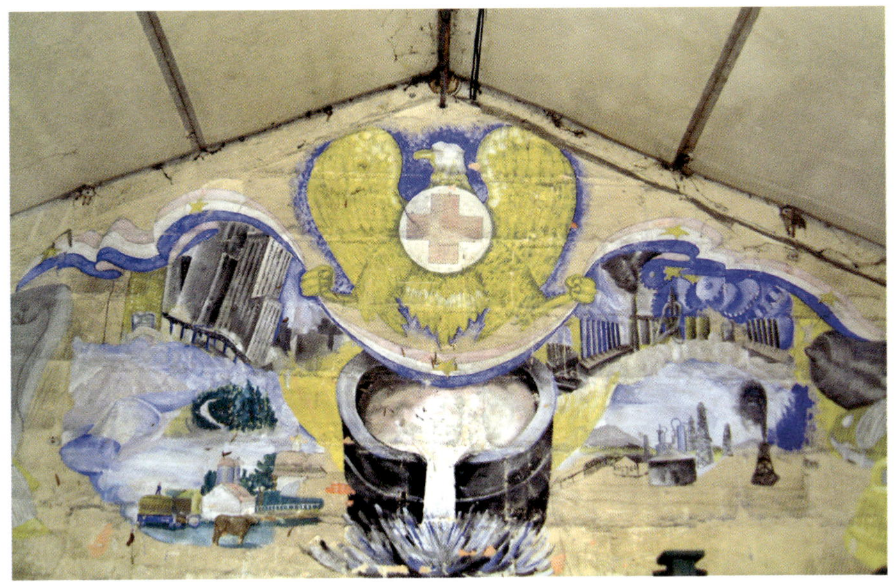

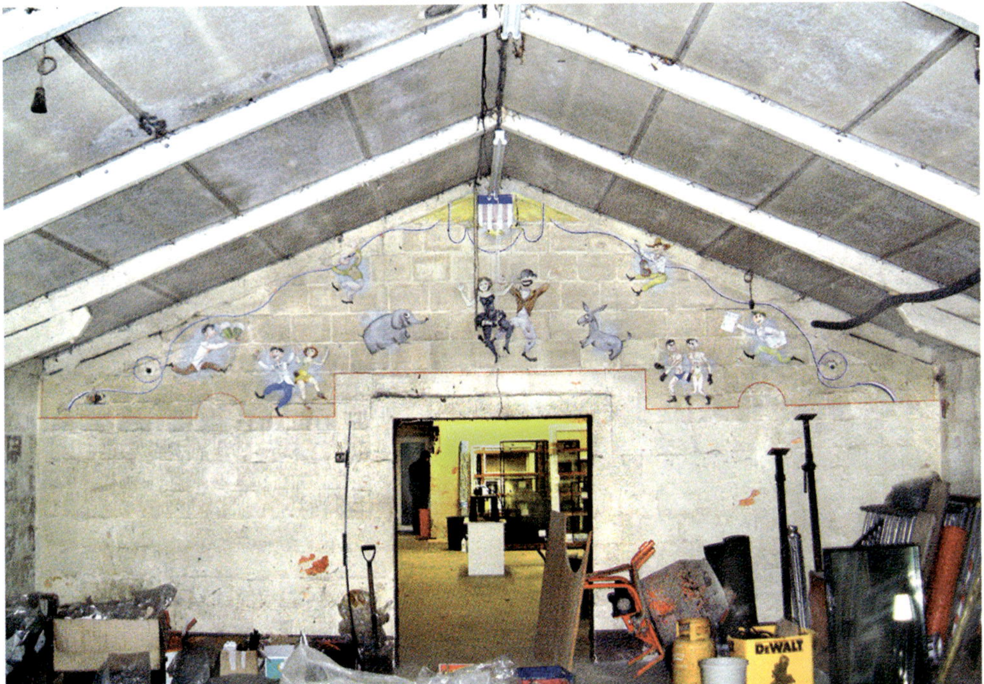

Ullenwood, Gloucestershire,
**USAAF 62nd General
Hospital, canteen building**
Top: Left – **Exterior of Former
Canteen**
Top: Right – **American Red
Cross mural**
Bottom: **Central wall**
(© R J C Thomas)

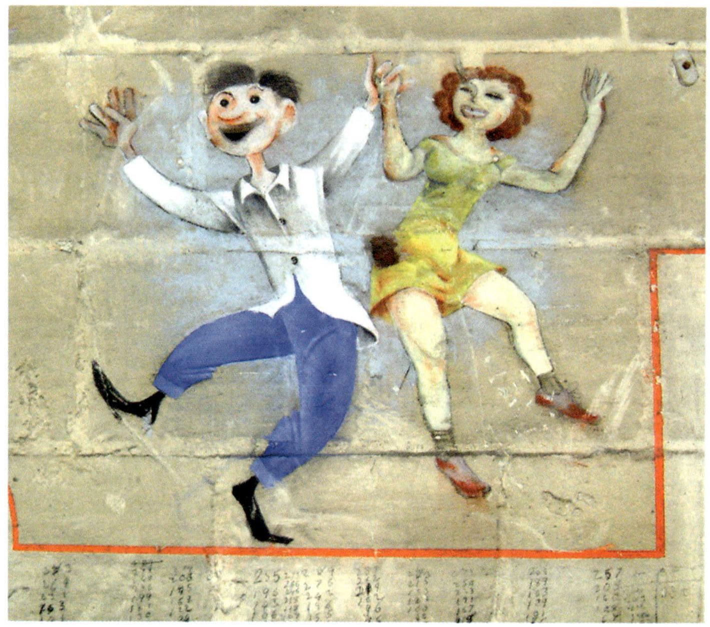

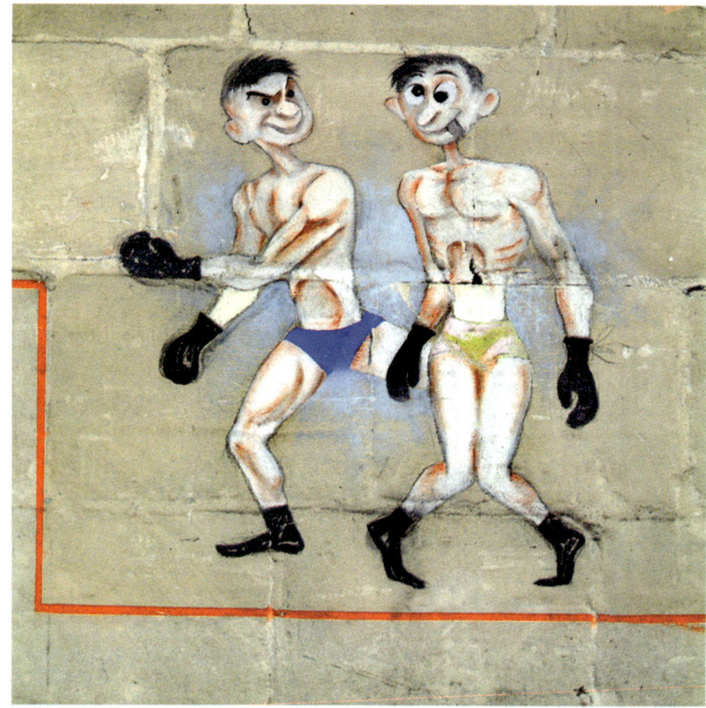

Ullenwood, Gloucestershire, USAAF 62nd General Hospital, canteen building
Top: **Couple dancing the 'Jitterbug';** *Bottom:* **Boxers (© R J C Thomas)**

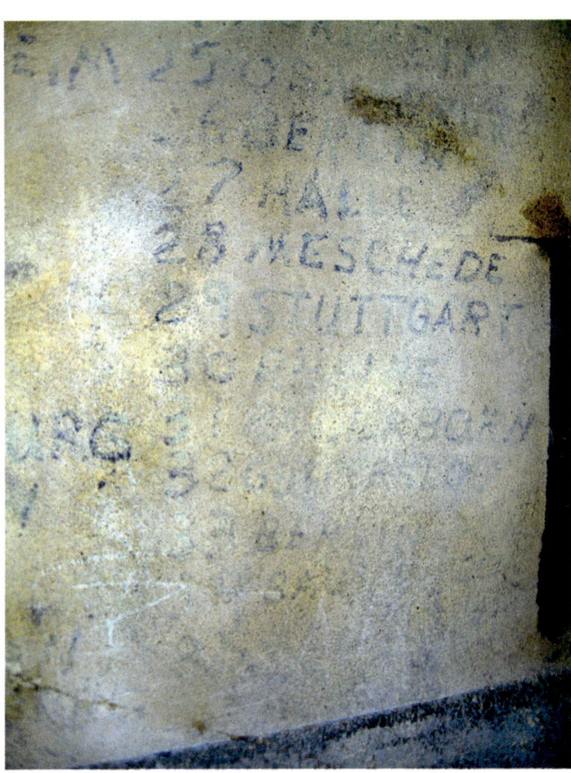

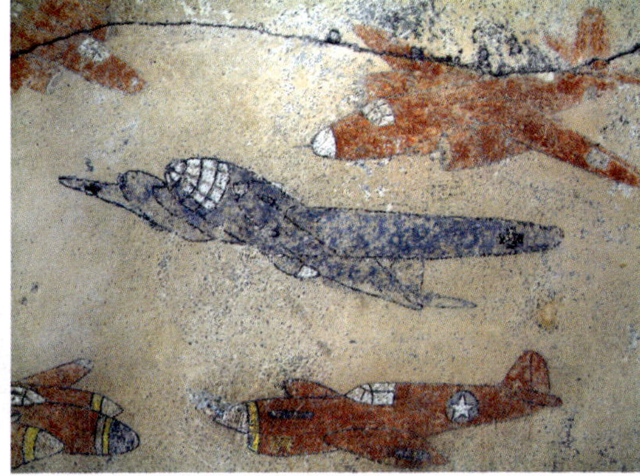

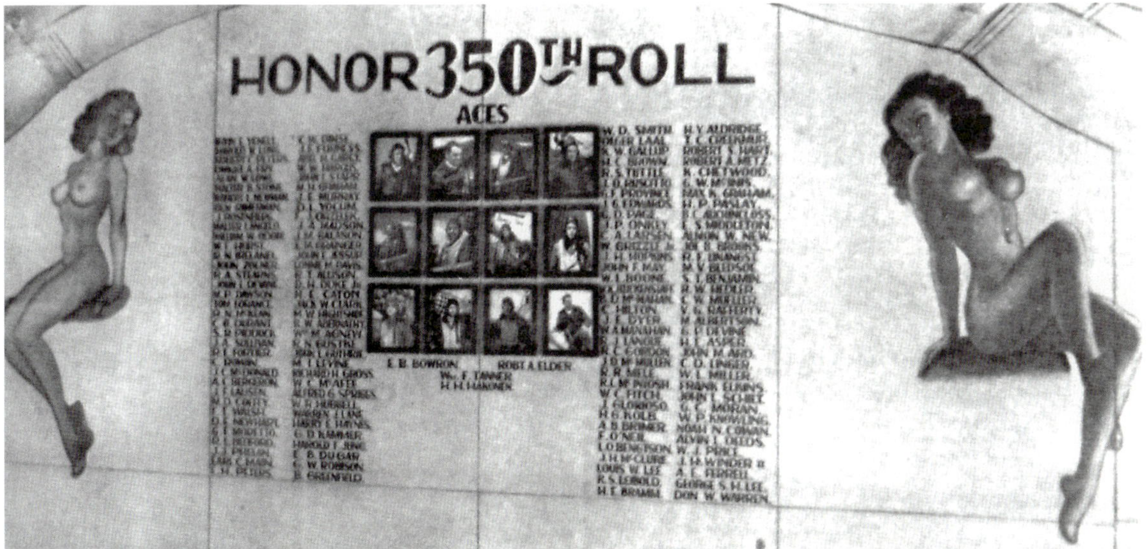

RAF Raydon, Essex (Station 157). The 'Honor Roll 350th Fighter Squadron', 353rd Fighter Group, 8th USAAF was originally displayed on the gable wall of the unit's Briefing Hut, flanked by a pair of painted nude female figures. A further pair of female figures was situated at the opposite end of the hut. Reputedly the hut was later used to house pigs and it was at this stage that the figures painted on fibreboard were removed to preserve them. Although their removal and preservation was well intended, the four figures are no longer associated with the 'Honor Roll' and as such, have lost their historic context.
Above: The Honor Roll 350th Roll Aces in its original position (© IWM)

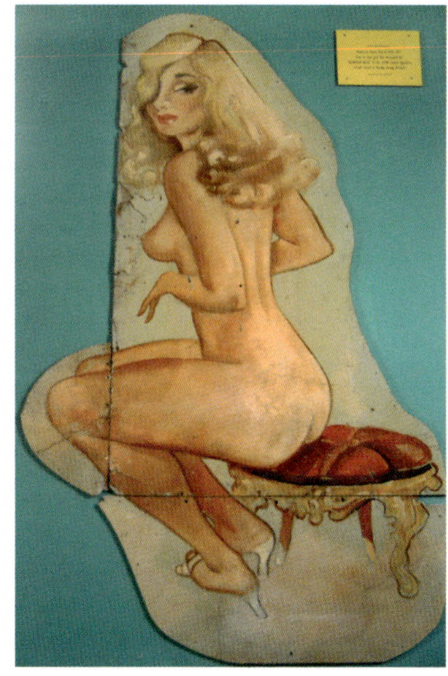

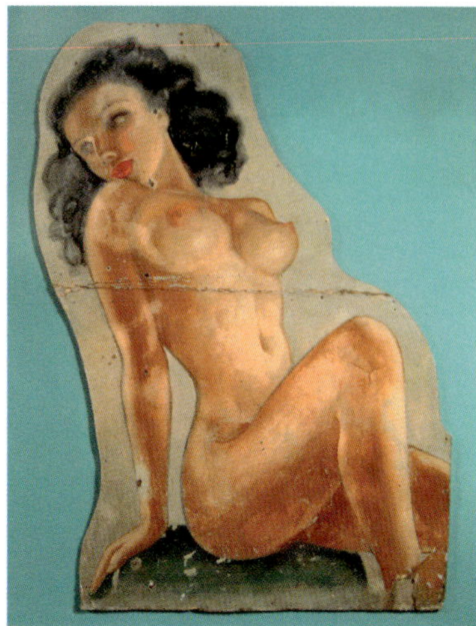

RAF Raydon, Essex (Station 157). The 'Honor Roll' Four figures, out of context (© R J C Thomas)

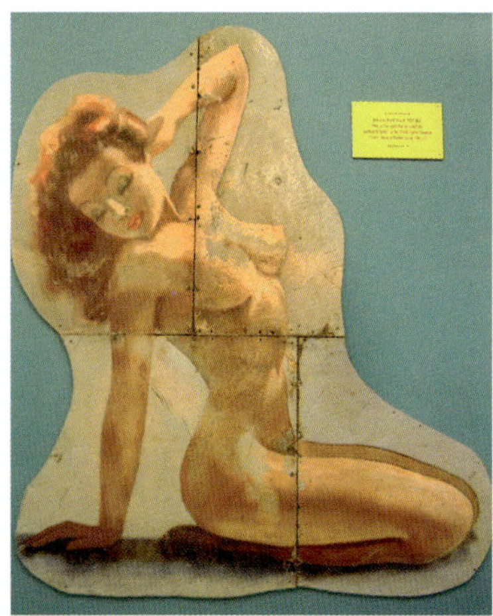

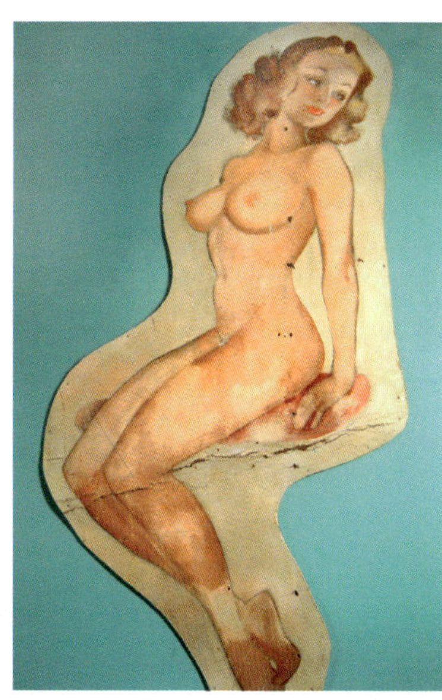

Inspiration for many of the female figures was taken from the pin-up art of various magazines and books like *Esquire*, *Beauty Parade*, *Petty Folio*, *Silk Stocking Stories*, *Movie Merry-Go-Round* and *Life* painted or drawn by Art Frahm, George Petty, Rolf Armstrong, Alberto Vargas, Earl Moran, Gil Elvgren, and Peter Driben. What is often not appreciated is that a number of the pin-up artists were women including Zoe Mozert, Joyce Ballantyne and Pearl Frush. Nevertheless, George Petty and Alberto Vargas were the most influential of artists; George Petty's stunningly smooth stylish simplicity was particularly popular, and was the inspiration for the nose art of the Memphis Belle, made famous by William Wyler's remarkable wartime documentary of the same name.

This diversity of expression continued with the presence of American units in the UK during the period of the Cold War. Although styles changed, as the influences changed and the cultural backgrounds of American servicemen became more diverse, many of the same themes are evident. Unit badges are a significant presence on USAF bases such as Upper Heyford (Oxfordshire) and Greenham Common (West Berkshire), while instruction drawings, graffiti and unofficial paintings exist in the private spaces amongst barracks and living quarters. An example of cultural influence is the Hispanic style and language of images at Greenham Common.

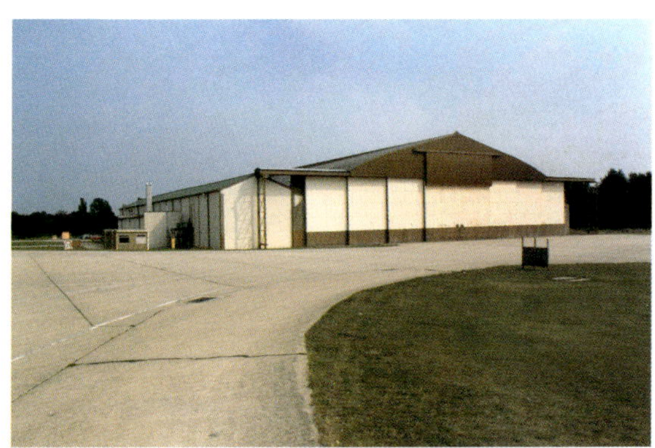

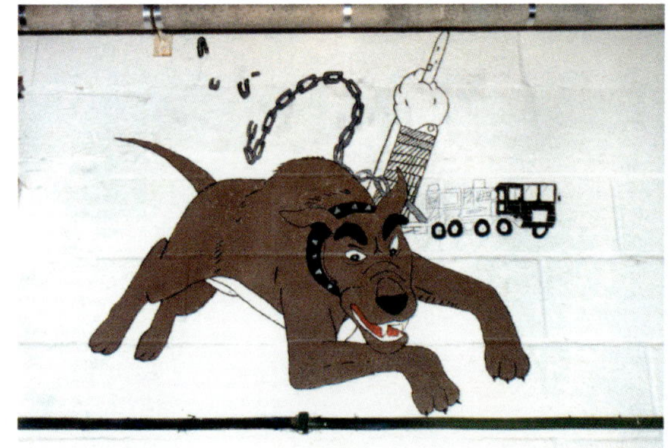

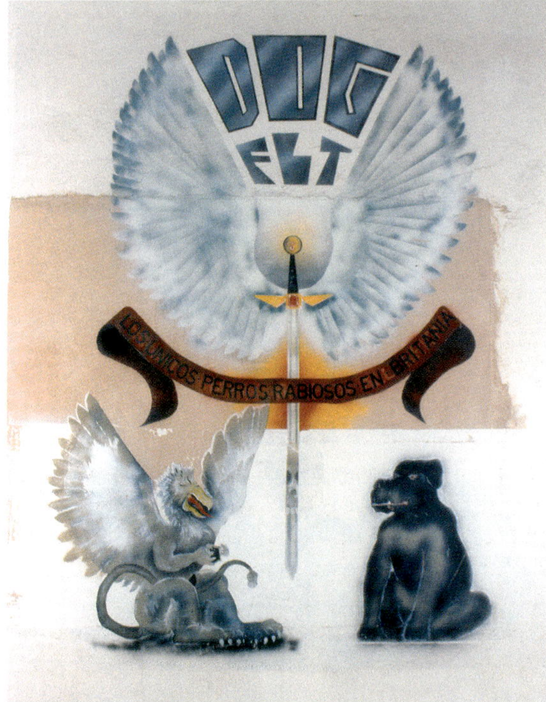

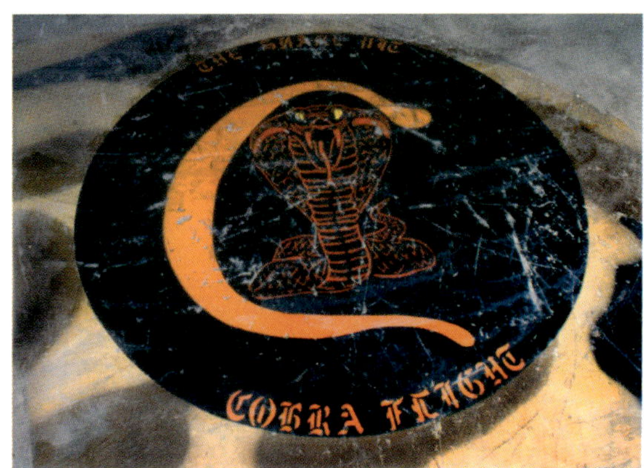

RAF Greenham Common, West Berkshire, cruise missiles were based here 1983–1991
Top: Left – Maintenance hangar 303
Top: Right – Dog Flight mural, locker room with an unfinished drawing of a missile launcher in the background (3041/17A © English Heritage)
Bottom: Left – Dog Flight Los Unicos Perros Rabiosos En Britania
Bottom: Right – Cobra Flight (© R J C Thomas)

HISTORY AND DEVELOPMENT

Although this collection concentrates on modern war art – that of the nineteenth and twentieth centuries – the use of martial emblems and symbols has a long history and was certainly in widespread use by the Ancient Greeks, Egyptians and the Romans. In the earlier medieval period war art was used to identify troops, display wealth, power and status, and to invoke fear in the enemy. Powerful images of dragons and mythical beasts adorn Saxon and Viking artefacts and can be seen on the prows of ceremonial warships, while the Lindisfarne stone-carving included bas-relief depicting warriors armed with axes and swords, raiding the Lindisfarne monastery.

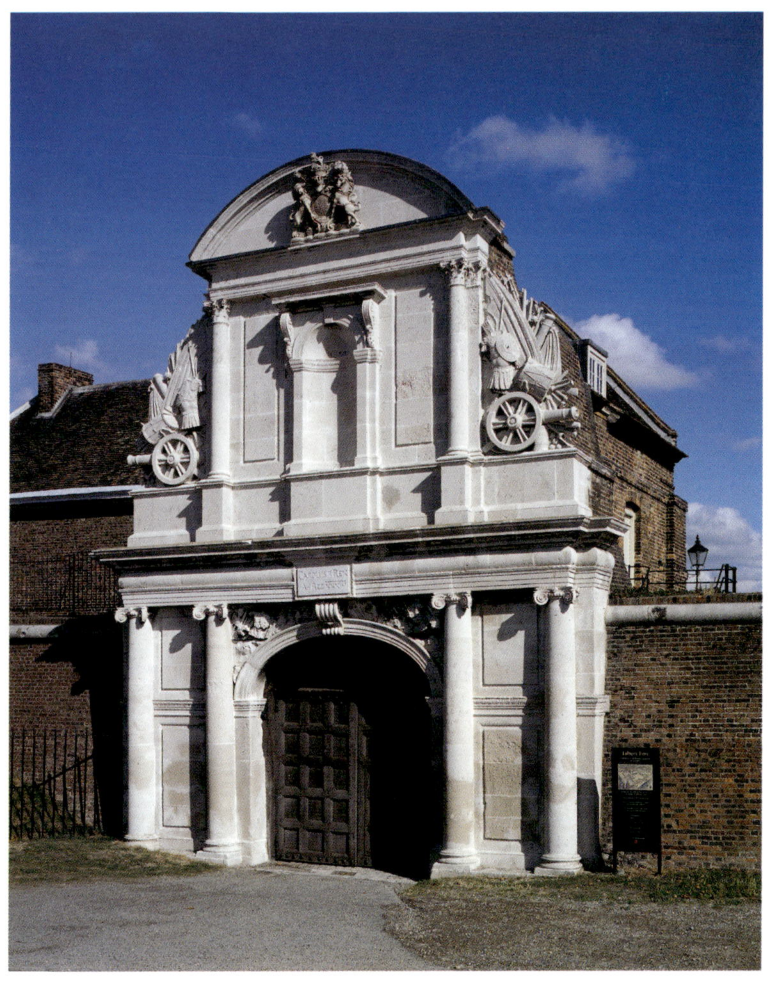

Tilbury Fort, Essex, the Water Gate (© English Heritage)

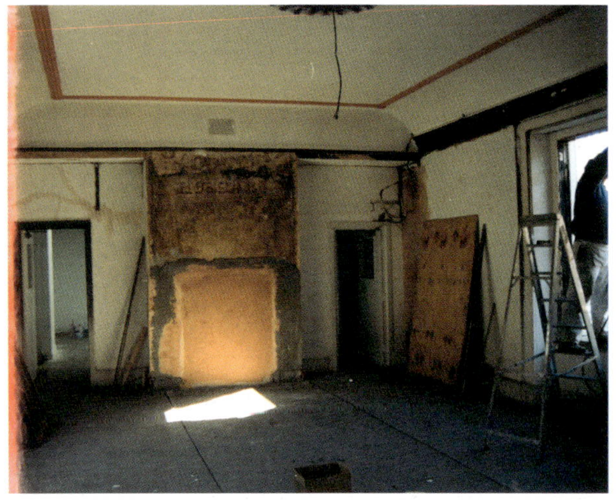

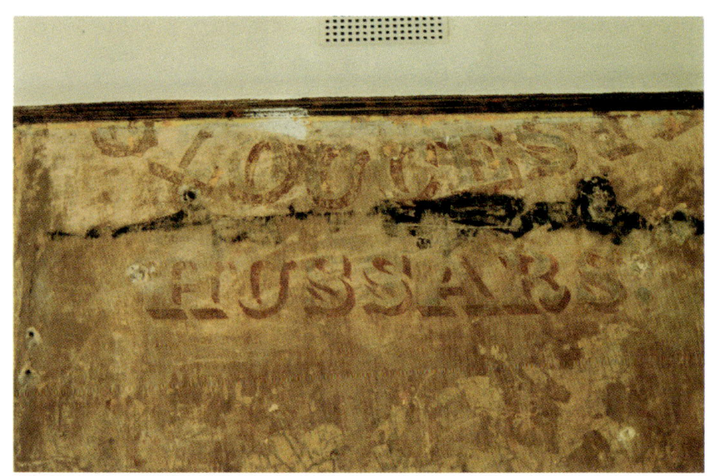

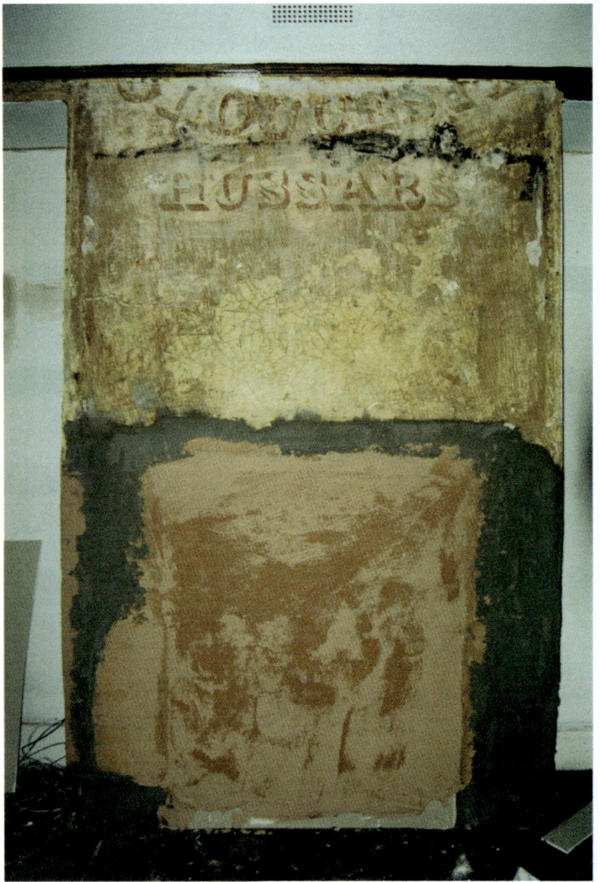

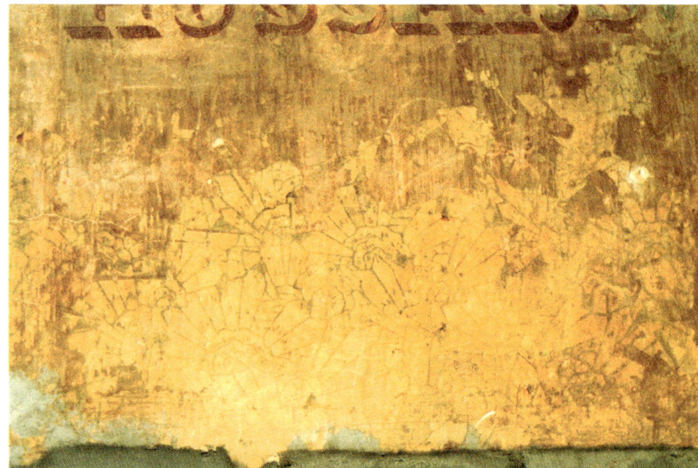

Chipping Sodbury, Gloucestershire, George Hotel, late eighteenth- or early nineteenth-century wall painting naming the (South) Gloucestershire Hussars was uncovered during restoration in 1996. The Hussars were one of a number of militia units raised in South Gloucestershire, whose main purpose was as an anti invasion reserve against the French, although they were often used in a civil role such as the Bristol Bridge Riot of 1793 and the reform riots of 1831 (© South Gloucestershire Council)

Throughout the Middle Ages, the symbols of warfare applied to shields, flags and banners became increasingly stylised through the use of family heraldic devices. Large army units employed specific badges to symbolise regimental honour and individual loyalty to a fighting unit, while flags acted as rallying points on the field of battle. Within medieval Britain, conflict and the preparation for war occupied a central place in the lives of the aristocracy, demanding an increasing number of fortifications, which often combined defensive capabilities with extensive residential complexes. Very few examples of early medieval castle decoration survive, at Chepstow (Gwent) wall plaster in Marten's Tower is painted with red lines to resemble joints in ashlar masonry, similar painting was found in excavations at Okehampton Castle (Devon) (Kenyon 1990, 124). In the later Middle Ages, as heraldic and chivalric display became more fashionable, coats of arms were often applied to castle walls as a means of indicating status and ancestry of the owner. During early fifteenth-century alterations at Warkworth Castle (Northumberland) the Percy family adorned one of its towers with their lion symbol. At around the same time, Ralph, Lord Cromwell, Lord Treasurer to King Henry VI, was rebuilding Wingfield Manor (Derbyshire): here he embellished a gateway with his family and associated crest and the purses of the Lord Treasurer's office. Such brazen displays of 'vanity' were frowned upon during the Commonwealth and many examples of war art and coats-of-arms were destroyed by the puritans, but the restoration of Charles II witnessed a resurgence of highly visual heraldic devices, armorial emblems, royal crests and exuberant martial displays such as those on the gateways of Tilbury Fort (Essex) and Plymouth Citadel (Devon).

Examples from the eighteenth century are also generally restricted to grand gateways, such as the 1718 entrance to Chatham dockyard (Kent), which was originally adorned by George II's coat of arms (Coad 1989, 82), and of similar date the Royal Brass Foundry at the Royal Arsenal Woolwich. The dining hall of the Royal Naval College at Dartmouth (Devon), and the Great Hall at the Chelsea Barracks (London), both contain monumental schemes of wall painting by leading artists such as Thornhill and Verrio. Surviving graffiti from this period is quite rare, and primarily linked to places of incarceration, such as Portchester Castle (Hampshire), where the Norman keep was used as a prisoner of war camp during the Seven Years War (1756–63) and again at the end of the century during the French Revolutionary Wars. An analysis of the locations of these graffiti noted that it occurred in clusters, in rooms that were used to incarcerate prisoners who had committed some minor infringement of camp rules. Another group was found at the top of the keep's staircase where the natural light hit the wall, which was perhaps a place where prisoners met to sit and talk (Cunliffe and Garratt 1994, 68–9).

The tradition of applying sculptural royal coats of arms to gates and pediments continued into the late eighteenth and nineteenth centuries. During the 1790s, half a dozen large Coade stone reliefs depicting the royal coat of arms were ordered, one of which survives at the Wyvern Artillery Barracks, Exeter (Douet 1998, 87–8). Once in place they were often rendered in bright primary colours. Surviving nineteenth-century photographs and engravings of barrack interiors indicate that most were simply whitewashed, they were also crowded with rows of beds, dining tables, with equipment hung from walls, leaving little room for decoration. The survival of nineteenth-century war art is sparse and chiefly consists of eponymous graffito, although officially sanctioned stencilled instructions, room numbers, identification marks, magazine signs and wall decorations such as stencilled friezes do survive in many Victorian forts. Poor levels of literacy amongst soldiers must be a reason for this, but discipline amongst the small 'regular' British Army should not be overlooked; officers and sergeants would not have approved of unofficial artwork or doodlings on their pristine barrack room walls. However, the scarcity of nineteenth-century soldier's art and graffiti may also be illusory, as the British Army was primarily used to police the Empire and a large proportion of the soldier's time was spent abroad, away from the stifling discipline of their home depots, and it may be there that creative opportunity presented itself. Other transient groups

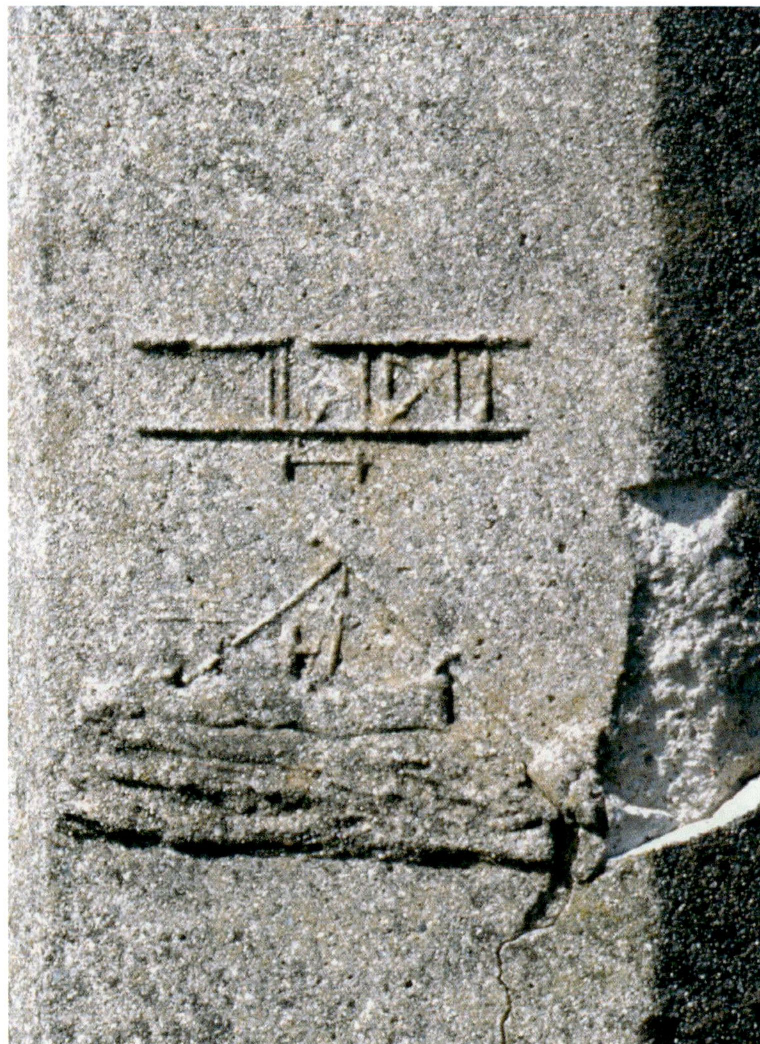

Tregantle Fort, Cornwall, early twentieth-century bas relief on pillar (© R J C Thomas)

produced portable folk art in the form of scrimshaw, worked bone and ivory, which is a well-known product of nineteenth-century mariners, many of whom were drawn from the same social classes as the army. Many pieces of fine scrimshaw work were also produced by French prisoners interned during the Napoleonic Wars – some of these may have been produced by officers during their forced idleness.

EXPLORING TWENTIETH-CENTURY WAR ART

THE FIRST WORLD WAR

Amongst the squalor of the front lines of the Western Front, where the priority was survival, there is little evidence of attempts to make the living environment more homely, with the exception perhaps of photographs of home or a sweetheart. In the less threatened rear areas, where the troops were safer and had some free time, more elaborate work was possible. Much of northern France is underlain by chalk bedrock and beneath many towns caves were used as billets and hospitals. In this environment, the readily workable chalk walls were carved with images of animals, patriotic and religious symbols and unit badges; even chapels and altars were hewn from the rock. Good examples are accessible in the Dragon's cave on the Chemin des Dames overlooking the Aisne valley and in the caves of Confrécourt near Soissons (Saunders 2002a, 41). Subterranean wall art was produced by all of the major fighting nations on the Western Front. In the German fortresses surrounding Metz are many fine murals, both patriotic and humorous, painted by serving soldiers, including Willy Reue (1893–1962) and Ernst Koch who were to become well-known artists after the war (www.braunn.chez.tiscali.fr). Towards the end of the war the mood changed and scenes depict the hardships of soldiers sitting down to a meal of potatoes and a skeletal civilian in oversized clothes, reflecting the food shortages at home.

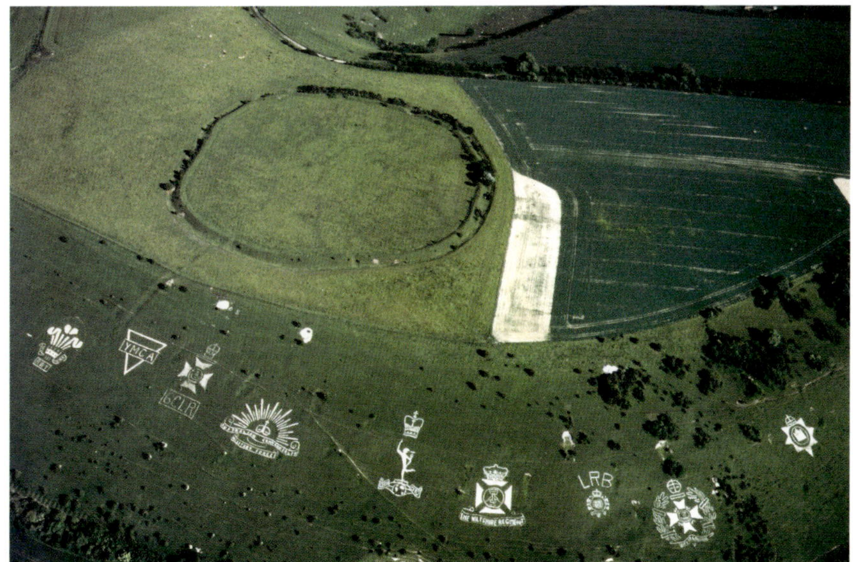

Fovant, Wiltshire. During the First World War a series of chalk figures were cut into the Chalk Downs above Fovant by soldiers undergoing training in the area. Units who cut badges included battalions from the London Regiment and Australian troops. During the inter-war period some became overgrown and after the outbreak of war in 1939 others were covered over to prevent their use as navigation markers by the Luftwaffe. Subsequently some of the badges were re-cut and others added to commemorate the local Home Guard and the 50th anniversary of the Royal Corps of Signals. They are protected as a Scheduled Monument. Also visible in this view is the prehistoric hillfort of Chiselbury (© Crown copyright NMR 18037/10)

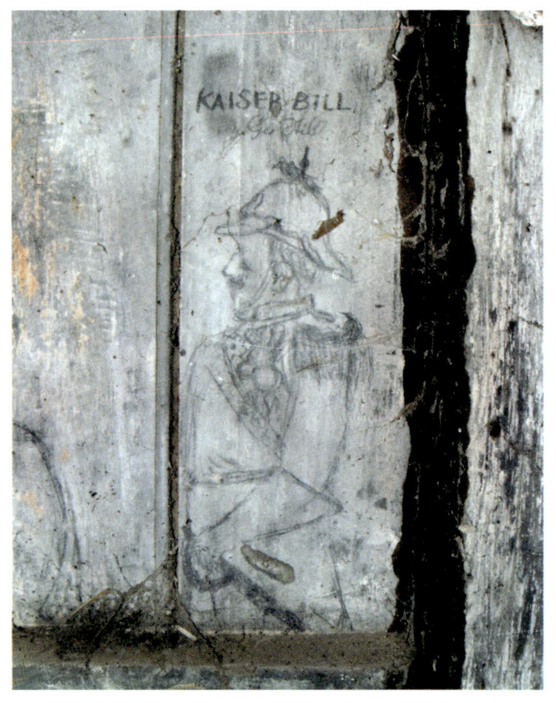
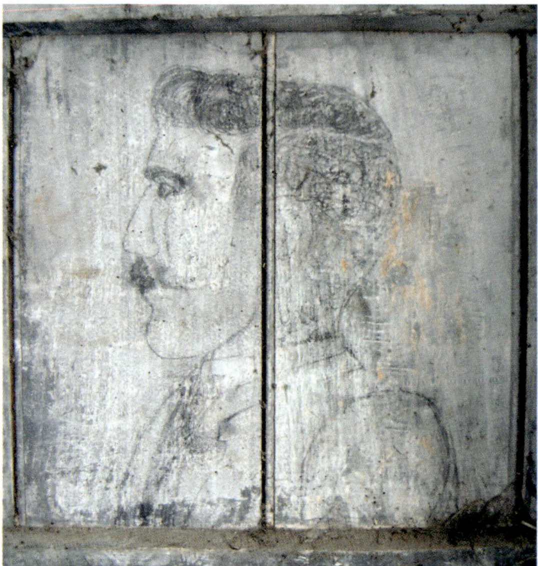

Wigmore Abbey, Herefordshire
Left: A rare surviving sketch from the First World War of Kaiser Bill (Wilhelm II) – it was probably drawn by British troops billeted at the farm
Right: Pencil sketch of a man's head
(© R J C Thomas)

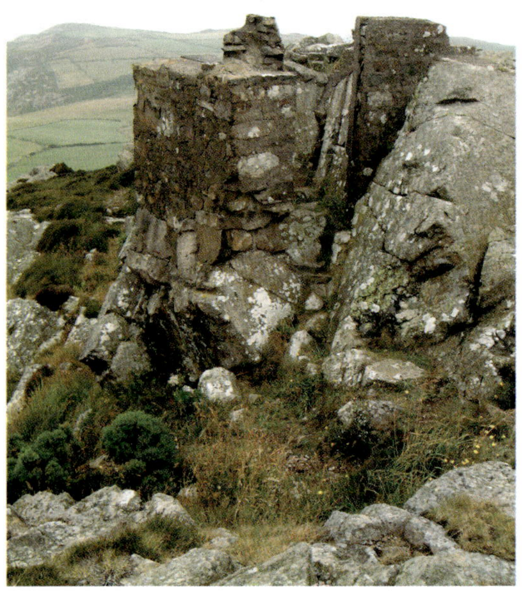
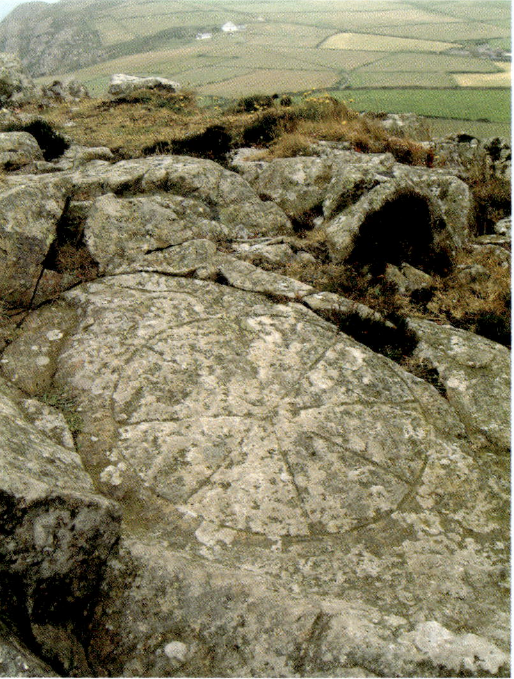

Garn Fawr, Fishguard, Pembrokeshire, First World War coast watcher's post
Left: Coast watcher's post
Right: Carved compass on rock
(© R J C Thomas)

Garn Fawr, Fishguard, Pembrokeshire, First World War coast watcher's post
Top: J J W Calderon Commander RN, D J W Edwardes Deputy CW RN 1914–15
Bottom: Builders J Thomas and Pritchard
(© R J C Thomas)

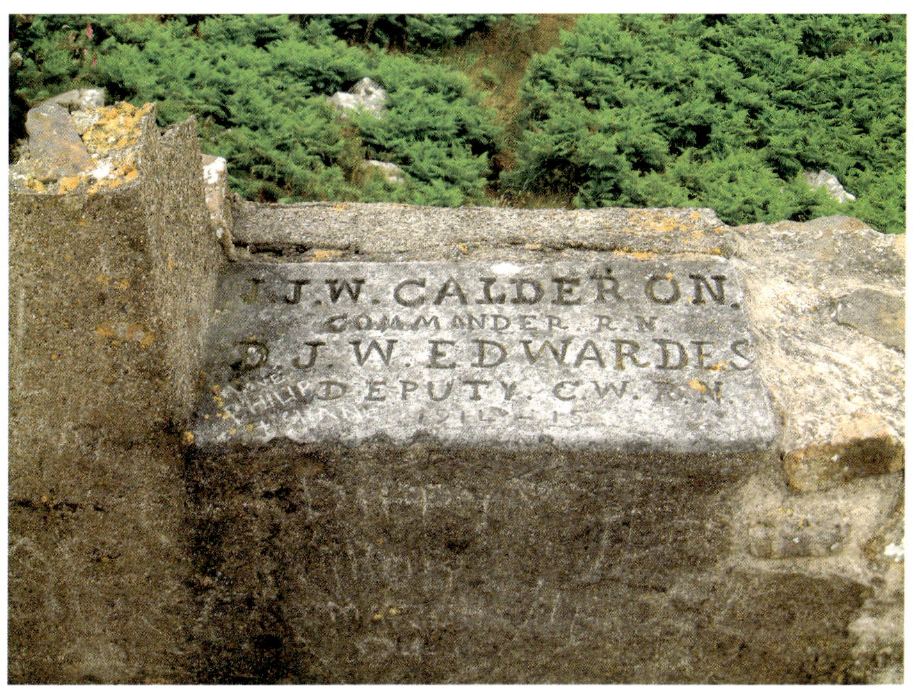

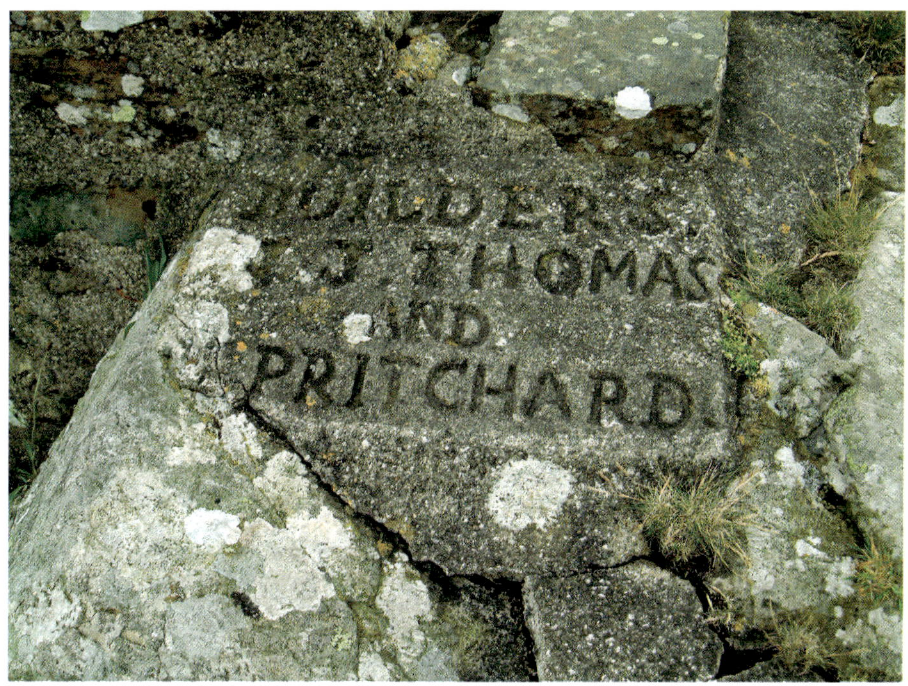

In Britain, there are few surviving examples of Great War soldiers' art in military buildings, and the graffiti of conscientious objectors at Richmond Castle (North Yorkshire) is a rare example of what may have been commonplace. This absence may be explained by the passage of time and subsequent reuse of structures; it may also be accounted for by the widespread use of prefabricated timber huts during the war, most of which no longer survive. Occupation of most camps was also generally transitory, during training or on route to one of the battle fronts. On the home front recognition of the relationship between productivity – not to mention health – and decent working conditions resulted in the common areas of newer armaments factories, such as canteens, being 'spruced up' through painting and often simple decoration. Some of the larger factories had their own theatres, where various forms of music hall show were performed by the workers. As part of their sets they might include elaborate back-drops probably painted by the more artistic amongst them.

Better known artwork from this conflict, but beyond the scope of this book, is the vast range of Trench Art (for more information see books by Jane Kimball 2004 and Nicholas Saunders 2002b). Some was produced by soldiers from spent war *matériel*, but it also includes commercially manufactured items produced as souvenirs for the troops and post-war battlefield tourists.

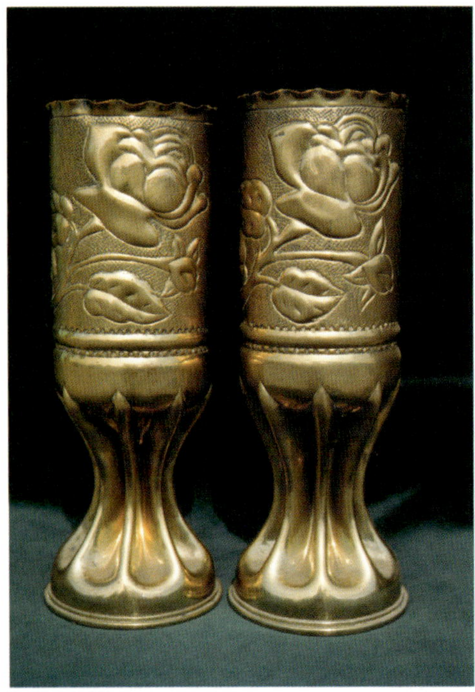

Two corseted artillery shell case vases with art nouveau decoration (© Nicholas J Saunders)

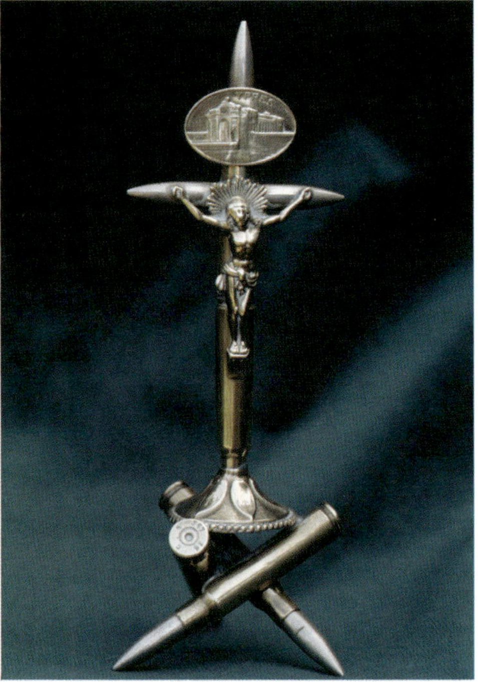

Bullet crucifix mounted on a tripod of three German Mauser rounds with memorial plaque attached showing the Menin gate, Ypres, and thus dating the piece to sometime after 1927 (© Nicholas J Saunders)

THE SECOND WORLD WAR

Troops on active service, or frontline aircrew, were generally freed from some of the minor regulations of soldiering. Either through attempts to adapt to local conditions or because of difficulties in supply lines, uniform regulations were also sometimes relaxed. Similarly, the painting of images on aircraft or vehicles, which would be forbidden during peace time was at least tolerated. One aspect of this greater freedom was the increasing use of symbols on the new engines of war, in particular aircraft and armoured vehicles, to identify national allegiances and lower unit formations. Crews also began to add their own emblems to individualise and identify standard and mass-produced machines. On campaign, men's lives not only depended on the reliable functioning of their vehicle; it also became their home. Images also took on a superstitious importance for aircrew, with rituals and good luck charms appearing as other means of coping with the repeated exposure to danger (Ward 1951, 287–9).

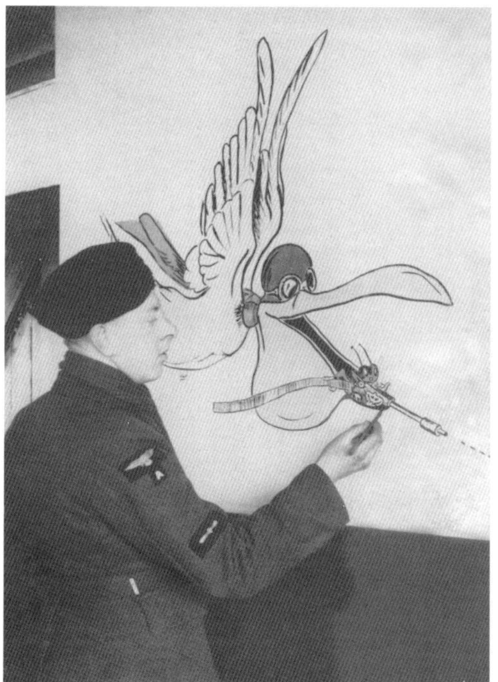 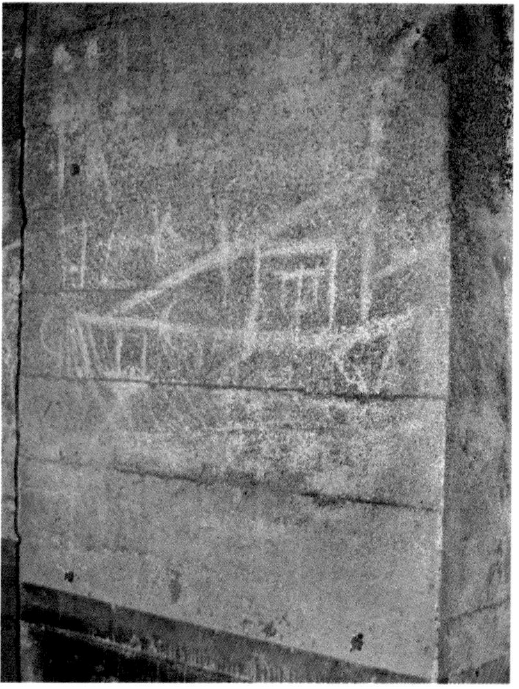

Left: **RAF Biggin Hill, Kent, 1943. Painting by leading Aircraftsman Harry Parnham in the Officer's Mess of 611 Squadron (© Harry Parnham via Aldon Ferguson)**
Right: **Craster, Northumberland Coastal Defence Chain Home Low radar station operations block, fishing smack scratched onto a wall (© R J C Thomas)**

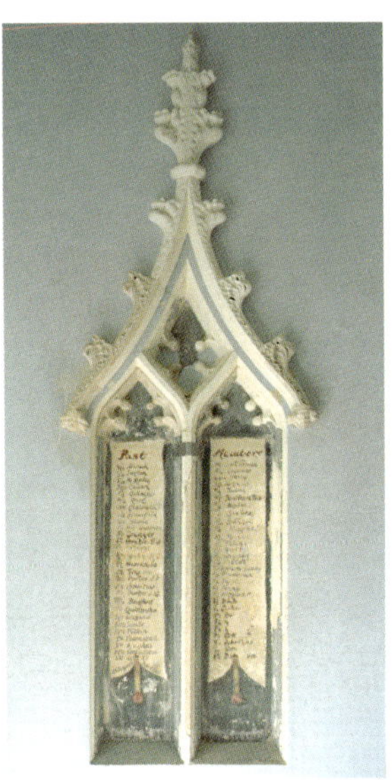

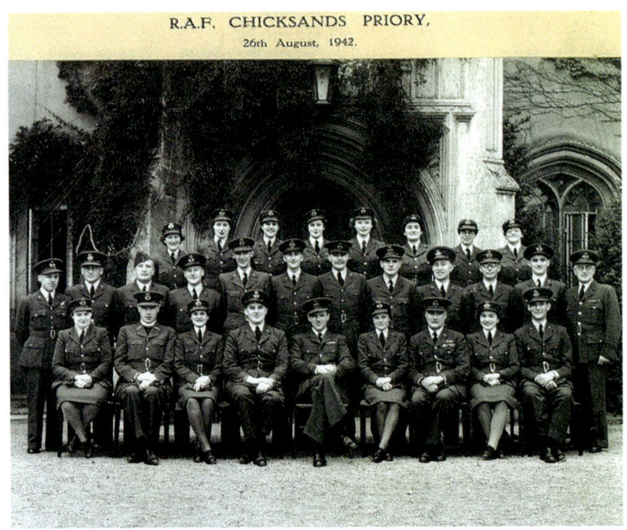

RAF Chicksands, Bedfordshire. *Above:* **During the Second World War Chicksands priory was used as a Y Station to intercept German wireless signals. A painted panel recording the names of wartime personnel was discovered during decorating work in 2005. Detail of the panel with names (AA0533454 © English Heritage)**
Below: **Wartime photograph showing some of the personnel whose names are recorded on the panel (© Crown copyright)**

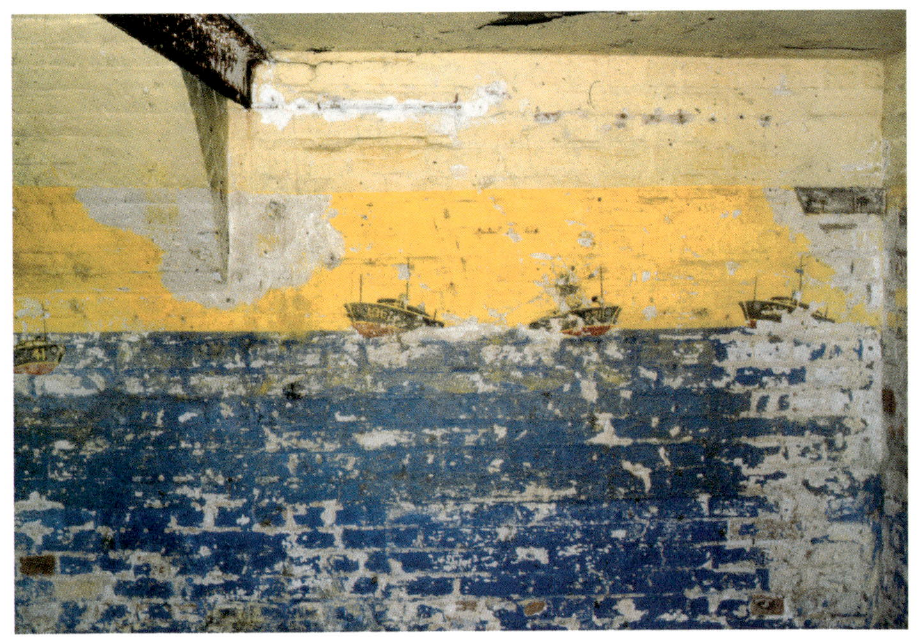

Newhaven Fort, East Sussex,
Air Sea Rescue Launches – 41, 106,
2711, and 2300
(© R J C Thomas)

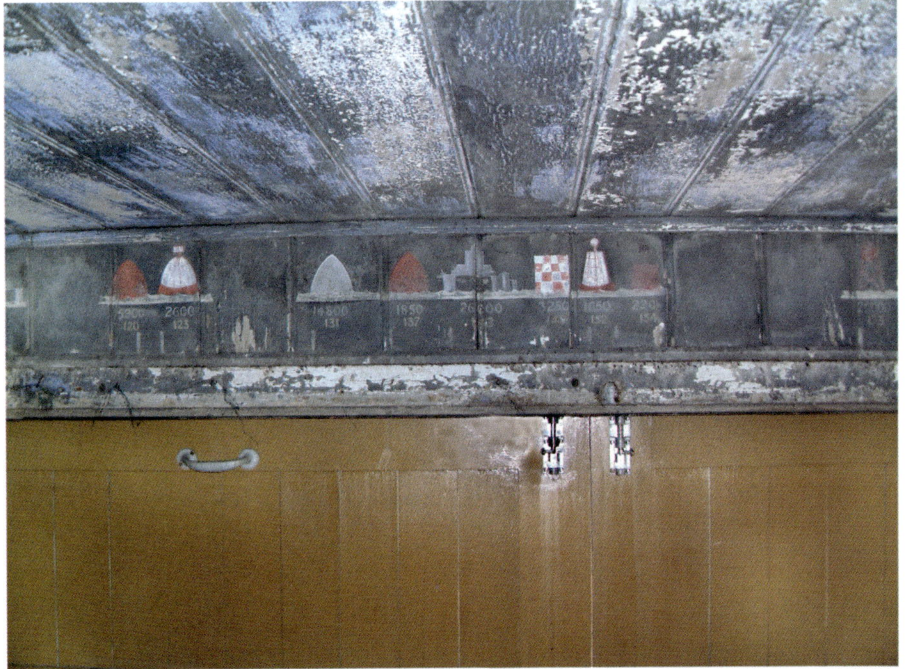

Landguard Fort, Suffolk
Battery Observation Post:
gunnery range and bearing marks –
range is shown above and bearing
beneath. The building in the
middle is Roughs Tower,
a Maunsell fort, an offshore
anti-aircraft battery
(© R J C Thomas)

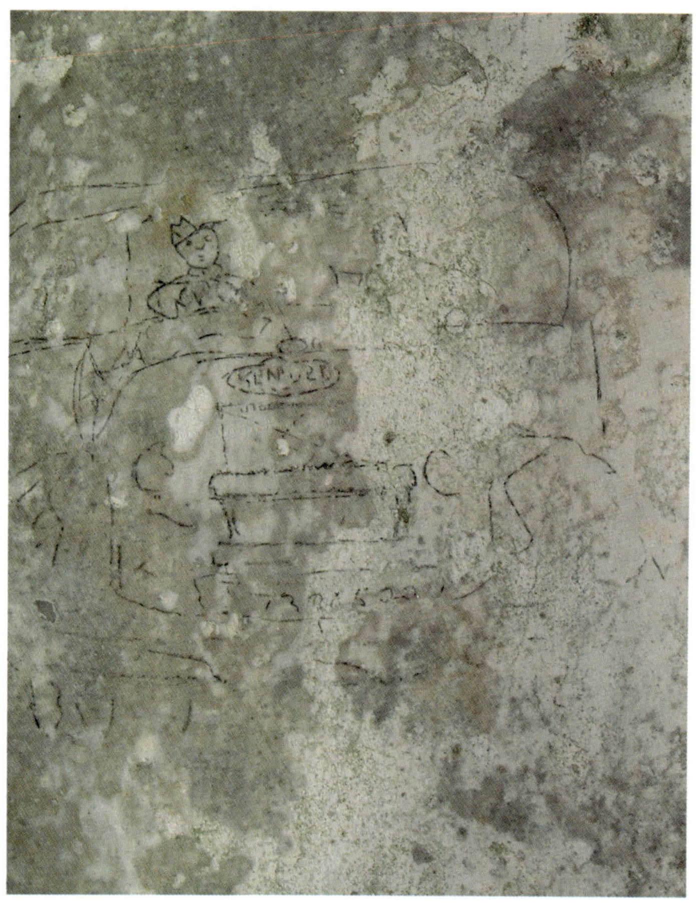

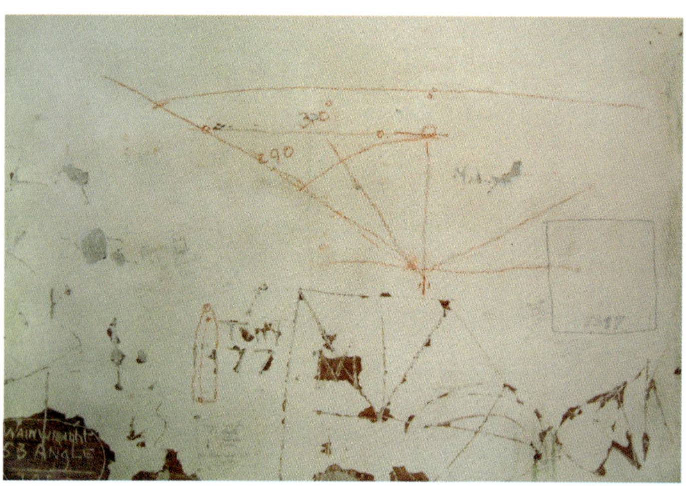

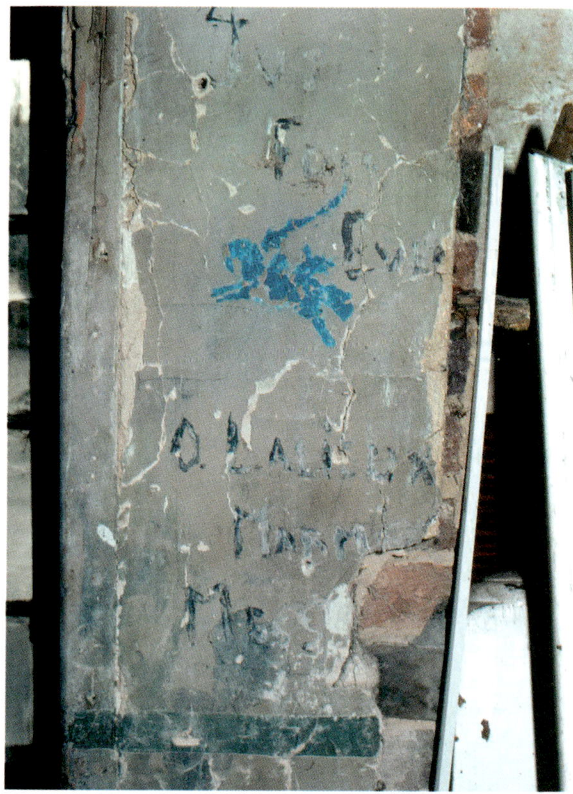

Fulbeck Hall, Lincolnshire
Pegasus badge of the Dutch airborne division, who acted as guides during the airborne assault on the bridges at Arnhem in September 1944

Chapel Bay Fort, Angle, Pembrokeshire
Top: Left – Casemate Shelter No 1, soldiers driving a truck, seen through whitewash
Bottom: Left – 12 pounder shell store, gunnery instruction probably Second World War
(© R J C Thomas)

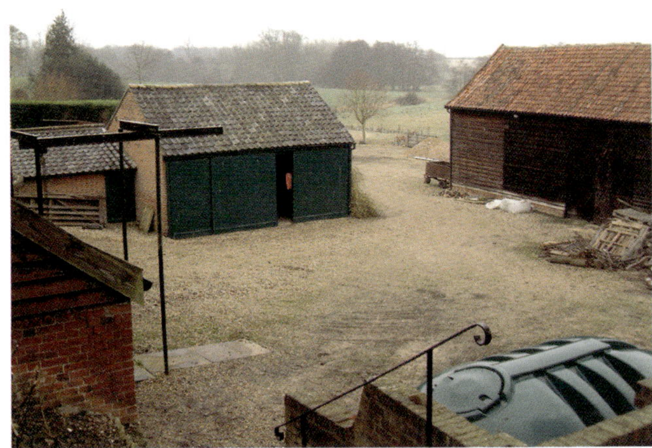

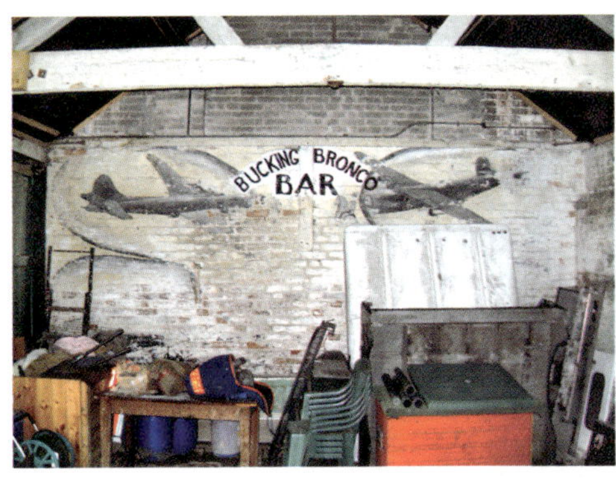

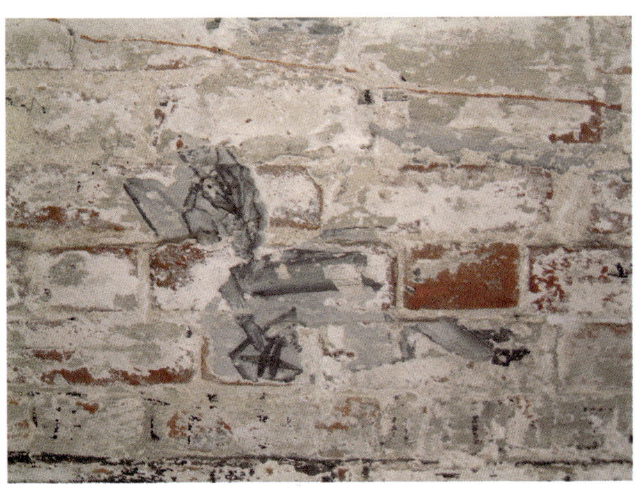

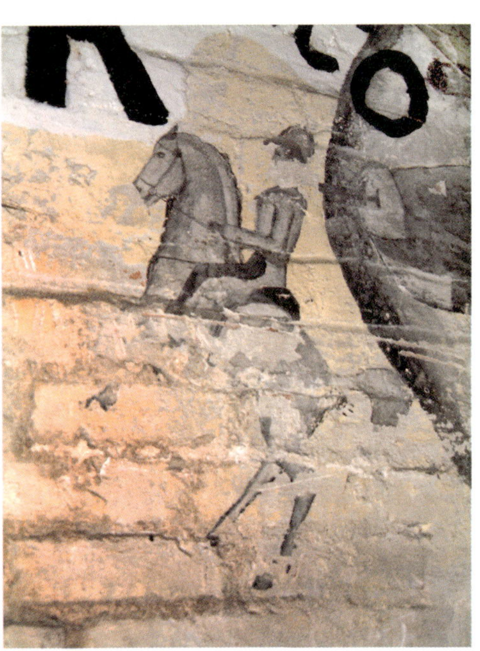

Ditchington Hall, Norfolk, USAAF officers' mess and sick quarters
Top: Left – **The farm yard view, the small building to the rear was used as a bar**
Top: Right – **South wall, 'Bucking Bronco Bar'**
Bottom: Left – **Airman dreaming**
Middle: Right – **Detail of rider**
Bottom: Right – **North wall, new or futuristic aircraft**
(© R J C Thomas)

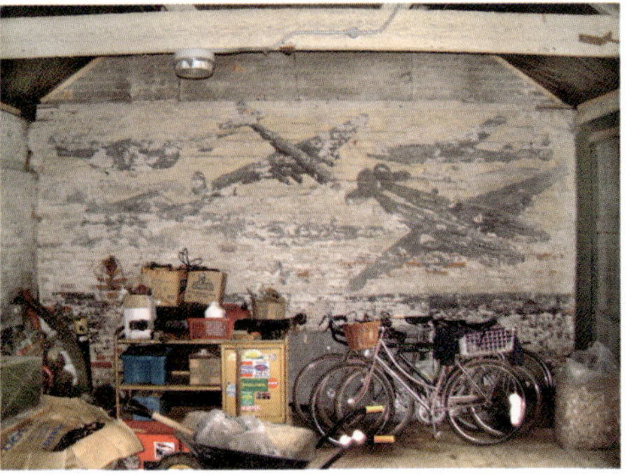

Photographs of the campaign in northern Europe after D-Day often show allied vehicles with names or other images. German vehicles were rarely similarly adorned, except perhaps for an unofficial unit badge, while on Soviet tanks contemporary photographs often depict patriotic slogans such as 'To the front for the rout of fascism' or 'We defend the conquests of October' crudely painted on their turrets.

A comparable official attitude appears to have been taken towards the application of murals to the walls of military buildings. In such a tightly regulated environment the walls were usually painted in gloss paint, but might be brightened by officially placed posters, often designed by influential artists of the day (Cantwell 1989), to deliver propaganda. During the war, officially sanctioned propaganda posters came to the fore amongst most of the combatant powers, which might be reinforced by slogans painted for example on factory walls. Murals are most commonly encountered in the many temporary airfields and camps that were built across the country. None of these establishments had a long military tradition and neither did most of their personnel who were volunteers or conscripts for the duration of the war.

Murals are commonly found in communal areas, such as canteens or institutes that might also be used for dances and other social functions. At Fowlmere (Cambridgeshire), a satellite airfield for RAF Duxford, a mural survives on the wall of a farm building. In most instances the painters of murals are unknown. However, at RAF Fowlmere it is known that the painting was executed by Robert Hofton, an Aircraftsman serving with 19 Squadron who was asked to decorate the barn for a Christmas party in 1940. It was originally painted using airfield paint and 100 octane aviation fuel. Over 50 years later, in 1993, he returned to repaint the image (*Cambridge Evening News* 1993, 1).

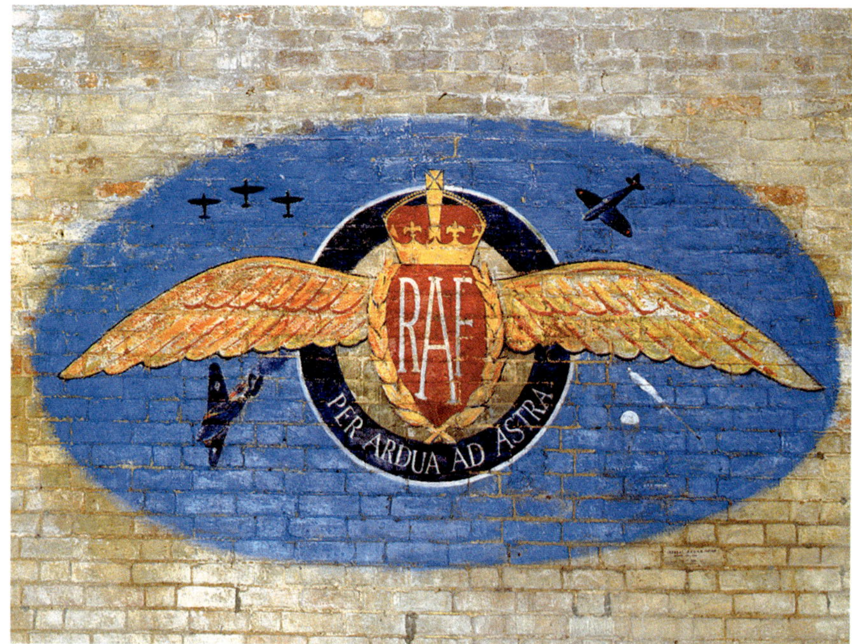

RAF Fowlmere, Cambridgeshire. Mural painted by Aircraftsman Robert Hofton in a farm building in preparation for a Christmas party in 1940. At the time Hofton was serving with 19 Squadron which during 1940 had distinguished itself during the withdrawal of the British Expeditionary Force from Dunkirk and during the Battle of Britain (© English Heritage AA051483)

THE COLD WAR

In Britain, following the end of the Second World War and with the return to peace time soldiering and spit and polish standards, there appears to have been an absence of war art within military establishments. The images from the Second World War survived because they were often located in temporary wartime bases that were abandoned in the late 1940s. During the 1950s, with the return of United States forces to counter the Soviet threat, there is some contemporary photographic evidence for

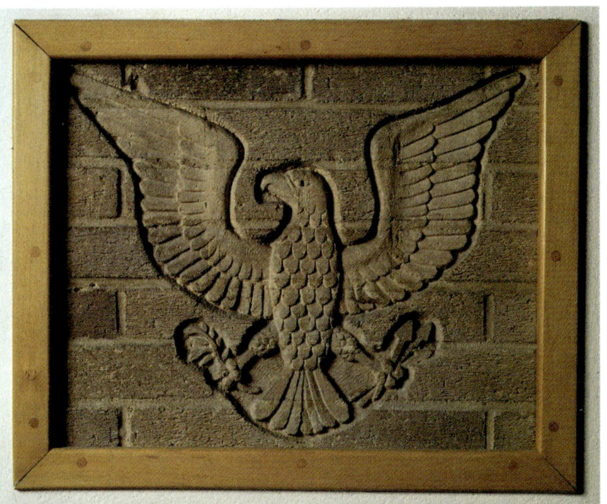

RAF Upper Heyford, Oxfordshire, club, brick reliefs probably dating to the 1950s
Top: **United States eagle (AA541122)**
Bottom: Left **– John Bull (AA054123)**
Bottom: Right **– Uncle Sam (AA054124)**
(© English Heritage)

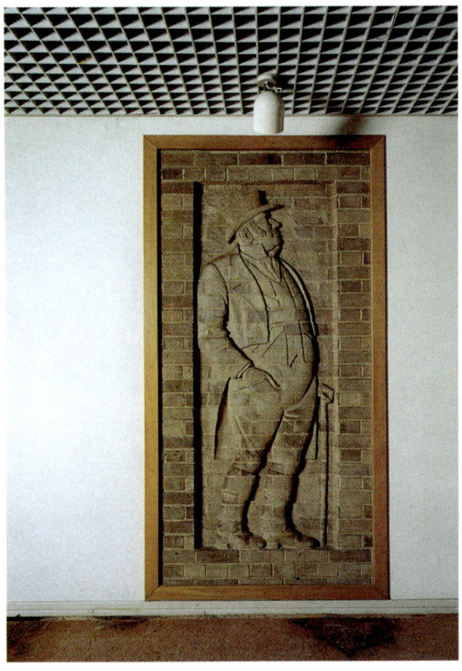

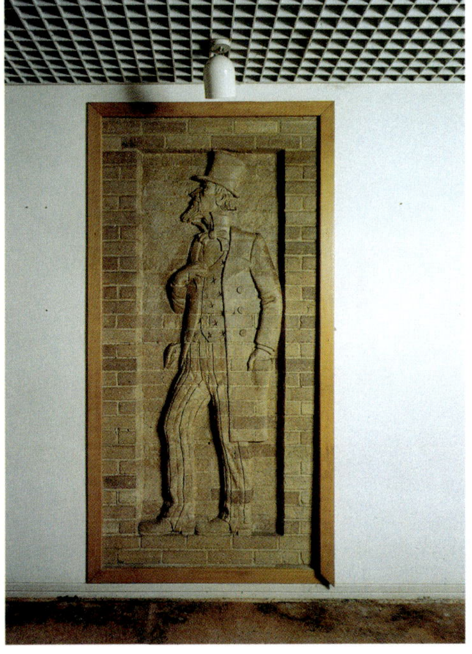

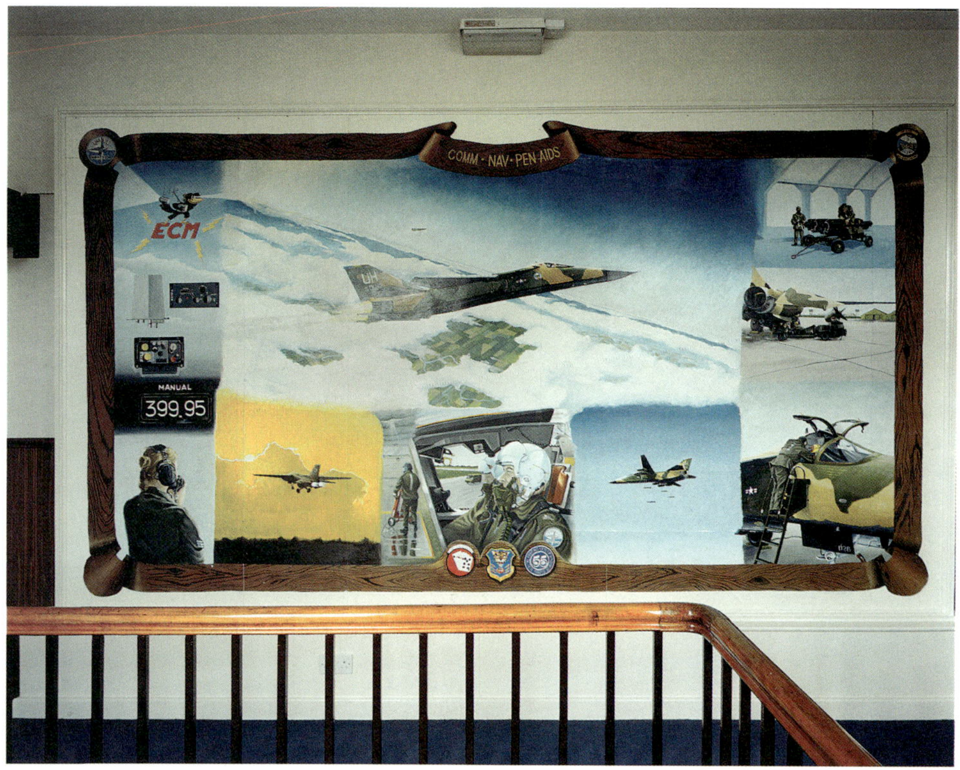

RAF Upper Heyford, Oxfordshire, former Station Offices (52), F-111 mural by Kenneth B Gore (1978–79), moved from Building 300 (AA051444 © English Heritage)

the reappearance of war art; however, little is known to survive from this era. Instead, the greatest survival of war art in Britain is associated with the Unites States Air Force, dating from the 1980s and early 1990s. The great variety of images that are encountered reflects both a visually-aware generation and a culture where street art and graffiti had become a part of everyday life. Some war art on American bases was officially encouraged to reinforce the *esprit de corps*, while other work was at least condoned.

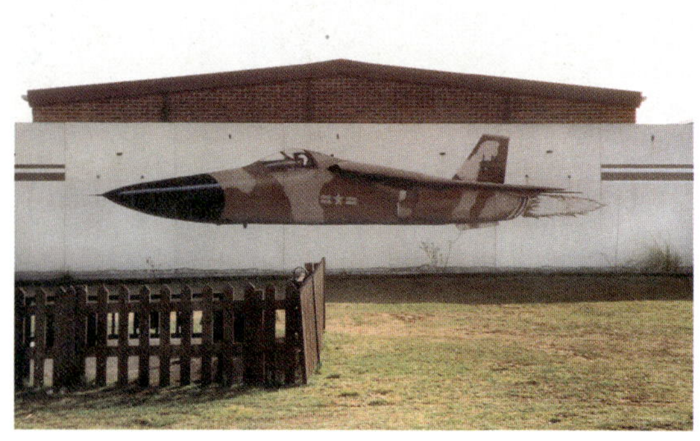

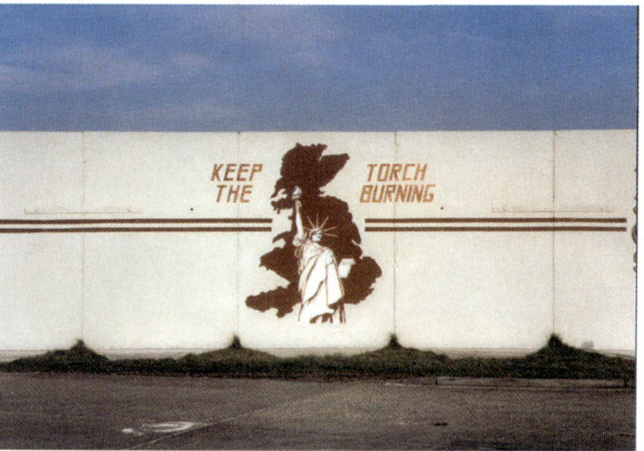

RAF Lakenheath, Suffolk, home of the USAF's 48th Fight Wing 'Liberty Wing'
Left: F111 on blast wall
Right: Keep the torch burning
(© Raymond Towler)

RAF Lakenheath, Suffolk, home of the USAF's 48th Fight Wing 'Liberty Wing'
Top: Left – The Liberty Club (© R J C Thomas)
Top: Right – Proud of Lakenheath (© Raymond Towler)
Middle: Spread the word prevent FOD (Foreign Object Damage) (© Raymond Towler)

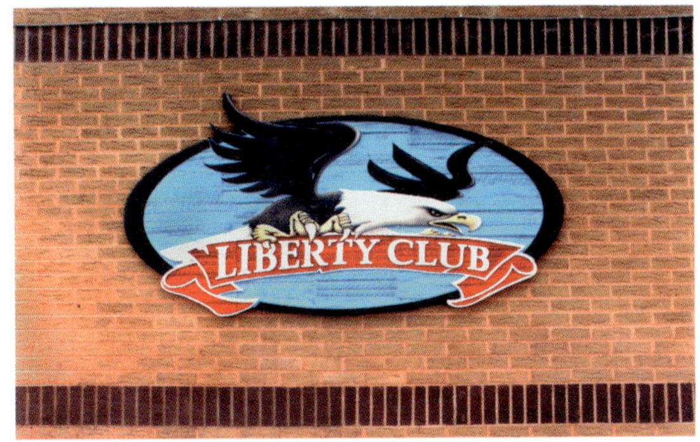

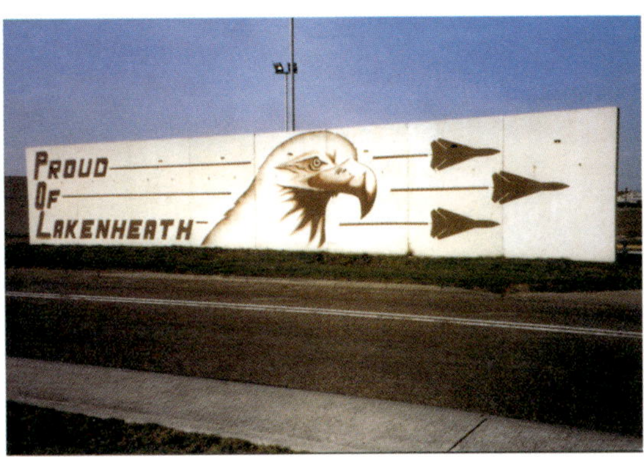

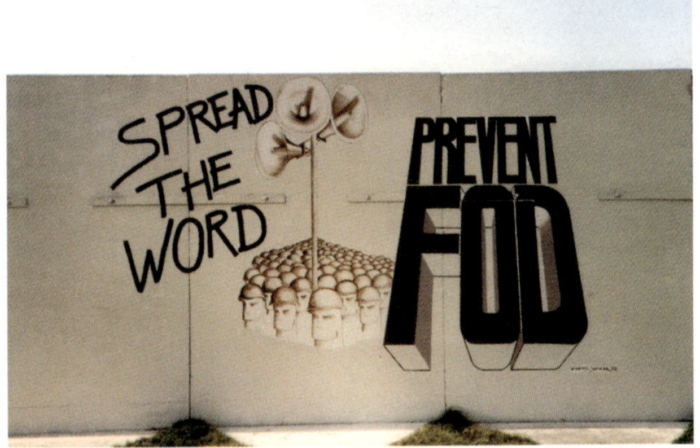

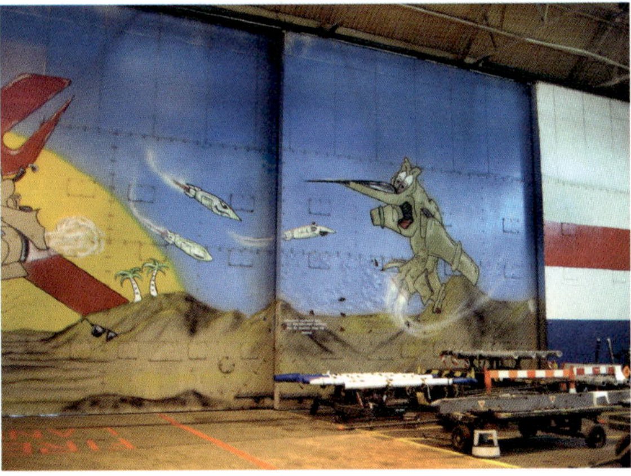

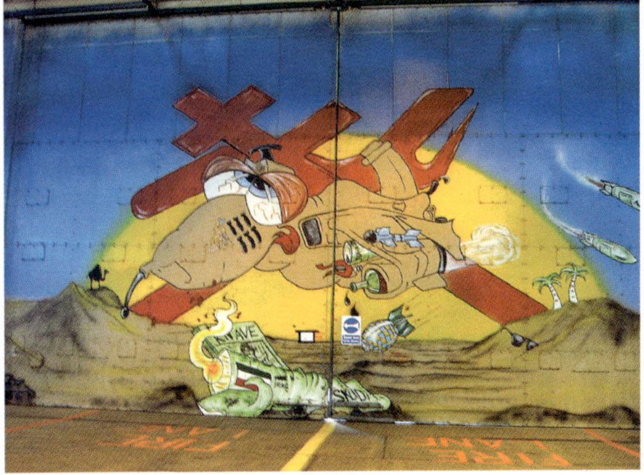

RAF Coltishall, Norfolk, spray paint artwork on hangar doors dating from the first Gulf War 1991
Left: Jaguar being attacked by Iraqi missiles (© Aldon Ferguson)
Right: Tired Jaguar, to the rear is cross of Lorraine, the badge of No.41 Squadron (© Aldon Ferguson)

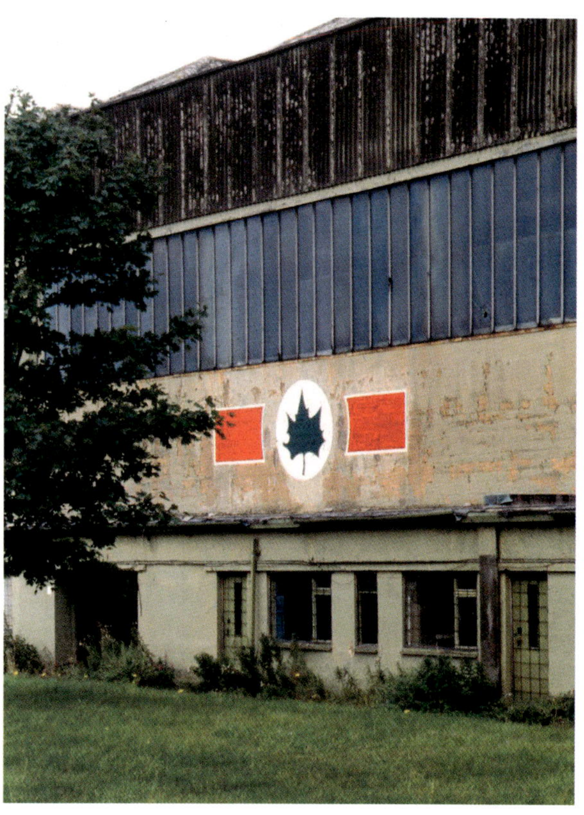

RAF Binbrook, Lincolnshire,
former Lightning interceptor base
Top: Maple leaf emblem
of 5 Squadron
Bottom: English Electric
Lightning of the Lightning Training Flight
(© R J C Thomas)

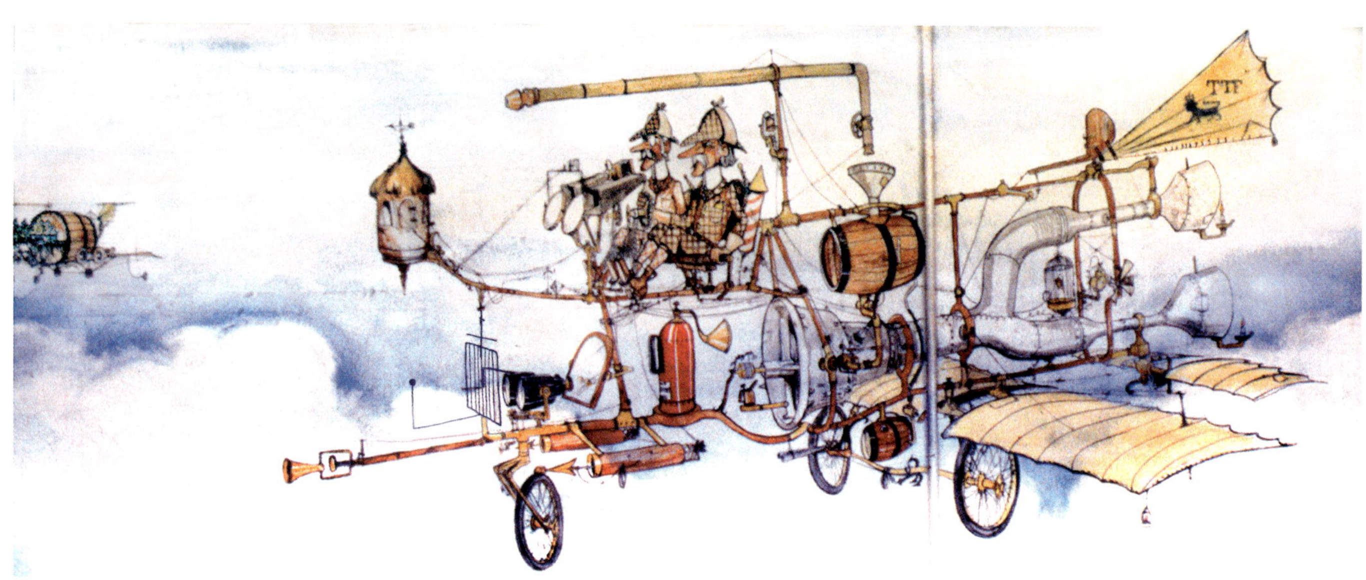

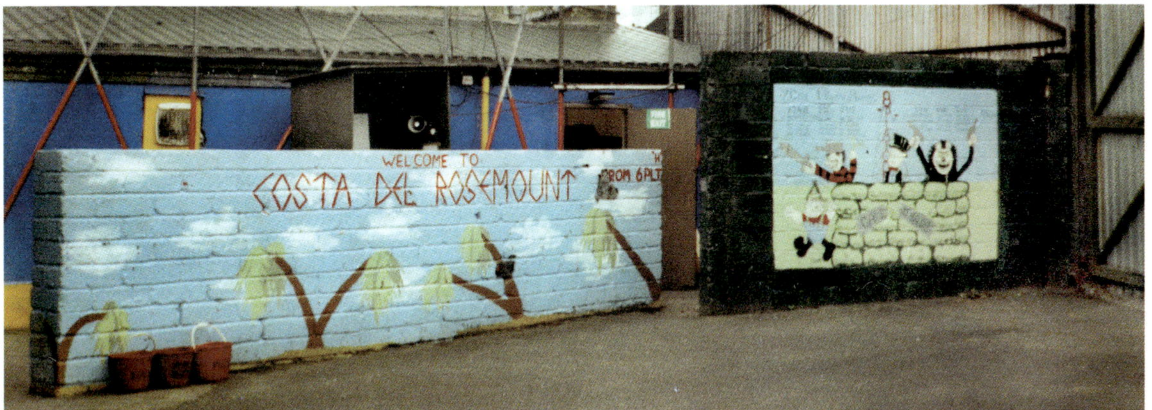

Top: **Londonderry, murals by British troops inside the yard of the Rosemount police station**
Bottom: **Cowabunga, mural by troops of the Royal Hampshire Regiment, Northern Ireland**
(© Ian Evans)

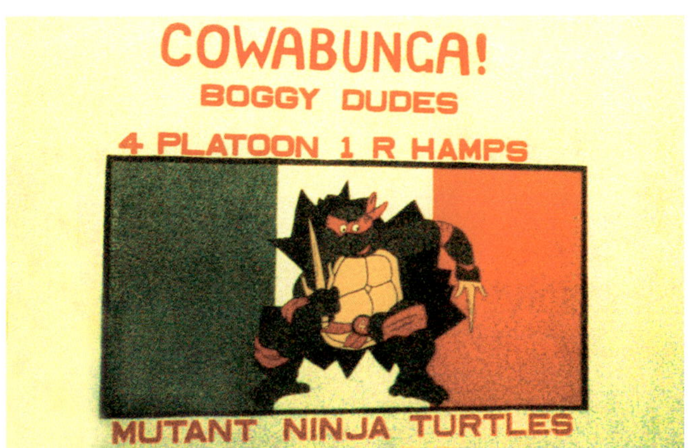

Murals of this date are also found on some RAF bases, but they tend to be restricted to unit emblems within hangers or other technical buildings. There are also examples in Northern Ireland.

PROJECT WARRIOR AND THE 1980s

It is acknowledged that it is a soldier's loyalty to immediate comrades that will sustain him or her in the heat of battle, rather than higher political ideals. Faithfulness is reinforced by training, and the teaching of history and heritage reflected through the heraldry of war, links an individual to the heroic deeds of past members of the unit.

In the late 1970s, in the United States Air Force, it was recognised that due to many formations simply being designated a number, and also because of the constant movement of personnel, that there was poor emotional bonding between service personnel and their unit. Both these factors coupled with the low morale in the services after the Vietnam War were leading to poor group cohesion, which could potentially have devastating results in combat. This period was also marked by a decline in relations with the Soviet Union and a massive increase in defence spending. Attempts to address the problem of morale were initiated under *Project Warrior,* one strand of which was to use history and heritage to foster *esprit de corps.* This was achieved by taught courses, the creation of base history rooms and the reintroduction of the iconic wartime A2 leather flying jacket for frontline personnel (Glines 1993, 60–5). These jackets were famously decorated with unit patches and mottoes, often corresponding with those on the sides of aircraft.

In the past, during wartime the authorities had often turned a blind eye to aircraft nose art only insisting that it should be removed when aircraft returned to their peace time bases; however, in 1970 during the Vietnam War individual aircraft markings were outlawed. This policy was reversed during the 1980s, when as part of *Project Warrior,* nose art was officially encouraged, Strategic Air Command naming their programme *Glossy Eagle.* The other side of official encouragement was the exertion of greater control, and a formal procedure was put in place to approve images; nudes and tasteless designs were forbidden (Ethell and Simonsen 1991, 173). It is in this context that many images were also applied to buildings.

In many situations murals arose from a group's desire to liven up uniformly decorated and furnished living areas and to reinforce their presence within a space. In February 1979, an air force newspaper, *The Vanguard,* reported that at RAF Upper Heyford a section of the 20th Munitions Maintenance Squadron had brightened up one of the dormitories with a wall-sized version of their unit patch, the design painted by AIC Randolph T Hinkle. Around the mural was written 'Home of the 20th Mun Maint Sq'. Later in accommodation block Building 485, an inter-war barracks, a mural in a common room identified it as the accommodation for the 20th Component Repair Squadron. On the first floor a pair of theatre masks and a quote in Italian, translating approximately as 'abandon hope all ye who enter here', the inscription at the entrance to hell as described Dante's *The Divine Comedy,* defined one of the living sections. In this particular building this section was uniquely decorated with murals in corridors and bedrooms, subjects

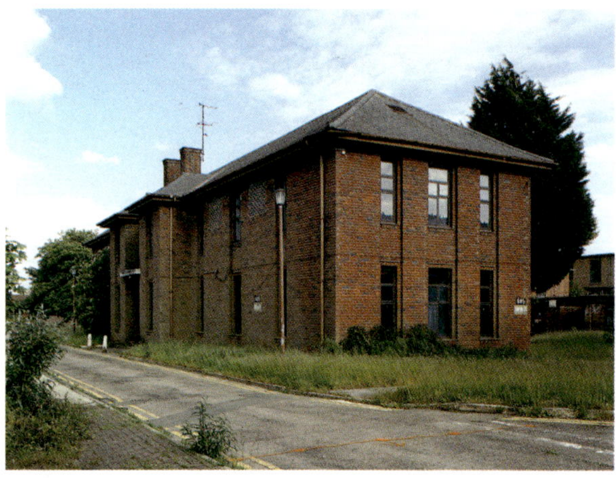

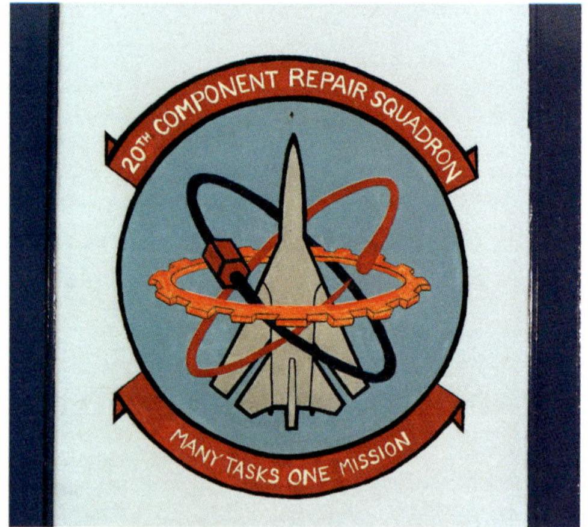

RAF Upper Heyford, Oxfordshire, Dormitory 485
Left: **Dormitory 485, 1920s barrack building, internally the original large open rooms have been divided into smaller single person bedrooms, externally some of the original openings have been blocked and new windows inserted (AA054119 © English Heritage)**
Right: **East side ground floor common room, 20th CRS (Component Repair Squadron) Many Tasks One Mission (AA051461 © English Heritage)**

RAF Upper Heyford, Oxfordshire, Dormitory 485
Top: Left – Entrance to west side first floor corridor, Italian quote from Dante's Inferno (AA051460)
Top: Right – West side first floor corridor, Judge Dredd (AA051464)
Middle: Left – West side first floor corridor, hatted Raven on Electronic Counter Measures pod 'Have pod will travel', Ed Wildner 1990 (AA051459)
Bottom: Left – West side first floor corridor, Doo Dah Man by Ed Wildner (AA051458)
Bottom: Right – West side first floor, bedroom, 'Always on Frequency Never a Random Jam' by Bill Campbell (AA051463)
(© English Heritage)

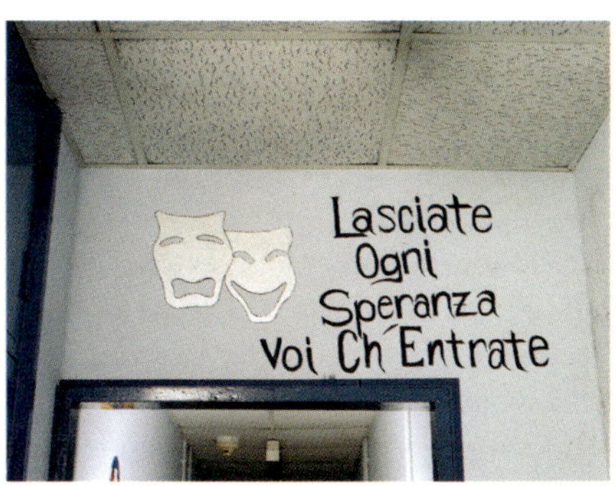

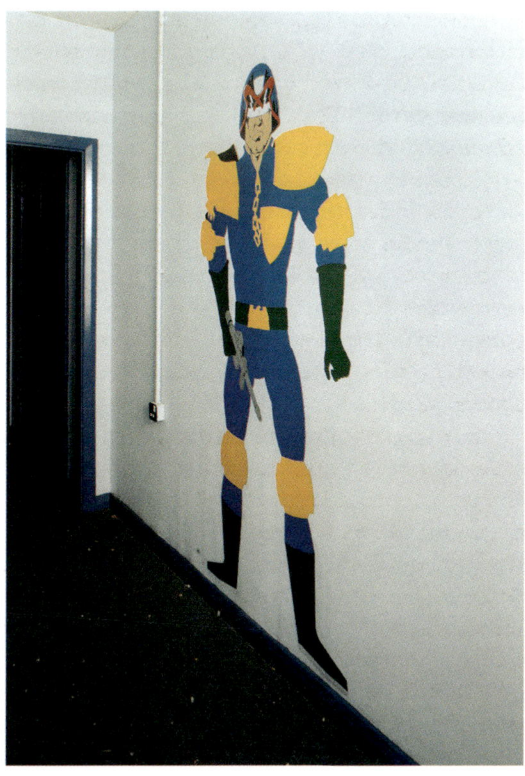

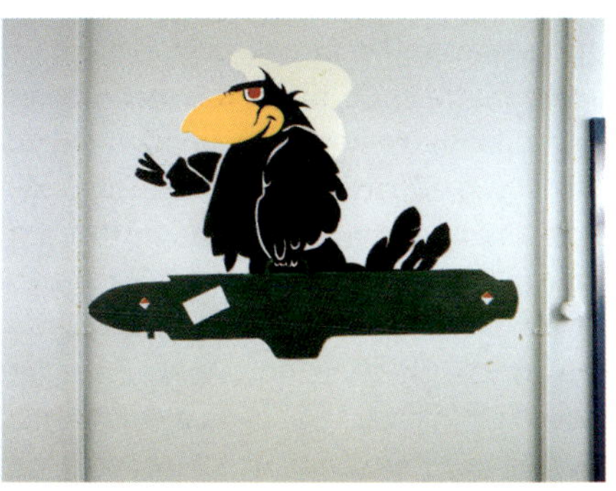

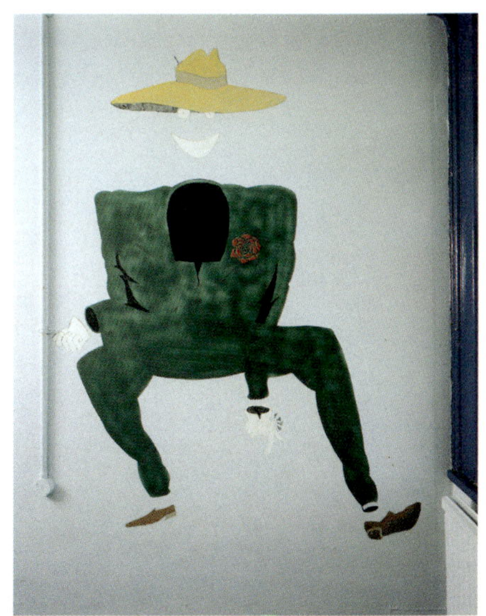

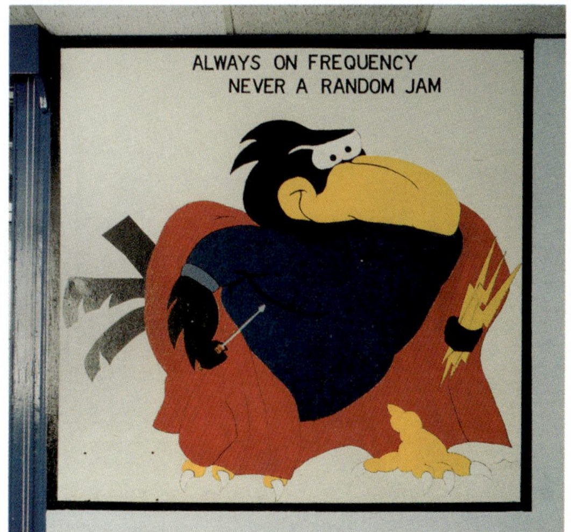

including *Judge Dredd*, cartoon Ravens, and the Doo Dah Man. An unfinished drawing of a Raven on an Electronic Counter Measure pod confirms the link between this living area and the Avionics Centre, Building 299, where most of this section worked. Other accommodation blocks in this complex were similarly decorated in the late 1980s and early 1990s, their accomplishment and topics indicative of the artists' cultural, educational and social backgrounds.

In the ammunition inspection building at RAF Bentwaters (Suffolk) there were large blank walls that were painted during airmen's spare time. The subjects of the paintings directly reflected this section's functions; some were designs on the floor and walls simply incorporating the word 'ammo'. Others were more elaborate and included a realistic portrayal of the unit's main aircraft type: an A-10 Thunderbolt nicknamed the Warthog. Another showed death in a contemporary olive drab uniform leaning on a conventional bomb while holding a large calibre 30 mm round used by the A-10's Gatling gun. On another wall a cartoon figure of a warthog is dressed as an ammunition inspector. This painting reveals considerable details about the working practices of the section and codes particular to that team. The figure holds an inspection stamp, adorned with a skull and feathers to make it easily distinguishable in the lockbox where they were stored. This decoration is so distinctive that it was probably identifiable to a known individual; below the AMMO troops' group identity is affirmed with their 'tag': IYAAYAS ('If you ain't AMMO you ain't shit'). The black painted corners of the ammunition box indicates that it is one that has been inspected, being one of the main functional activities within this room where the image appears. A similar warthog ammunition inspector can be seen a few miles away at the adjacent airfield of RAF Woodbridge, but this example is wearing a camouflaged jacket, possibly indicative of the introduction of a different style of uniform and date. One former United States airman posted to the bomb stores at RAF Bentwaters during the 1980s commented that the stories surrounding the paintings there were 'really kind of mundane', reflecting the fact that artwork could just liven up the monotony of military life, perhaps also satisfying a basic human need to personalise such undistinguished buildings.

In 1988, two of the six A-10 Thunderbolt squadrons based at Bentwaters and Woodbridge were transferred to RAF Alconbury (Cambridgeshire). In a former Second World War corrugated-iron Nissen

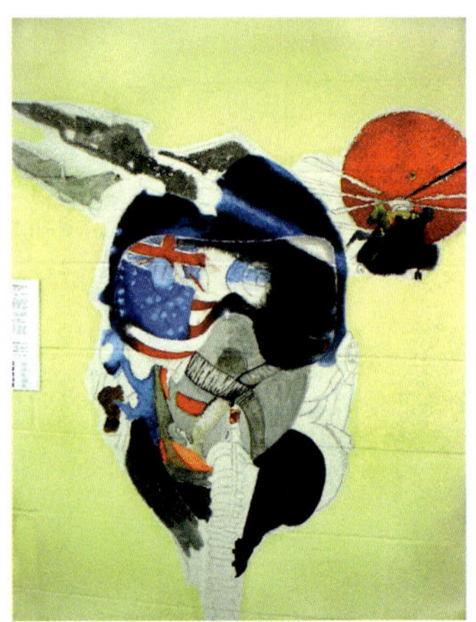
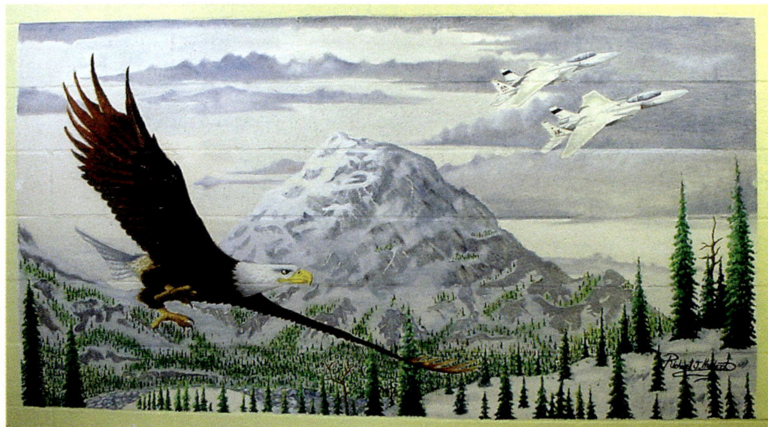

RAF Bentwaters, Suffolk, squadron office
Left: **Pilot's helmet (© Alistair Graham-Kerr)**
Right: **Painting of bald eagle and F15 'Eagles' by Robert J Herberd (AA054191 © English Heritage)**

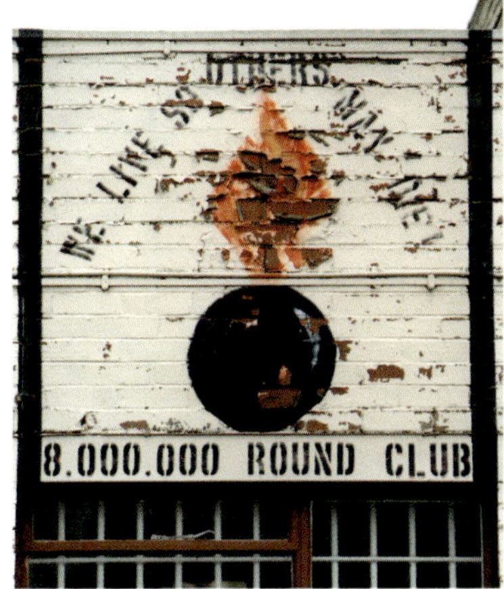

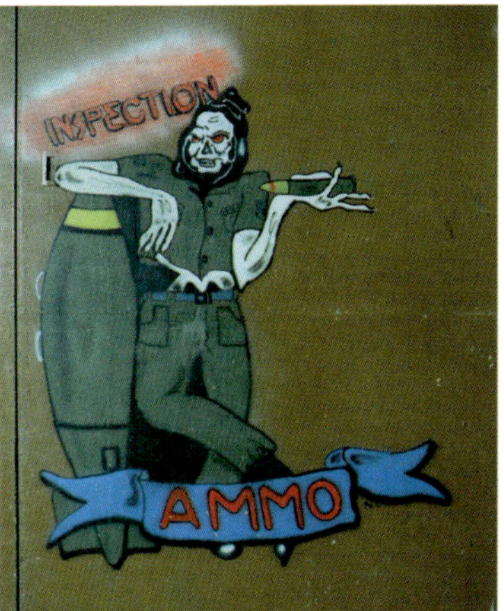

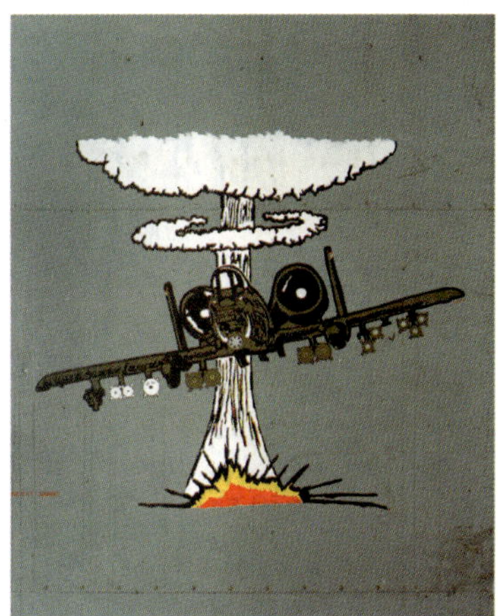

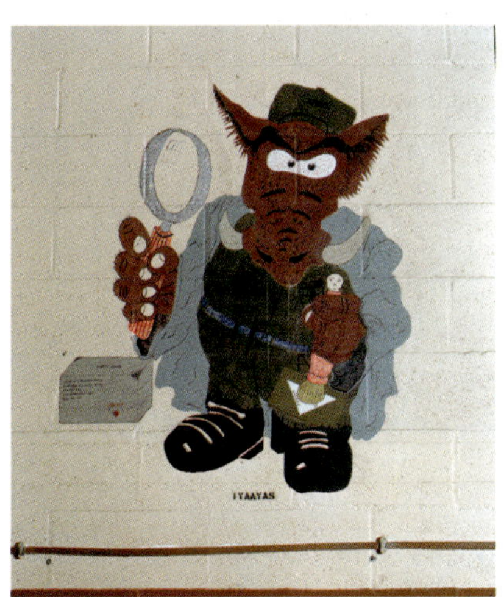

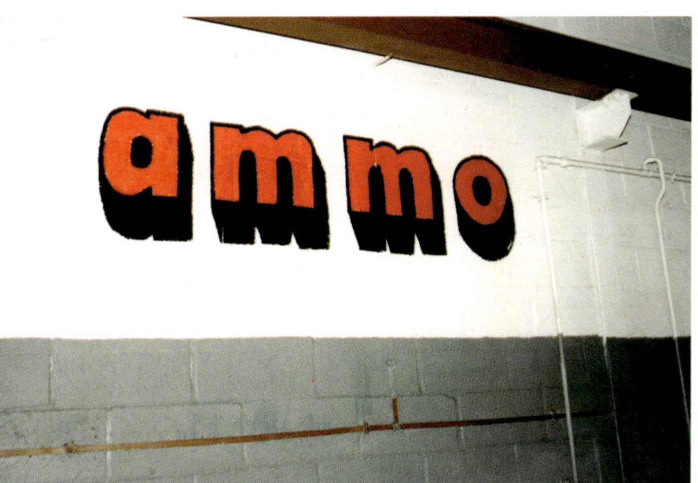

RAF Bentwaters, Suffolk, Weapons Inspection Building 437, 1980s artwork
Top: Left – 'We live so that others may die!' on the exterior wall (**AA021677** © **English Heritage**)
Top: Middle – 'Death' in a contemporary olive green uniform holding a large calibre cannon round, dated 1988 (**AA021681** © **English Heritage**)
Top: Right – Fairchild A-10 Thunderbolt, nicknamed the 'Warthog', signed by Poole 1989–91 (**AA021678** © **English Heritage**)
Bottom: Left – Warthog inspecting ammunition (**AA021680** © **English Heritage**)
Bottom: Right – Ammo (© **W D Cocroft**)

hut the pilots' mess of the 511th Tactical Fighter Wing 'The Vultures' was fitted out internally to resemble a half-timbered pub. The work of attaching mock beams to the walls and bar was probably carried out by members of the mess, whose names or nicknames are recorded on board in the hut. The image of the warthog to represent the A-10 was also common to their pilots and on one wall is a large marker pen

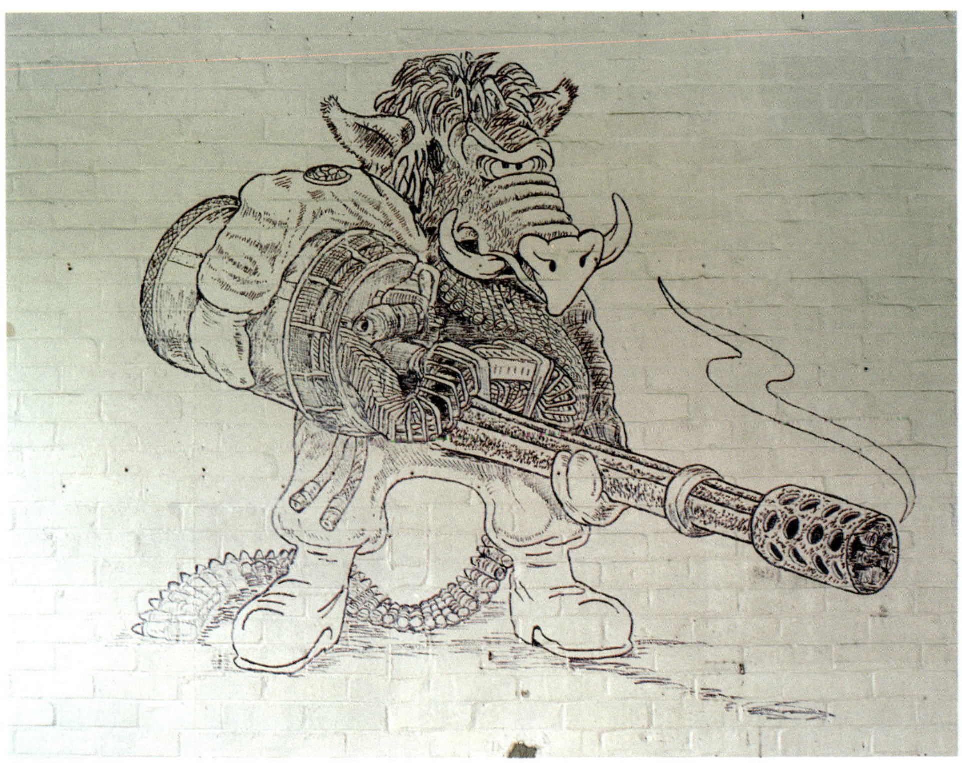

RAF Alconbury, Cambridgeshire, felt pen mural in the mess of 511th Tactical Fighter Squadron 'The Vultures'; this unit was equipped with A-10 aircraft nicknamed 'Warthogs' (AA023744 © English Heritage)

cartoon of a warthog holding a Gatling gun. Elsewhere on the base, in the munitions storage area under the control of the ammo troops, another warthog is depicted carrying a Gatling gun and a bomb.

The individualisation of aircraft through the use of nose art and naming had a beneficial effect on the ground crews' identification with and pride in the aircraft they were responsible for. During the 1980s, in USAF's Strategic Air Command, it was the ground crew, through their crew chief, who submitted the designs for nose art for approval (Ethell and Simonsen 1991, 179). The mechanism for selecting the nose art for the RF-4C McDonnell Phantom aircraft of the 10th Tactical Reconnaissance Wing aircraft at RAF Alconbury is unclear, although the ground crews' identification with the aircraft was reinforced by name plates attached to the Hardened Aircraft Shelters' doors, where the aircraft's nose art was often reproduced along with the name of the crew chief in charge of its maintenance. Subsequent to the departure of the A-10s in 1992, the base was occupied by the 39th Special Operations Wing transferred from RAF Woodbridge. It declared its possession of the airfield by the application of a large mural of a specially modified Lockheed MC-130P Hercules aircraft operated by the 352nd Special Operations Group. Not to be outdone, on the other side of the airfield the crews of the 17th Reconnaissance Wing, who maintained the high altitude TR-1A reconnaissance 'Dragon Lady' aircraft, incorporated a dragon design into a large mural in their refuelling building.

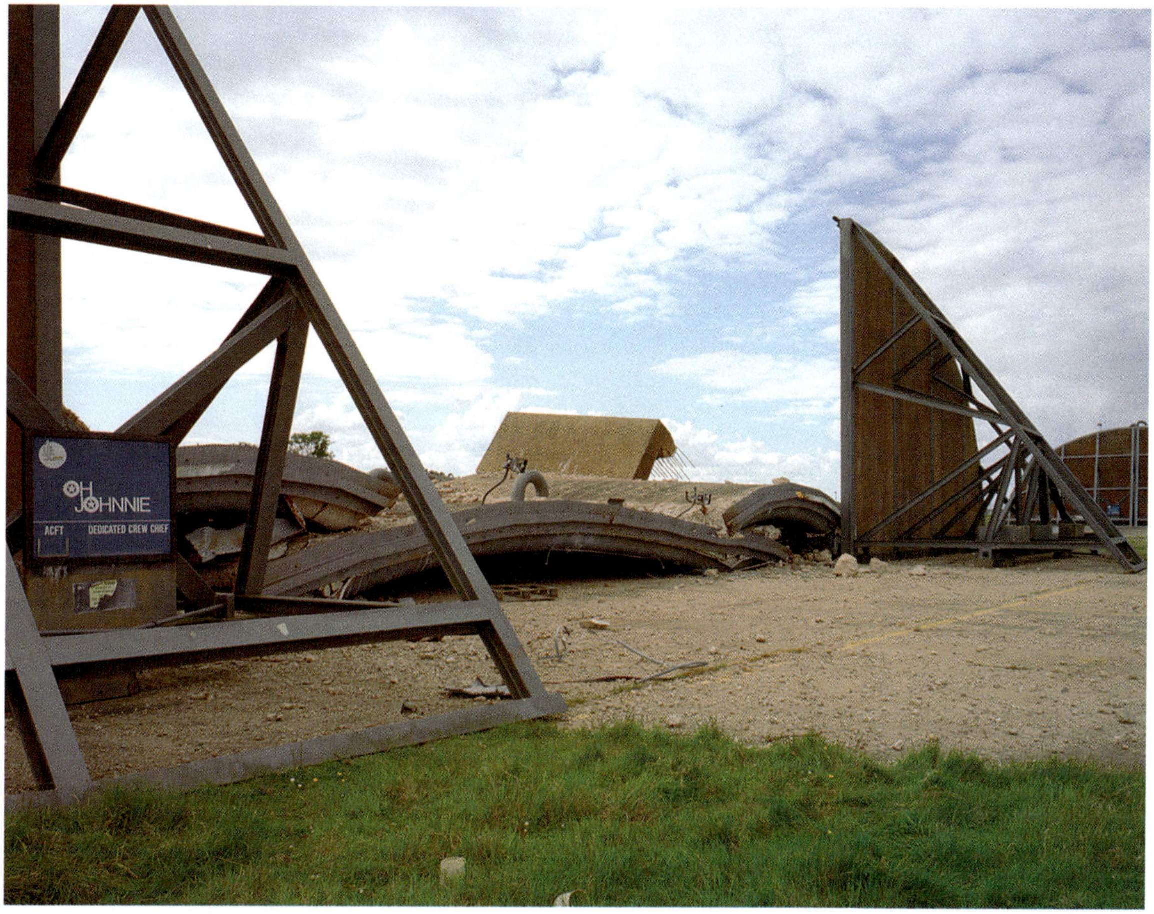

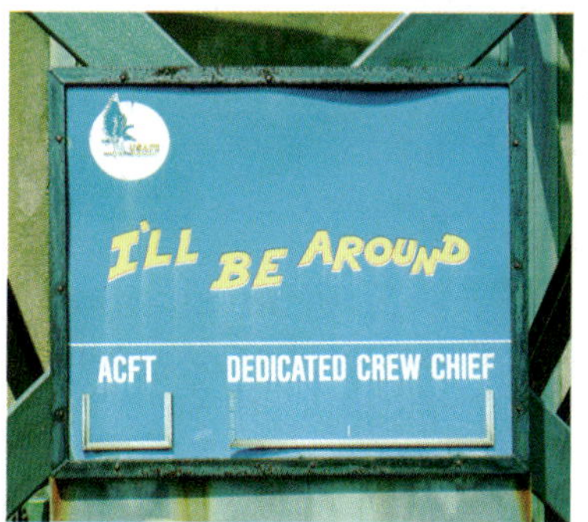

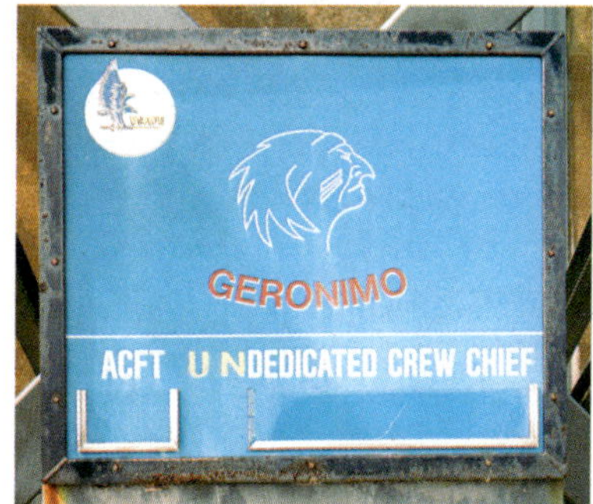

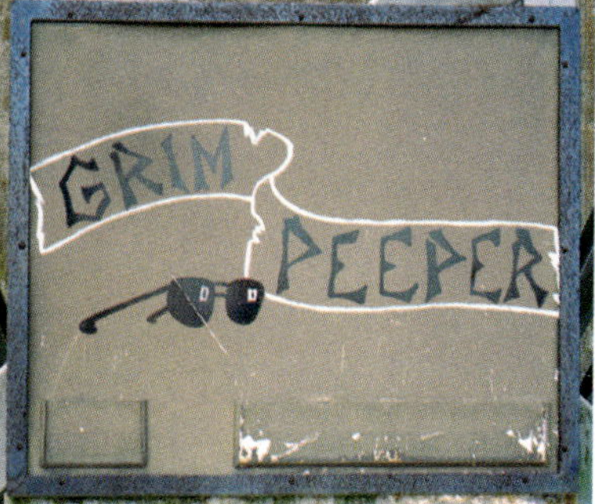

RAF Alconbury, Cambridgeshire, Crew boards on Hardened Aircraft Shelter doors (© English Heritage)
Top: 'Oh Johnnie' (AA023759)
Left: 'I'll be around' (AA023779)
Middle: 'Geronimo' (AA023780)
Right: 'Grim Peeper' (AA023781)

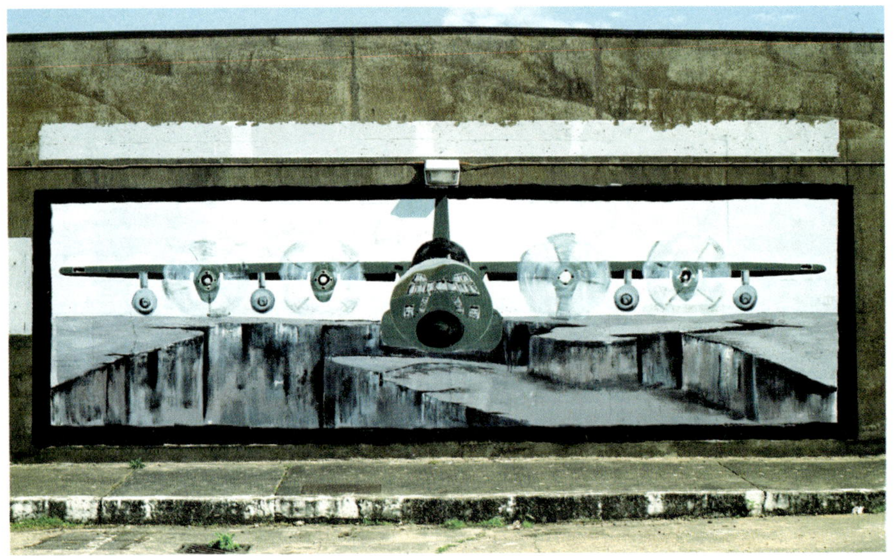

RAF Alconbury, Cambridgeshire, MC 130 H Combat Talon I of the 7th Special Operations Squadron, applied during the unit's occupation of the base 1992–94 (AA023755 © English Heritage)

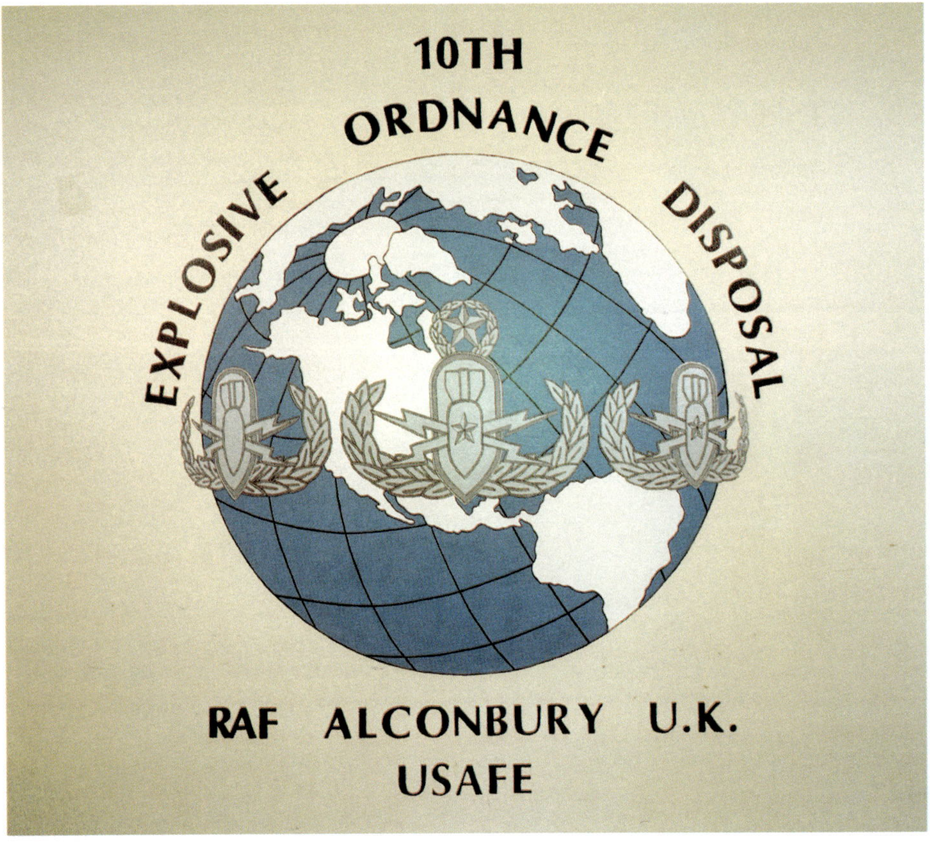

RAF Alconbury, Cambridgeshire, Building 250, 10th Explosive Ordnance Disposal badge (AA023745 © English Heritage)

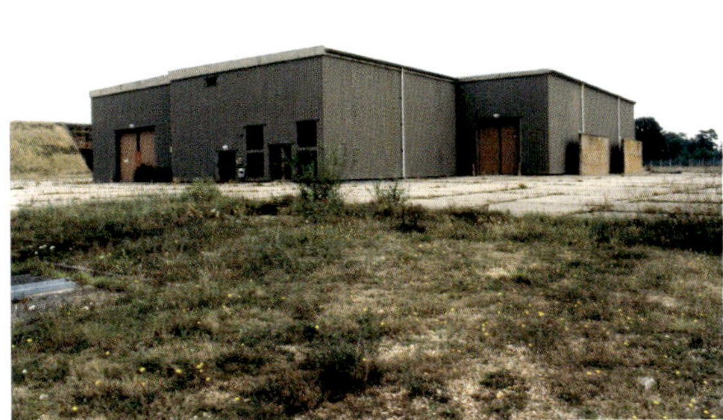 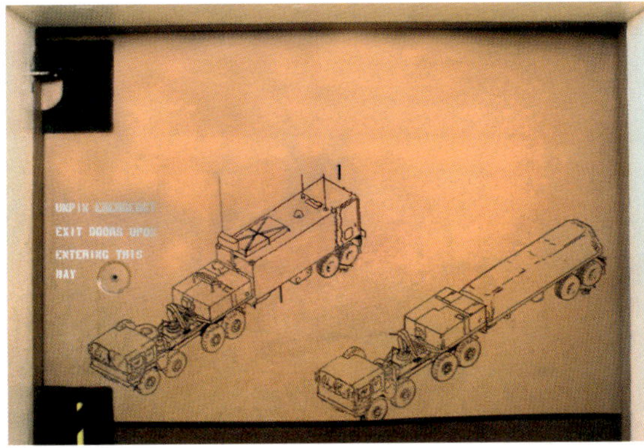

RAF Greenham Common, West Berkshire,
Left: **Integrated Maintenance Facility**
Right: **Realistic portrayals of cruise missile launch centre (LCC) and transporter erector launcher (TEL) vehicles (304M/21 © English Heritage)**

RAF Greenham Common, West Berkshire, Quick Reaction Alert shelter, 11th Tactical Missile Squadron decal (© R J C Thomas)

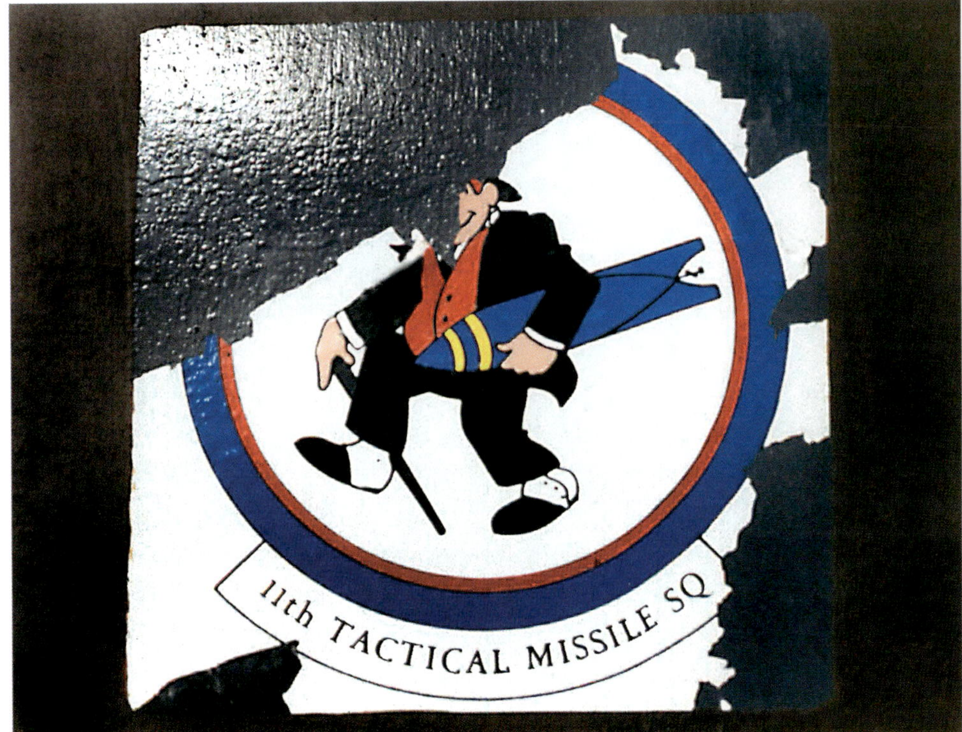

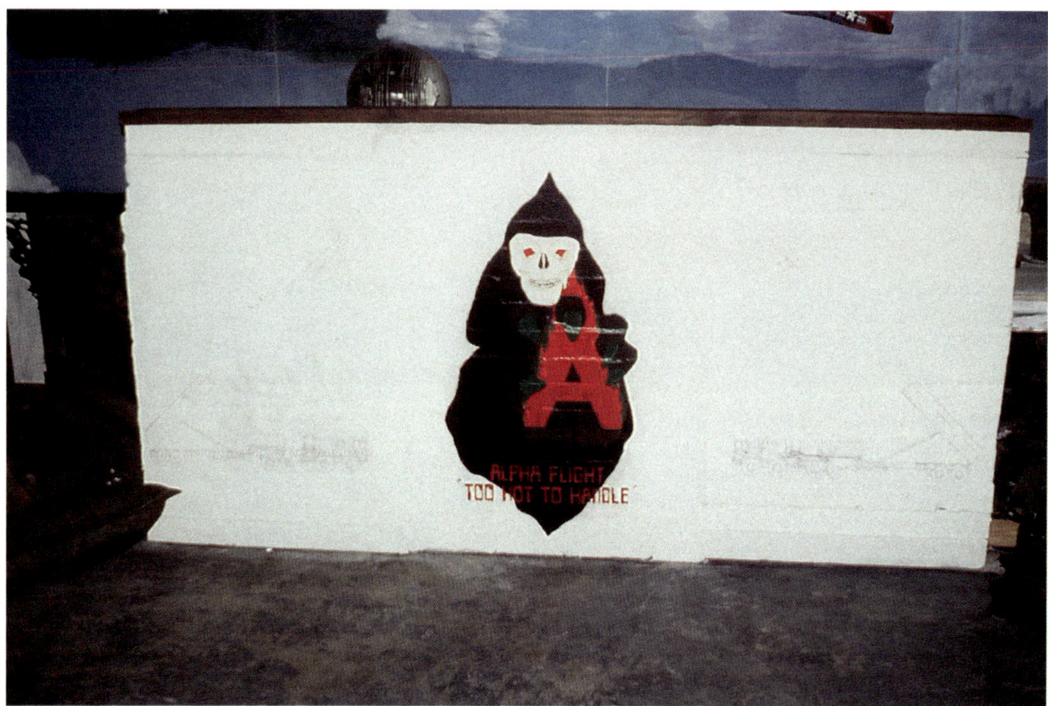

RAF Greenham
Common, West
Berkshire, Hangar 301
501st Tactical Missile
Wing A-Flight Alpha
Death's Head
(© Veronica Fiorato)

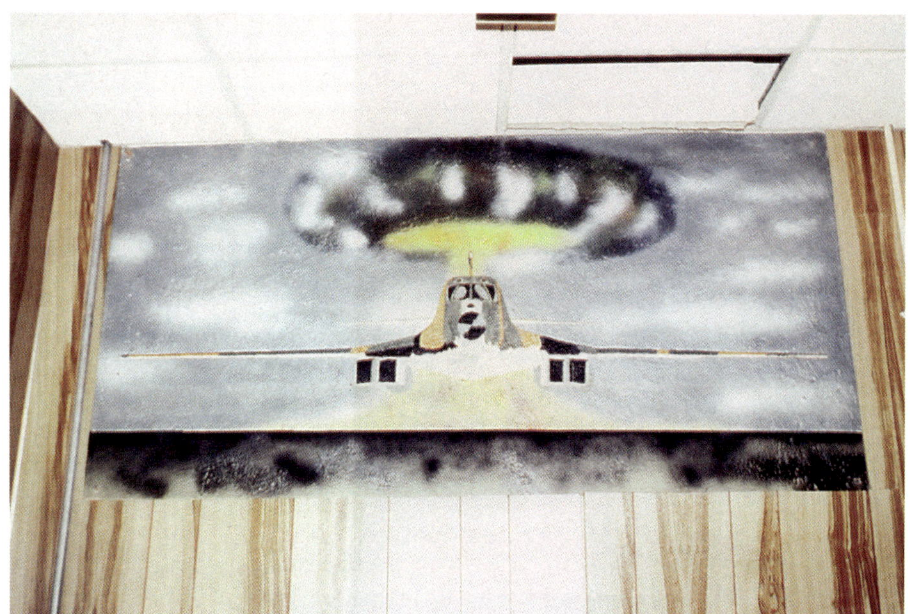

RAF Greenham Common,
West Berkshire, Warhead
Maintenance Building, B1B multi-role
strategic bomber introduced into
service during the 1980s
(© Veronica Fiorato)

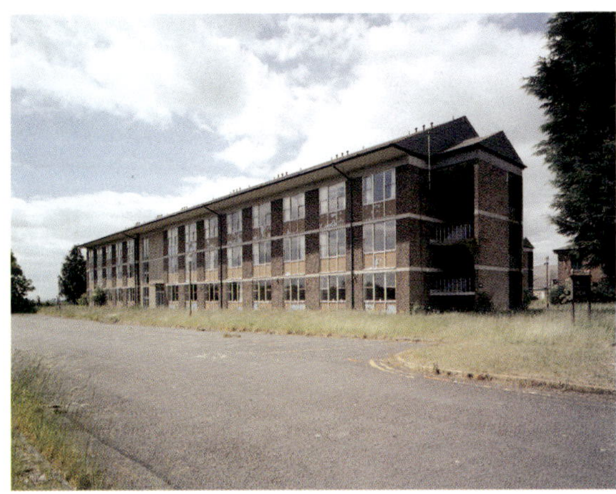

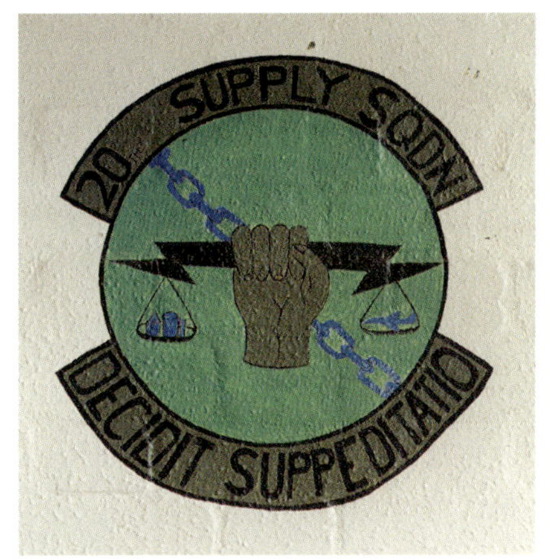

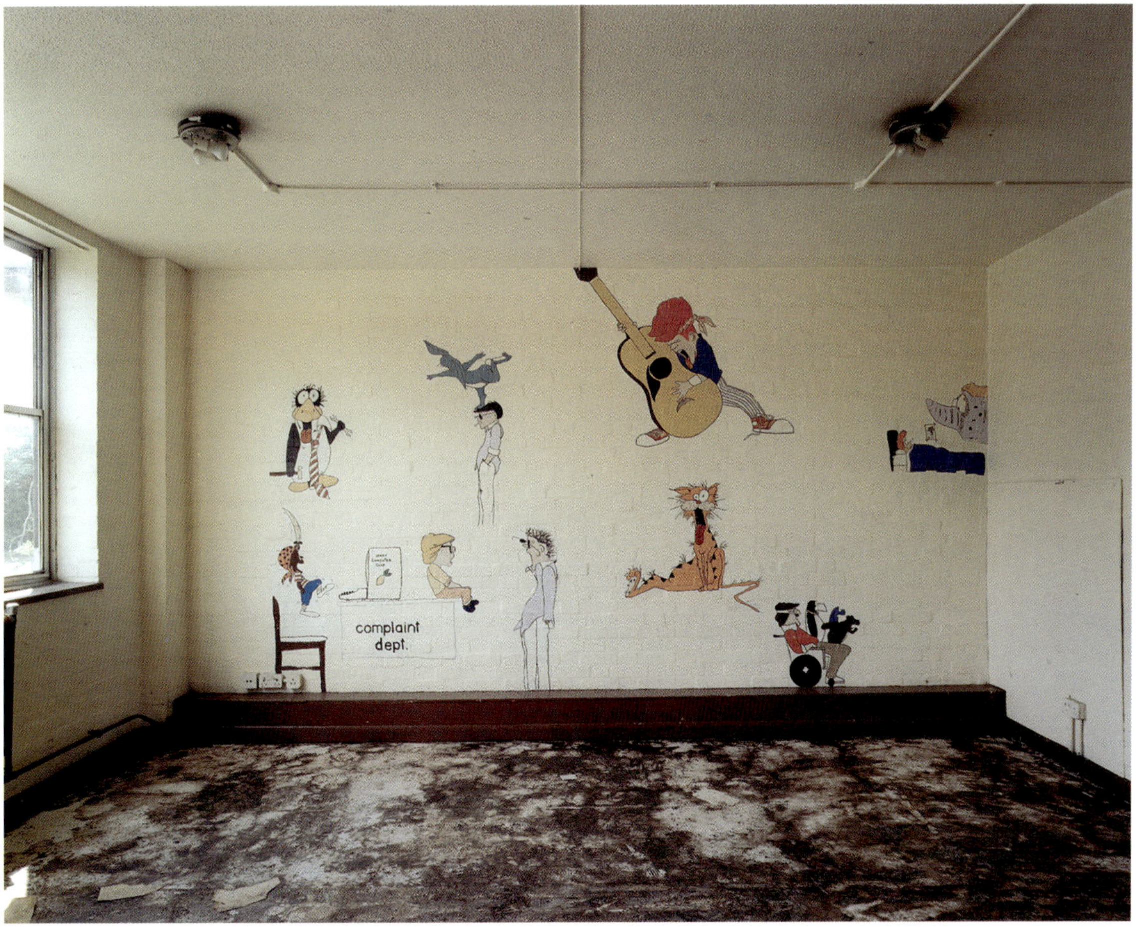

RAF Upper Heyford, Oxfordshire, Dormitory 446
Top: Left – Dormitory 446 (AA054117)
Top: Right – Entrance lobby north side ground floor 20th Supply Squadron badge (AA051473)
Bottom: North side ground floor, games room, cartoon characters from various American newspapers (AA054126)
(© English Heritage)

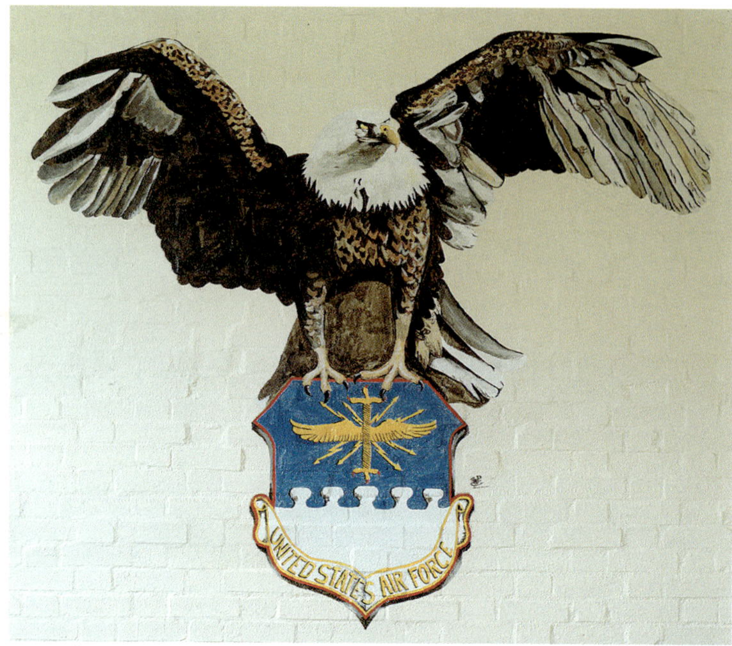

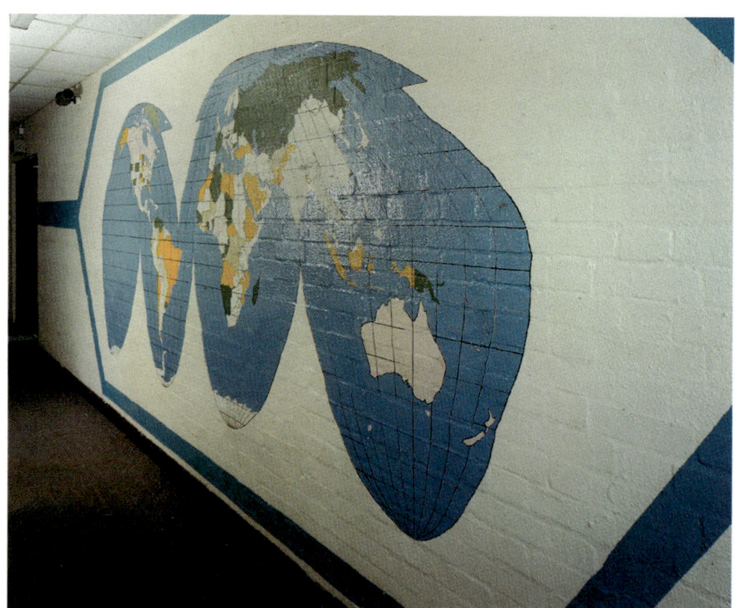

RAF Upper Heyford, Oxfordshire, Dormitory 446
Top: Entrance lobby south side ground floor, USAF shield and eagle badge, by Steve Wellever 1991 (AA051472)
Bottom: Ground floor south side corridor, world map (AA051465)
(© **English Heritage**)

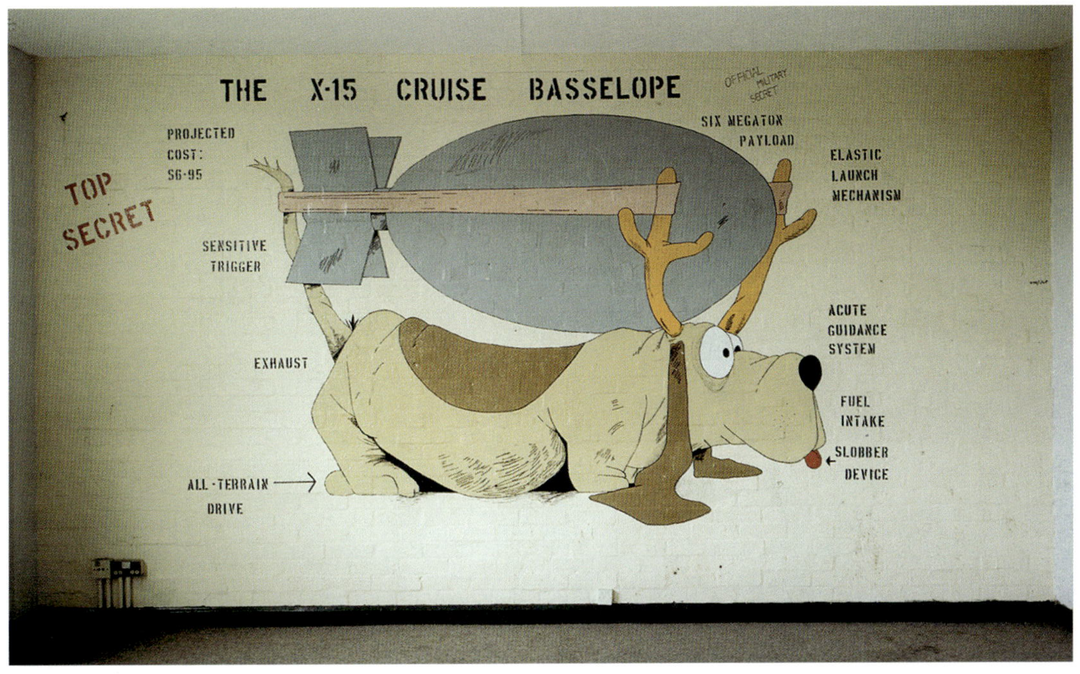

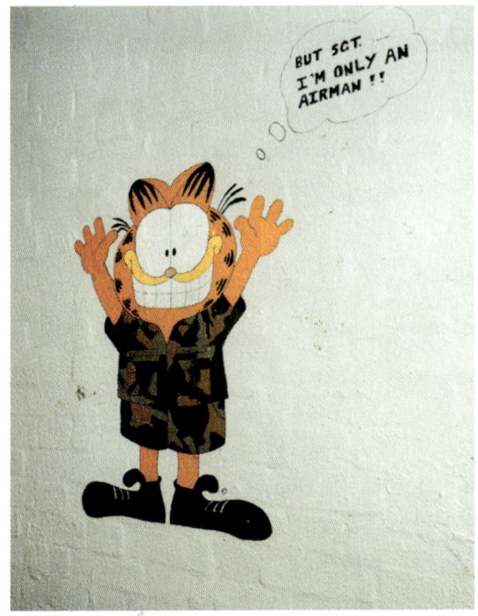

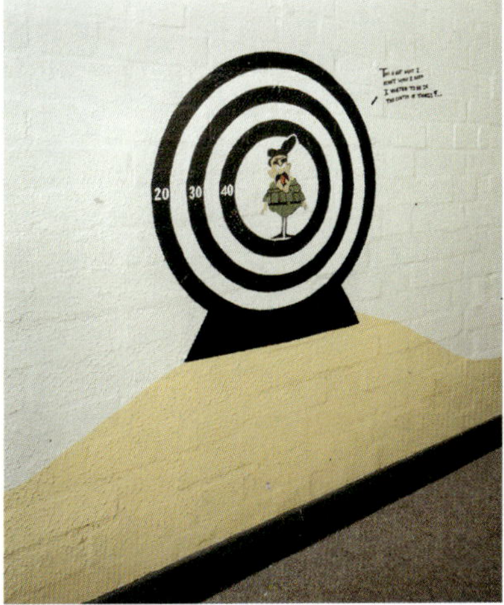

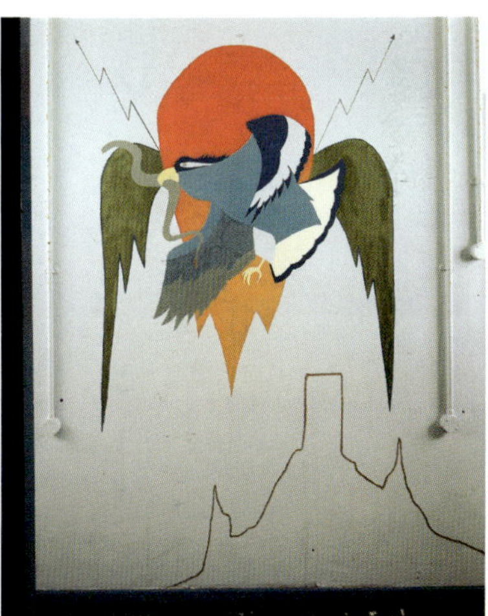

RAF Upper Heyford, Oxfordshire, Dormitory 446
Top: **North side first floor, games room, 'The X-15 Cruise Basselope' by F S (AA0514125)**
Bottom: Left – **North side first floor corridor, Garfield by F S (AA051467)**
Bottom: Middle – **North side first floor corridor, early 1990s Saddam Hussein cartoon 'This is not what I meant when I said I wanted to be the center of things!...' (detail). Also see context picture on p 8 (AA051468)**
Bottom: Right – **First floor, corridor, eagle with snake cartoon by Jim Cable 1992 (AA051474)**
(© **English Heritage**)

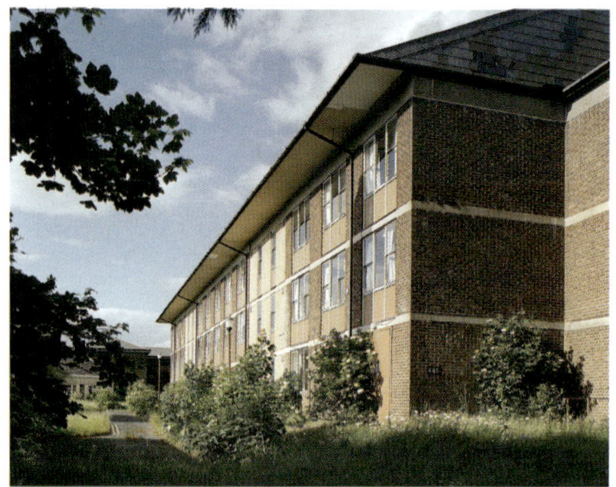

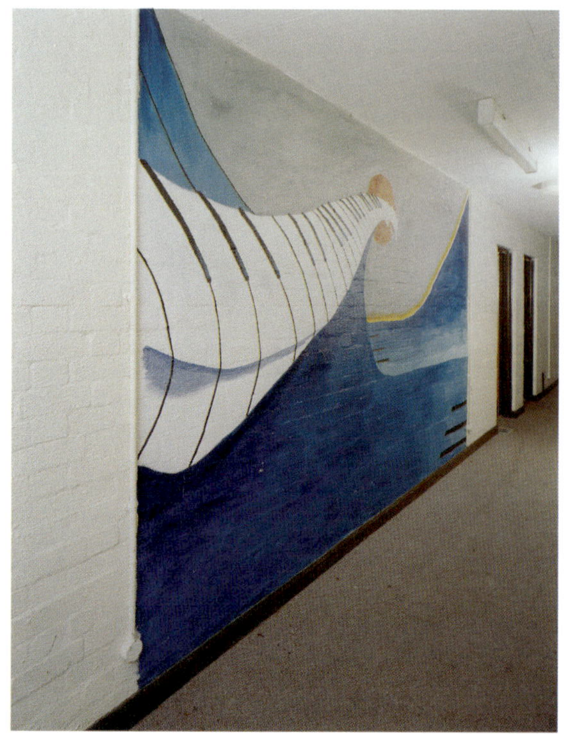

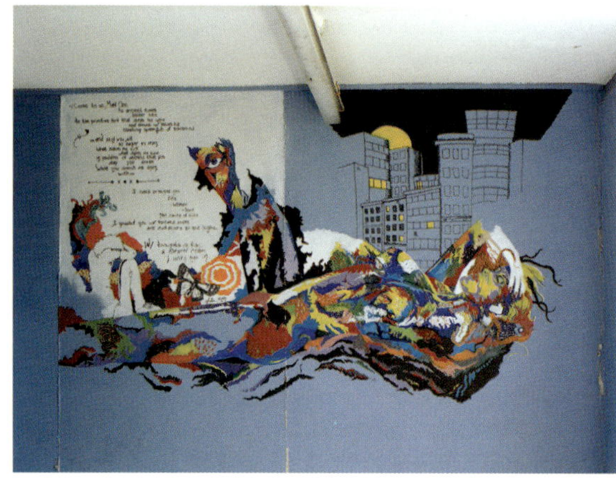

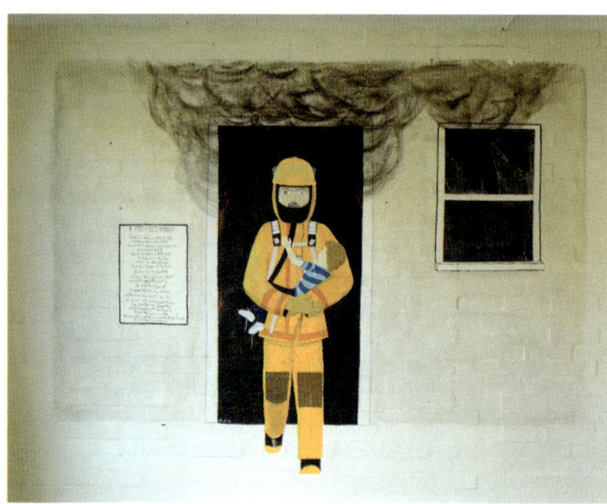

Upper Heyford, Oxfordshire, Dormitory 445
Top: Left – **Dormitory 445 (AA054118 © English Heritage)** *Top: Right* – **Ground floor corridor, mural perhaps inspired by the ink drawing of The Great Wave at Kanagana by Katsushika Hokusai (1760–1849) held by the Metropolitan Museum of Art New York (AA0541131 © English Heritage)** *Middle: Left* – **Ground floor, shower room with a surreal image of a woman with a verse, signed by Julia 1992 (AA054142 © English Heritage)** *Bottom: Left* – **Ground floor, 'A Fireman's Prayer' *'Dear God, when I am called to duty whenever flames may RAGE Give me the Serenity to save some lives whatever be its AGE Help me embrace a little child before it is too late or save an older person from the horror of fate Enable me to be alert and hear the weakest shout and quickly and efficiently to put the fire out I want to fill my calling and to give the best in me to guard my every neighbour and protect my property and if according to your will I am to lose my life Please bless with your protecting hands my children and my wife Amen'* signed 'R.A.T. May 93'. (AA054144 © English Heritage)**

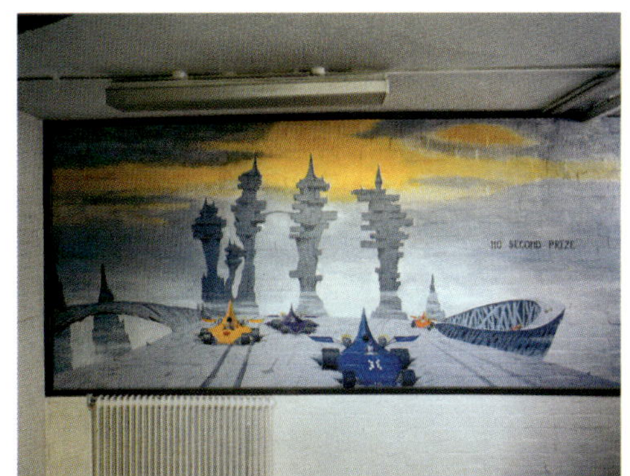

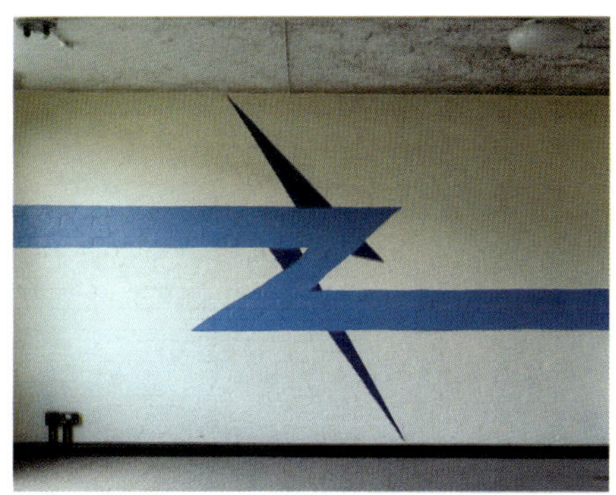

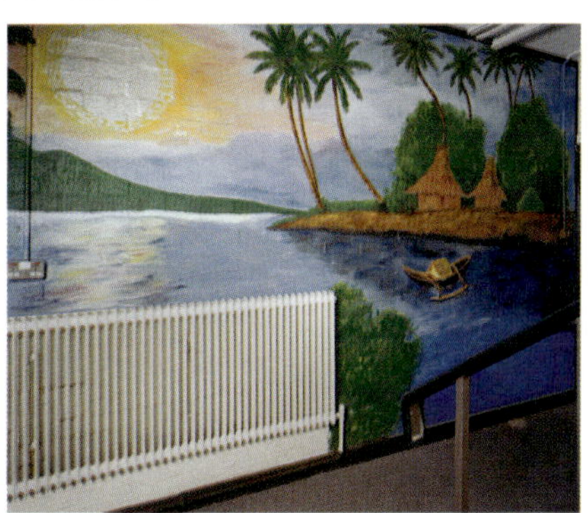

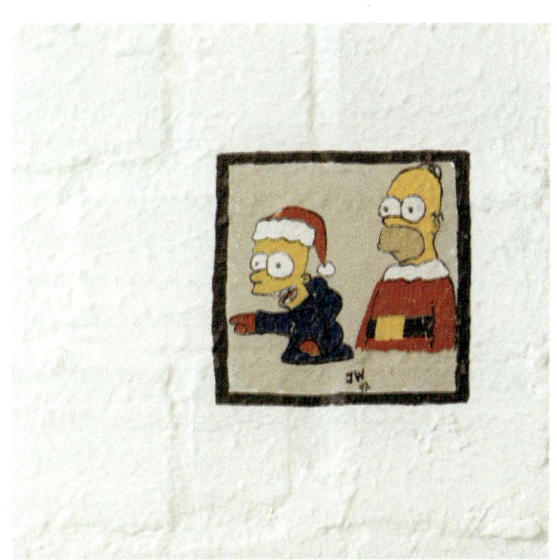

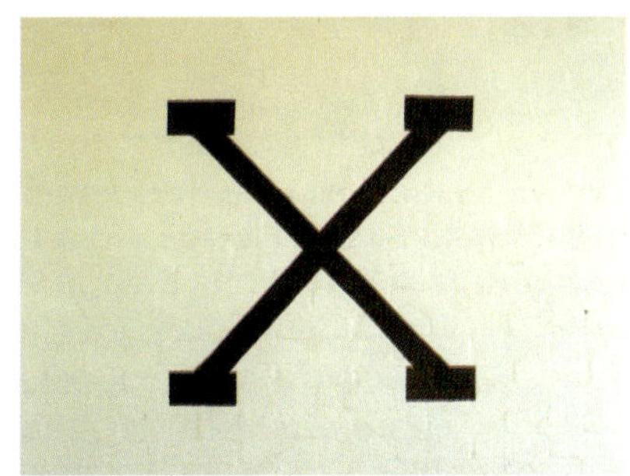

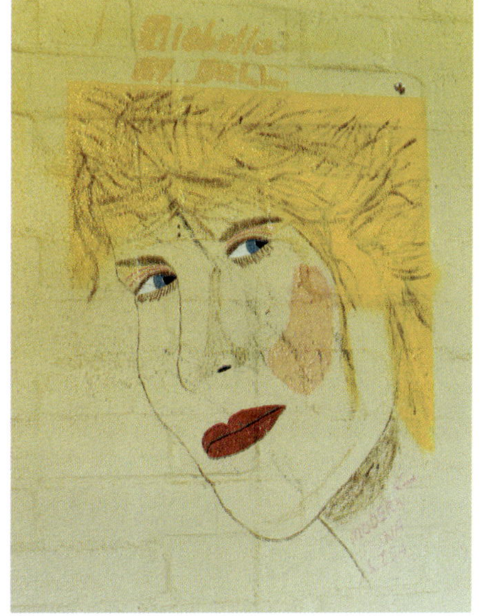

Upper Heyford, Oxfordshire, Dormitory 445
Top: Left – First floor landing, 'No Second Prize'
signed **RAT (AA054136)**
Top: Right – First floor lounge **(AA054129)**
Middle: Left – Ground floor stair lobby, by
'Steve Wellever 1991' **(AA054134)**
Middle: Right – Ground floor bedroom, Bart and
Homer Simpson, signed 'J W 92' **(AA054146)**
Bottom: Left – First floor bedroom **(AA054149)**
Bottom: Right – First Floor bedroom, 'Michelle
my bell Modern Mona Lisa' **(AA054141)**
(© **English Heritage**).

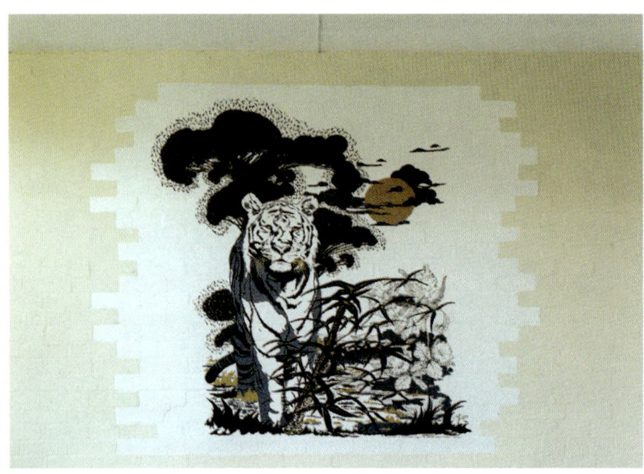

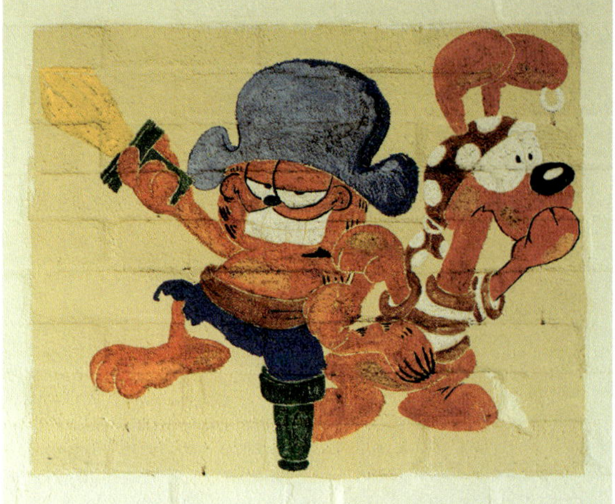

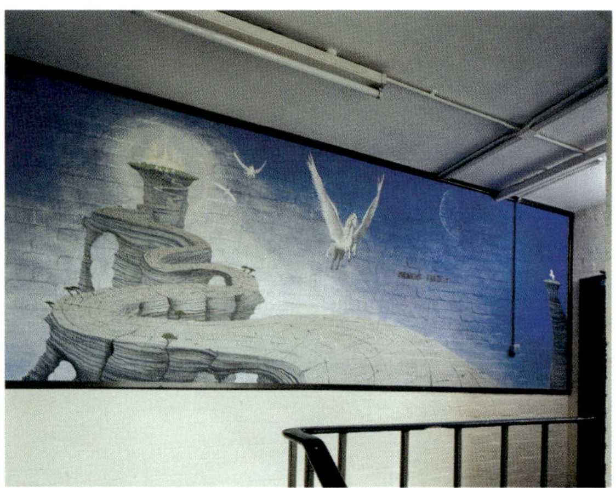

Upper Heyford, Oxfordshire, Dormitory 445
Top: Left – First floor bedroom (AA054147)
Top: Right – First floor bedroom, Garfield and Odie (AA054148)
Middle: Right – First floor landing ' Midnight Fantasy' (AA054140)
Bottom: Left – Second floor, common room, impressionistic painting of a tiger signed by Cindy L Monzaley, April 1992, 'I dedicate this to my Husband Tony & all the wonderful Friends in the Dorm! Thankyou!' (AA054127)
(© English Heritage)

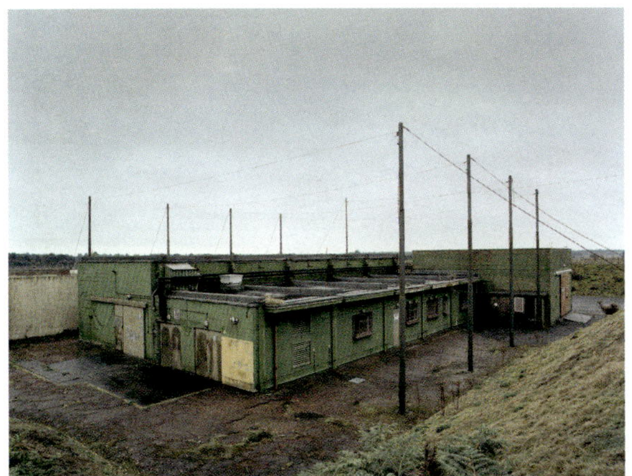

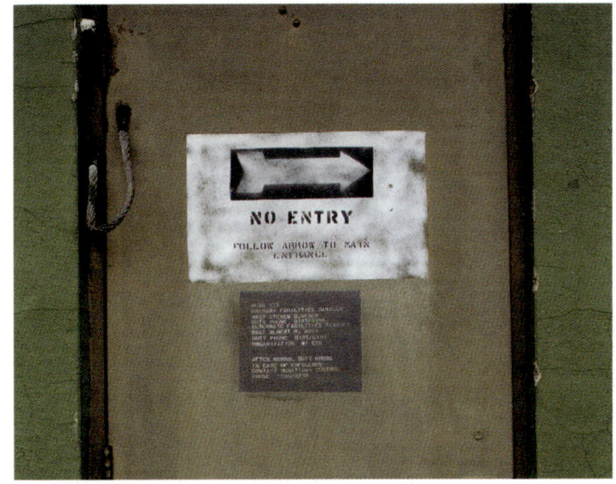

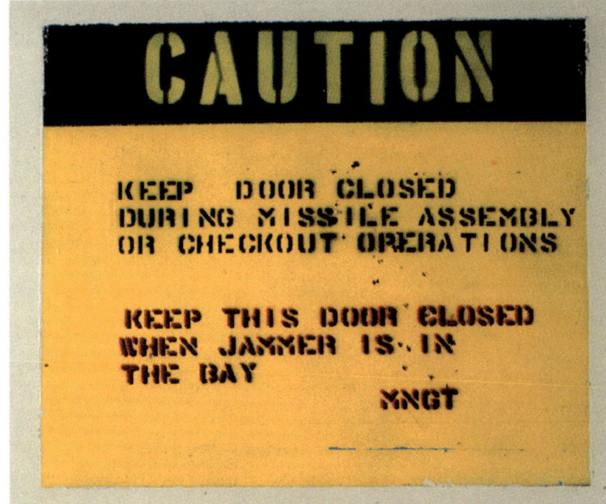

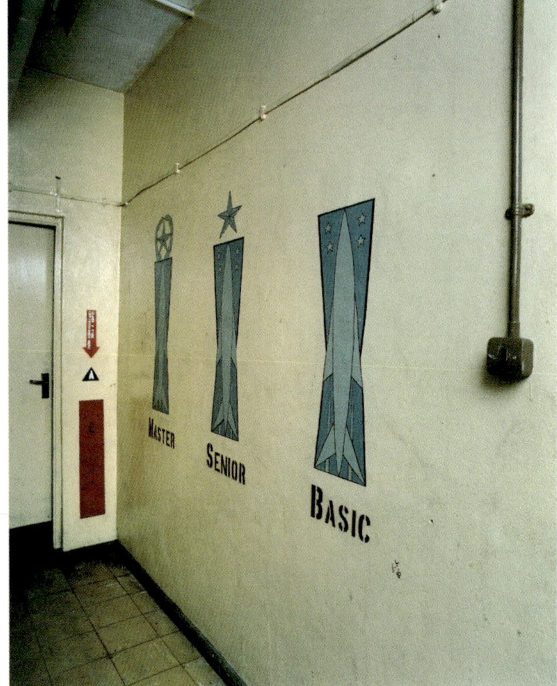

RAF Woodbridge, Suffolk
Top: Left – Missile Maintenance Building 277
(AA054155)
Top: Right – Personnel entry door (AA054156)
Bottom: Left – Blast door signage (AA054157)
Bottom: Right – Missile specialist badges
(AA054158)
(© English Heritage)

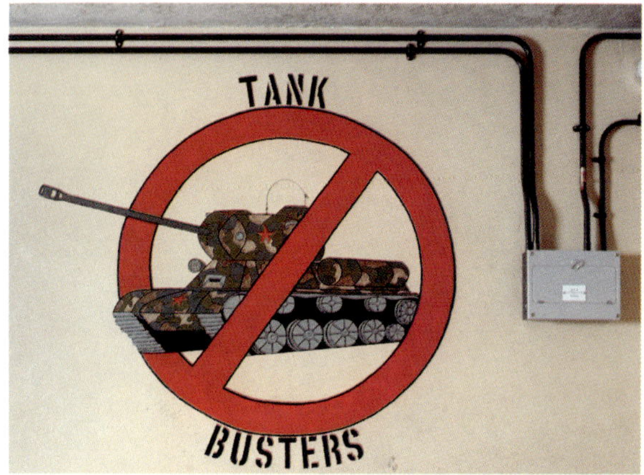

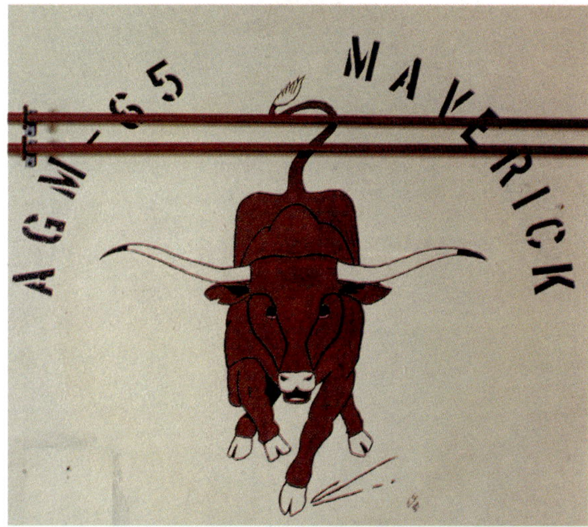

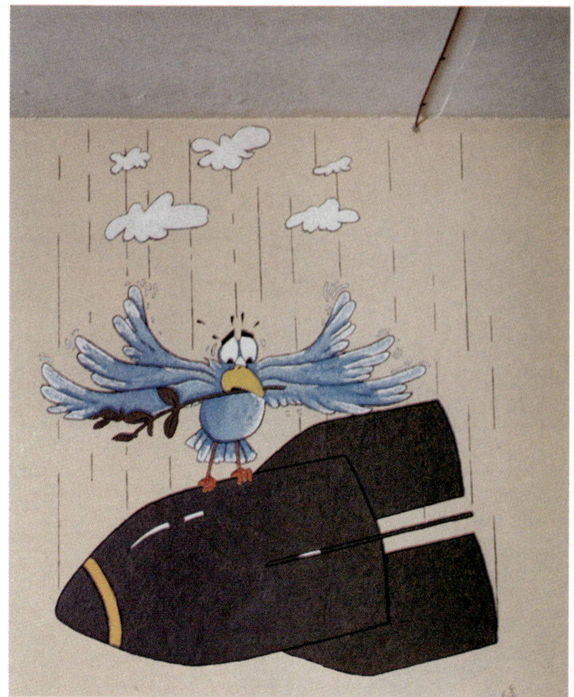

RAF Woodbridge, Suffolk
Top: Left – Tank Busters (AA054162)
Top: Right – Dove of peace, painted by ES 1985 (AA054163)
Middle: Left – AGM 65 Maverick, an allusion to a Hughes air-to-ground missile (AA054165)
(© English Heritage)
Bottom: Left – Signage indicating the use of both American and British voltage electrical systems
(© R J C Thomas)

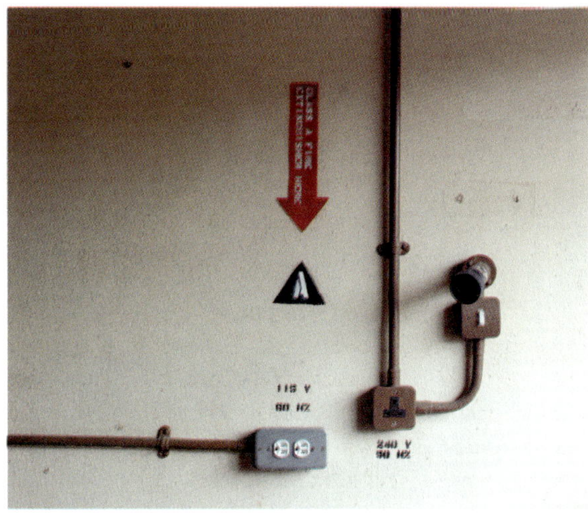

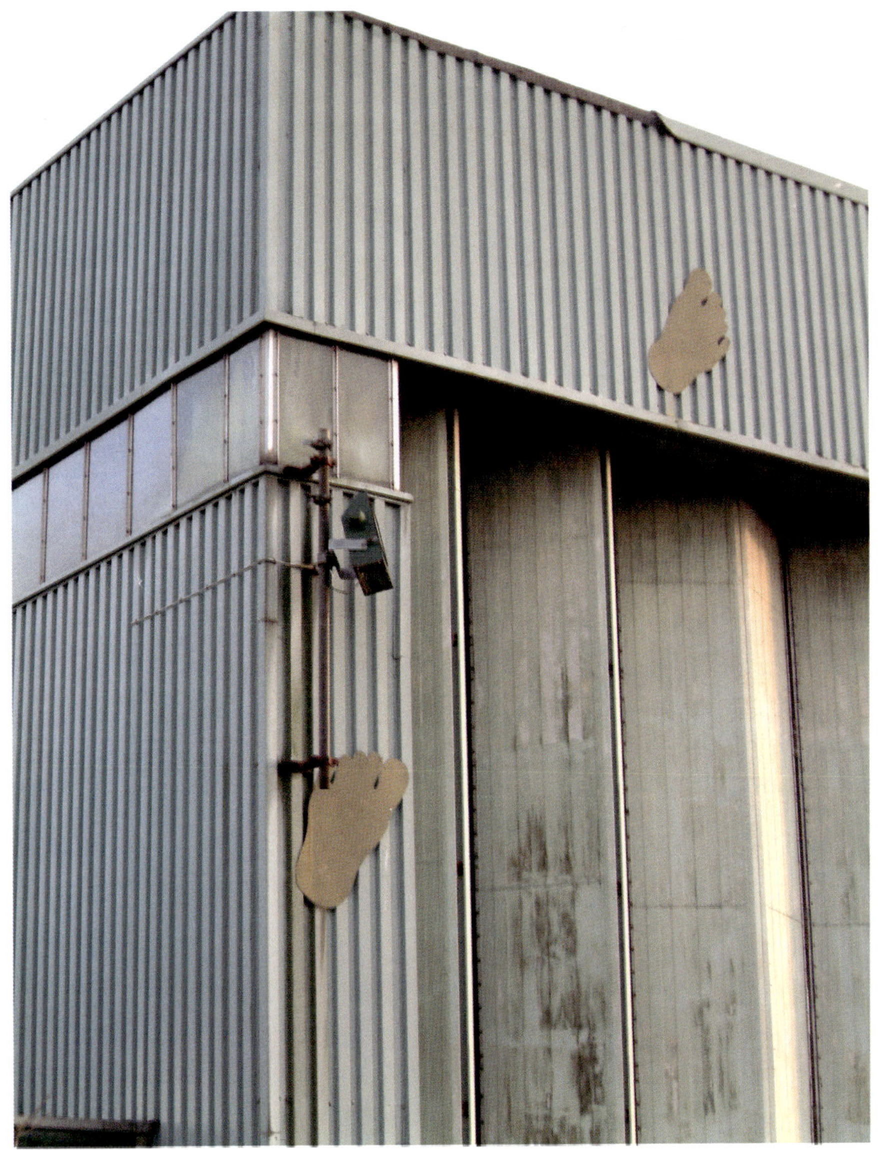

RAF Woodbridge, Suffolk, 667 SOMS Nose Docking Shed, Bigfoot foot prints (© R J C Thomas)

Also during the 1980s, RAF Greenham Common (West Berkshire) was remodelled to accept Ground Launched Cruise Missiles. In contrast to the reported low morale at Bentwaters, at Greenham Common, due to its high political profile, the missile troops were very proud of their work. This too finds expression through murals painted in operational areas. In a building occupied by the Security Police, who were responsible for base discipline, the murals were formal renditions of official badges. In contrast, in the workshops and restricted crew areas the images are less restrained, and in common with earlier murals,

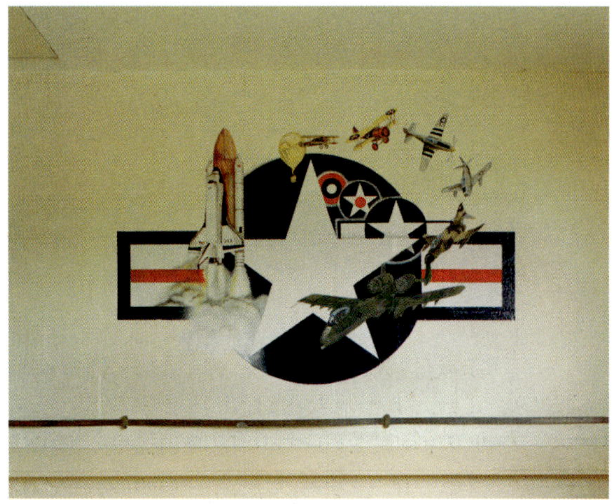
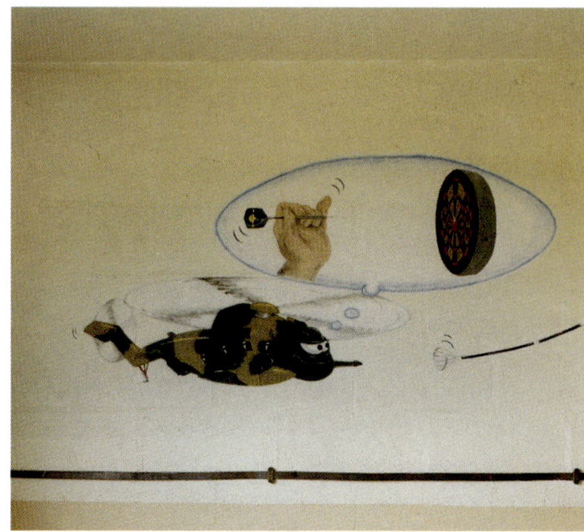

RAF Woodbridge, Suffolk, store building and workshops 296
Left: **History of American flight (AA054153 © English Heritage)**
Right: **Helicopter and dart board (AA054154 © English Heritage)**

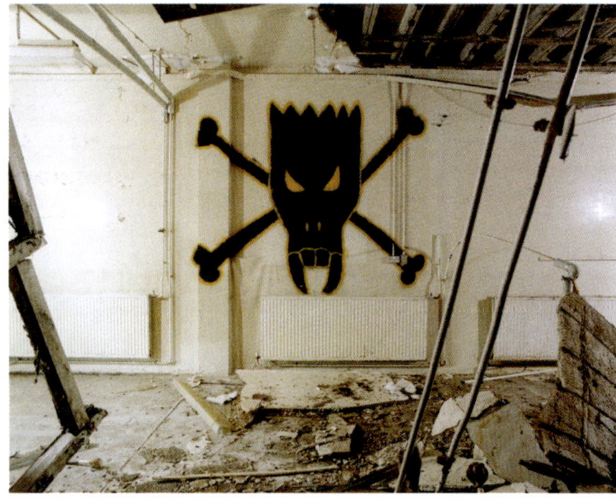
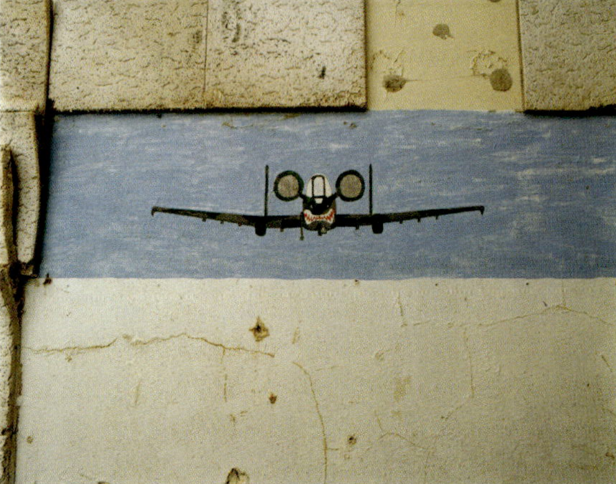

RAF Woodbridge, Suffolk, storage and handling building 259
Left: **Skull and cross bones (AA054171 © English Heritage)**
Right: **A10 Warthog (AA054172 © English Heritage)**

their style may be seen to be directly influenced by contemporary culture and graphic styles. Many of the images and themes are reminiscent of the material found in comic books of the time, such as *2000AD* and *Judge Dredd*. It was a style that many of the troops would have been familiar with, for example from magazines circulating around the base.

Some drawings at Greenham Common reflected in-jokes, such as a cartoon figure of a 'Smurf' in combat fatigues, reflecting the nickname of the troops based in the Special Maintenance Facility or SMF.

Some images of vehicles were so realistic that they may have been taken from contemporary training manuals, and were probably used for instructional purposes.

The missile unit at Greenham Common was divided into six flights, each designated by a letter (see p 29). A, or Alpha Flight, used a cloaked death's head motif clutching a letter A. D Flight, also known as 'Dog Flight', had a mural of a dog breaking loose from its chain with cruise missile launchers in the background. In common with a number of murals at Greenham Common it is unfinished. A motto in Spanish (LOS UNICOS PERROS RABIOSOS EN BRITANIA – The only mad dogs in Britain) below another Dog Flight mural reflects the changing cultural composition of the United States Air Force, with a gradually rising number of recruits of Hispanic origin entering the services.

In addition to the military's wish to improve morale, the inspiration for some of the murals may also be seen to come from contemporary American urban culture, where commissioned murals and graffiti on walls or subway cars, are a familiar part of city life. In Los Angeles, from at least the 1940s, Latino gangs marked their territories by 'Placas', or plaques, announcing their pride and strength to outsiders, a similar sentiment to many of the images in the semi-private areas on military bases. It is perhaps to Latino iconography that we also need to look to interpret some of the images found on 1980s USAF bases. In Western Europe, the skull as a symbol of death and corruption is well-known, and was incorporated into the badges of many famous cavalry and hussar regiments. In contrast, in Hispanic culture with its roots in South America, the skull is seen as a good luck charm, a protector from death, and symbol of rebirth (Bojorquez 2004). At Upper Heyford, a picture of the 'zoot suited' 'Doo Dah Man', may also be seen as an acknowledgement of the style of the sharply dressed Latino gangs of the 1940s.

So, on most bases a wide variety of images are encountered, including badges, renditions of contemporary cartoons and cartoons based on the unit's equipment and function. These themes give each base a distinctive identity or character. At Upper Heyford, a raven, the nickname for the EF-111a electronic countermeasures aircraft based there, is commonly incorporated into cartoons. Likewise, at bases where A-10s were deployed, images of heavily built warthogs are commonly found. At Greenham Common, aggressive and macabre images of unleashed dogs and death's heads reflect the cruise missile unit's preoccupations with their task.

VALUES AND MEANING

As we have seen, war art provides coded information about the ways in which space has been appropriated, used, and reused by a succession of its former occupants. It provides information on the value attached to those spaces, both at the time of occupation and subsequently. That occupation may either have been at a time of conflict, or in peace time, or both.

Areas of a military base, or rooms within a building, may have been used for training personnel resulting in the production of instructional drawings or text; signage perhaps. Some areas will have been secure and private, with restricted access; some areas will have served as public space. Access will have

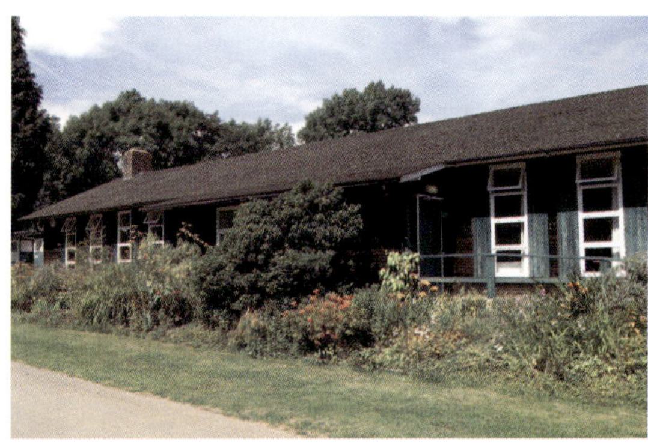

Sayers Croft, Ewhurst, Cranleigh, Surrey, murals painted by pupils and their teachers at a purpose-built wartime evacuee centre
Top: **Sayers Croft (DP016562)**
Bottom: Left **– Mural A designed by Arthur Davies (art master) and Len Davies (pupil) and painted by senior boys (DP016564)**
Bottom: Right **– Detail of camp life (DP016547) (© English Heritage)**

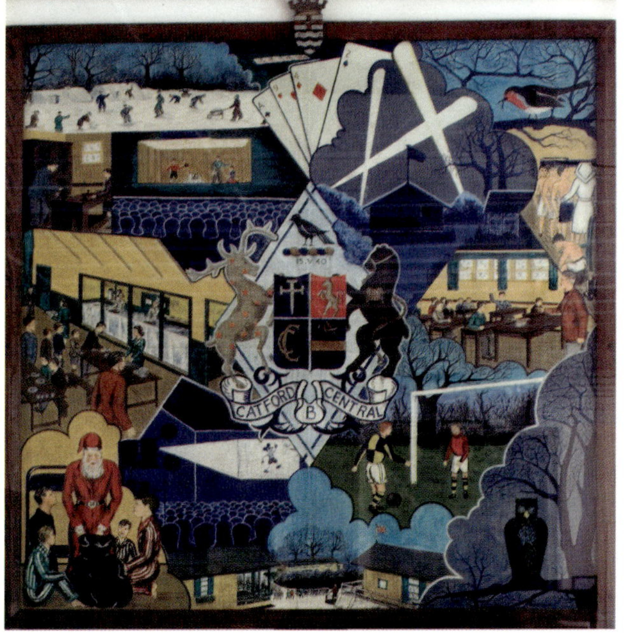

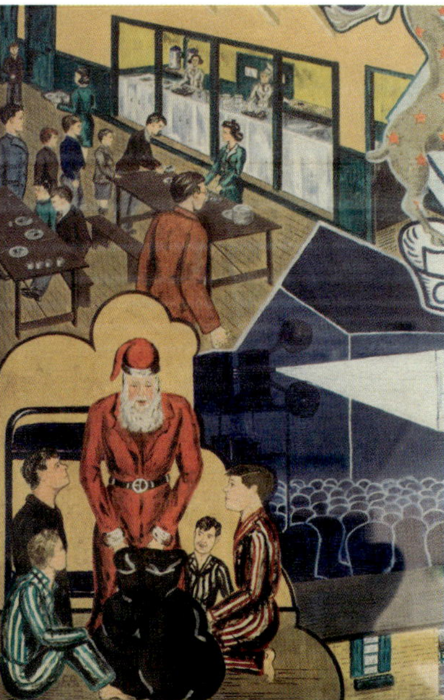

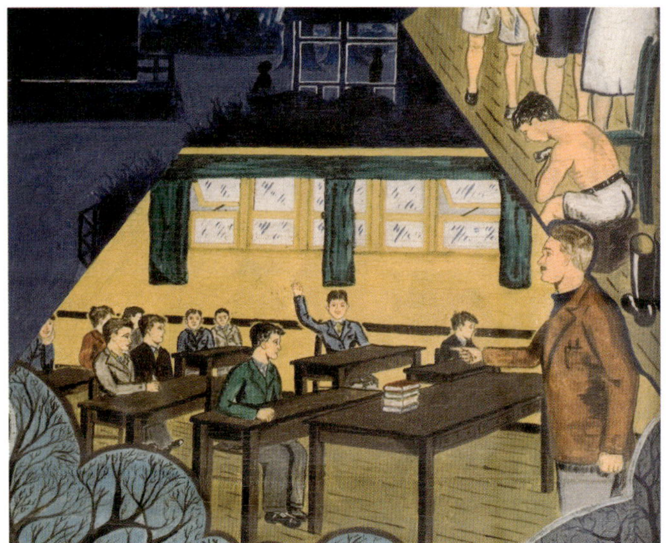

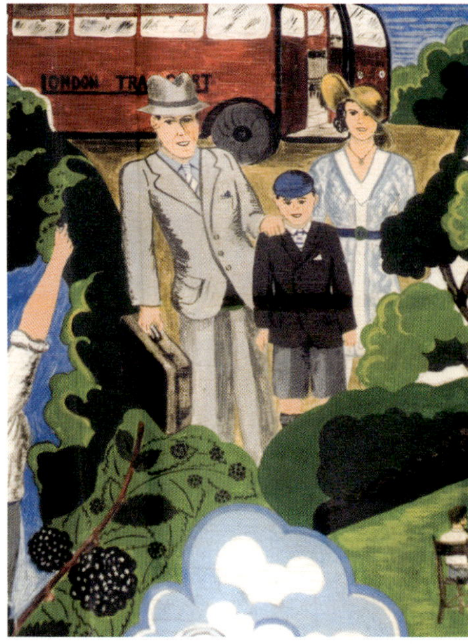

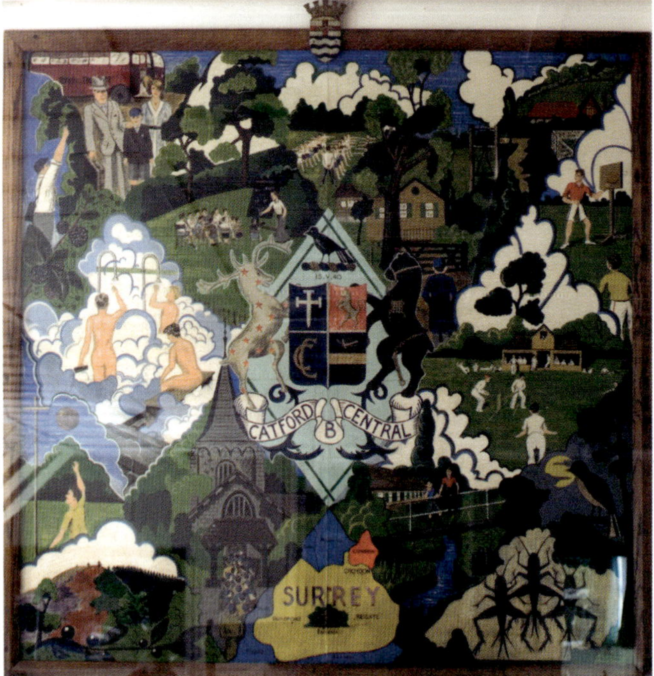

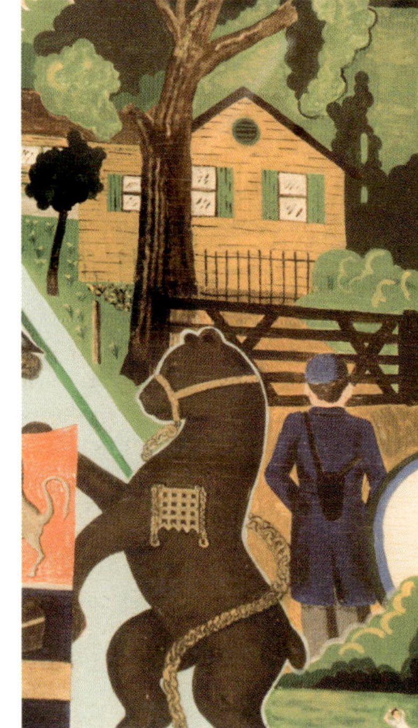

Sayers Croft, Ewhurst, Cranleigh, Surrey.
Top: Left – A wartime class room (DP016548)
Top: Right – An evacuee leaving his parents (DP016555)
Bottom: Left – Mural B designed by Arthur Davies (art master) and Walter Silcox (pupil) and painted by senior boys (DP016552)
Bottom: Right – An evacuee arrives at Sayers Croft (DP016557)
(© English Heritage)

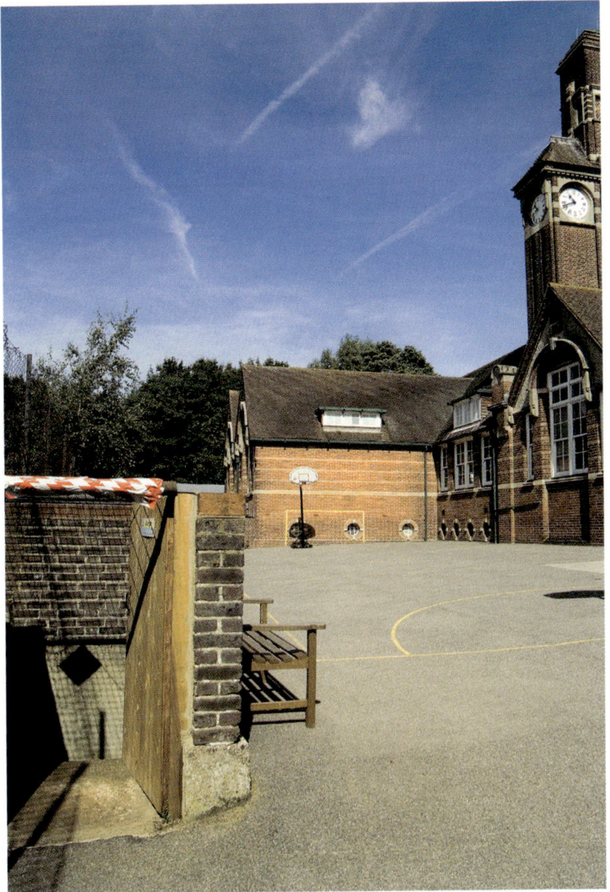

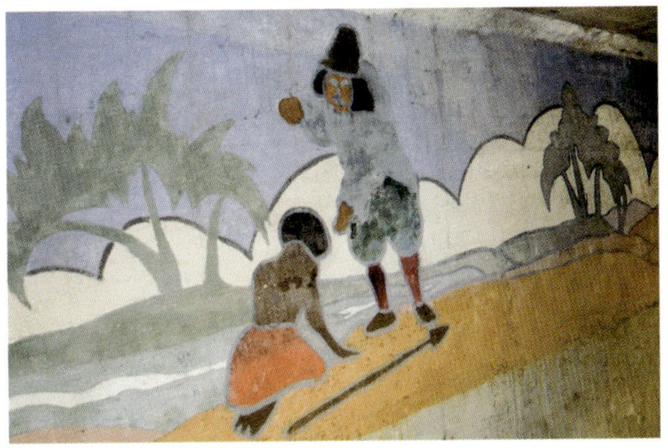

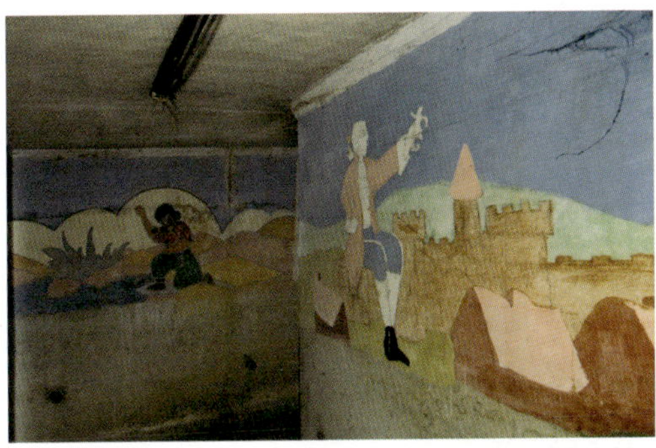

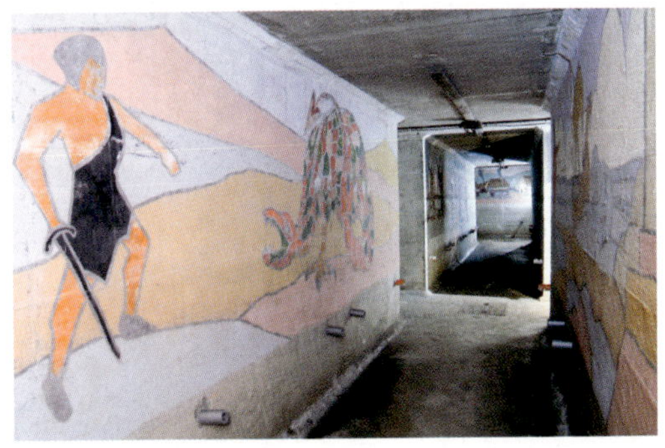

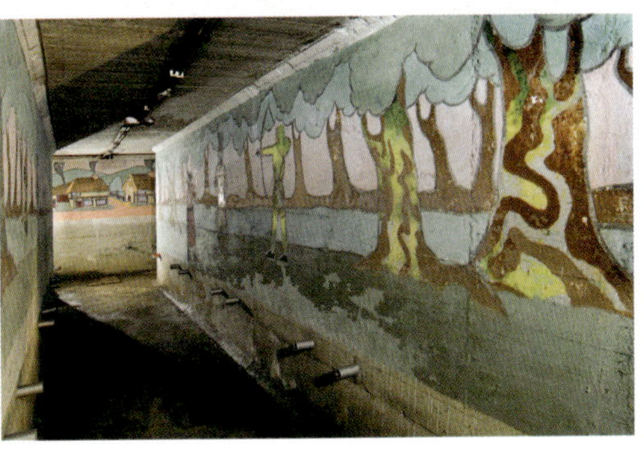

St John's School, Redhill, Surrey, Murals in a school air raid shelter have transformed potentially forbidding subterranean passages into a magical place.
Left – **St John's Primary School, the entrance to the air-raid shelter is to the left, and the shelter lies beneath the playground (DP016566)**
Right: From top – **Robinson Crusoe and Man Friday (DP016577)**
Gulliver (DP016573)
Murals in the tunnel complex (DP016588)
Robin Hood (DP016589)
(© English Heritage)

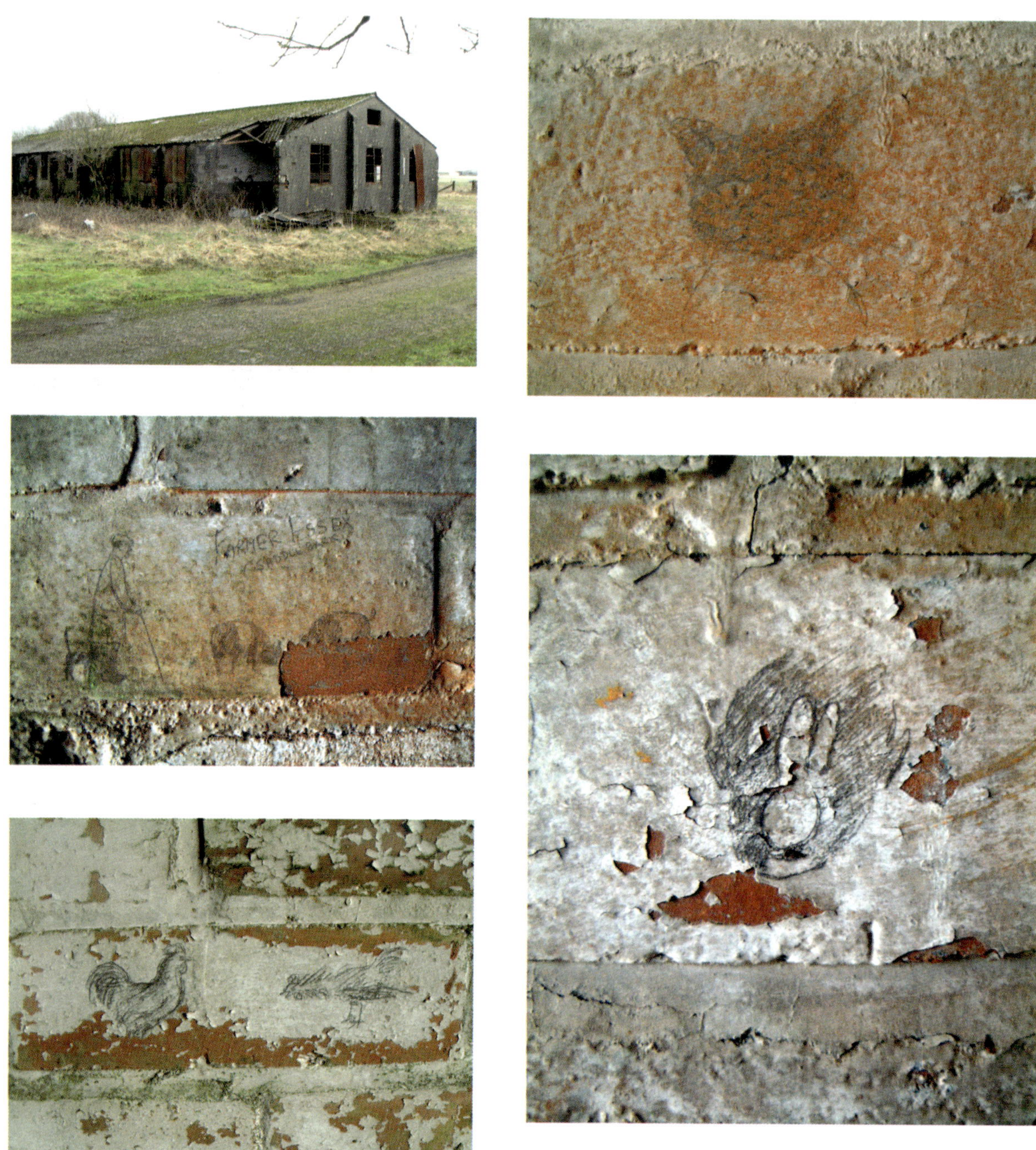

RAF Dunkeswell, Devon. *Top: Left* – No.18 Armoury maintenance; *Middle: Left* – Farmer Essex saddleback; *Bottom: Left* – Cock fighting; *Top: Right* – cat; *Bottom: Right* – Black and white minstrel (© R J C Thomas)

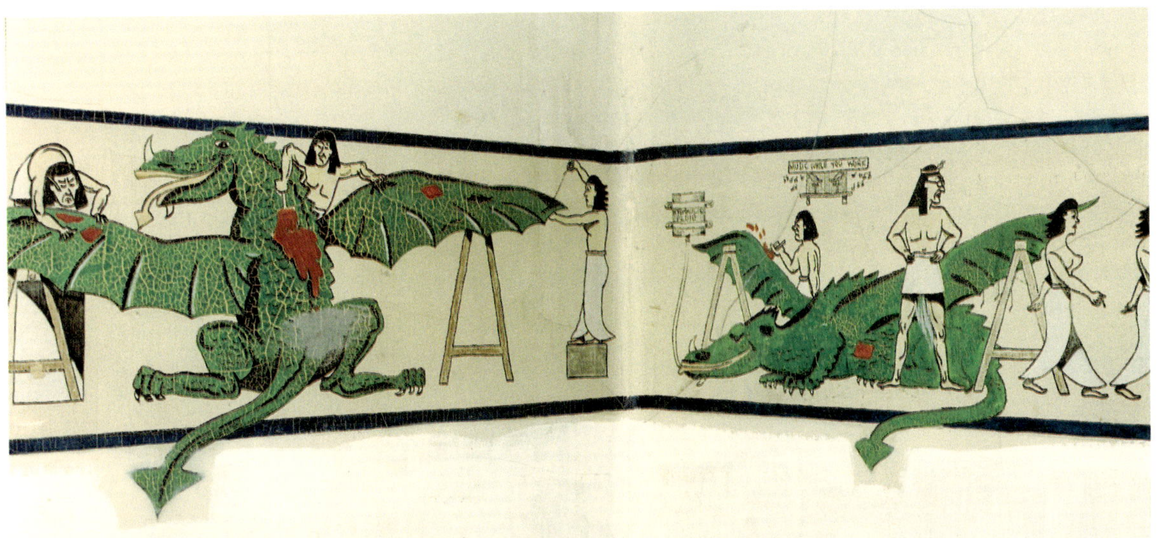

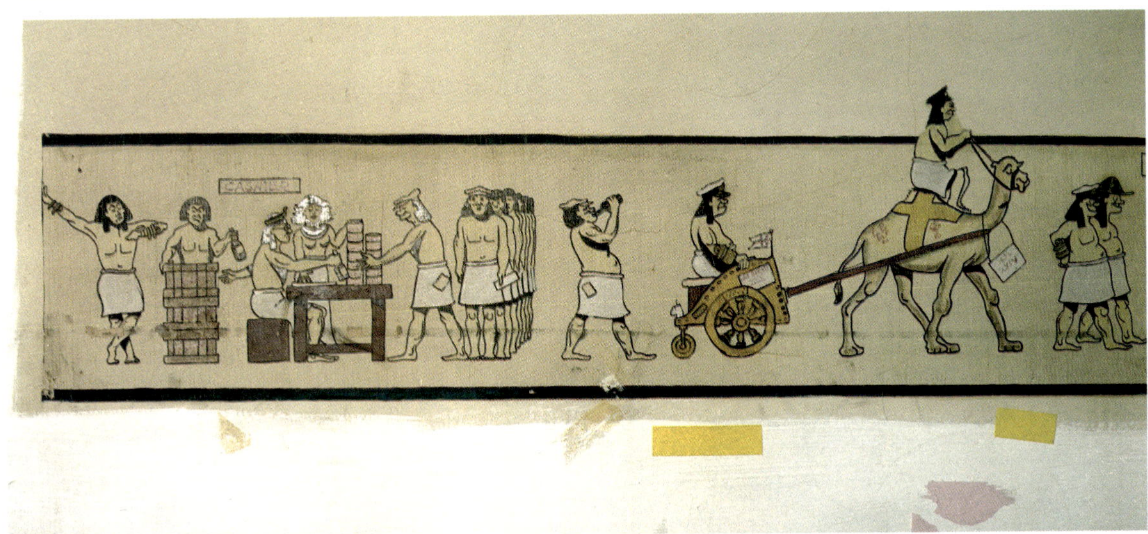

Donibristle Airfield, Fife, HMS Merlin, a repair depot for naval aircraft
Top: (SC44440 © Crown copyright RCAHMS)
Bottom: (SC924138 © Crown copyright RCAHMS)

influenced the degree to which art and signage was produced, to what extent it has remained, and the subject matter. Walls and surfaces will have been adorned for all of these reasons, and works that remain today will have significance for the opportunity they provide for interpretation and understanding of what often remain hidden and mysterious places. Artistic expression is thus part of the historic record; part of the archaeology of these military or militarised sites. It tells us about the culture prevalent amongst those who occupied the bases, the function of space within them, and about individuality, and about reuse.

We have noted how cultural differences can have an influence on artistic expression, and this is one reason why war art has such importance for interpreting the sites. On the one hand clear differences in style are evident between war art on Royal Air Force bases, sites occupied by the United States Air Force, and by the conscript Soviet army in the former East Germany. All three categories of war art are characteristic of the cultures and political systems from which they derive, and detailed study may reveal other more localised (regional) variations in style or execution. A further contrast can be seen between military war art and artistic interventions created by the protest community in opposition to the presence and potential use of nuclear arms. At its most obvious this can include painted fence posts and spiral graffiti close to the cruise missile area at Greenham Common (West Berkshire). But more sophisticated and

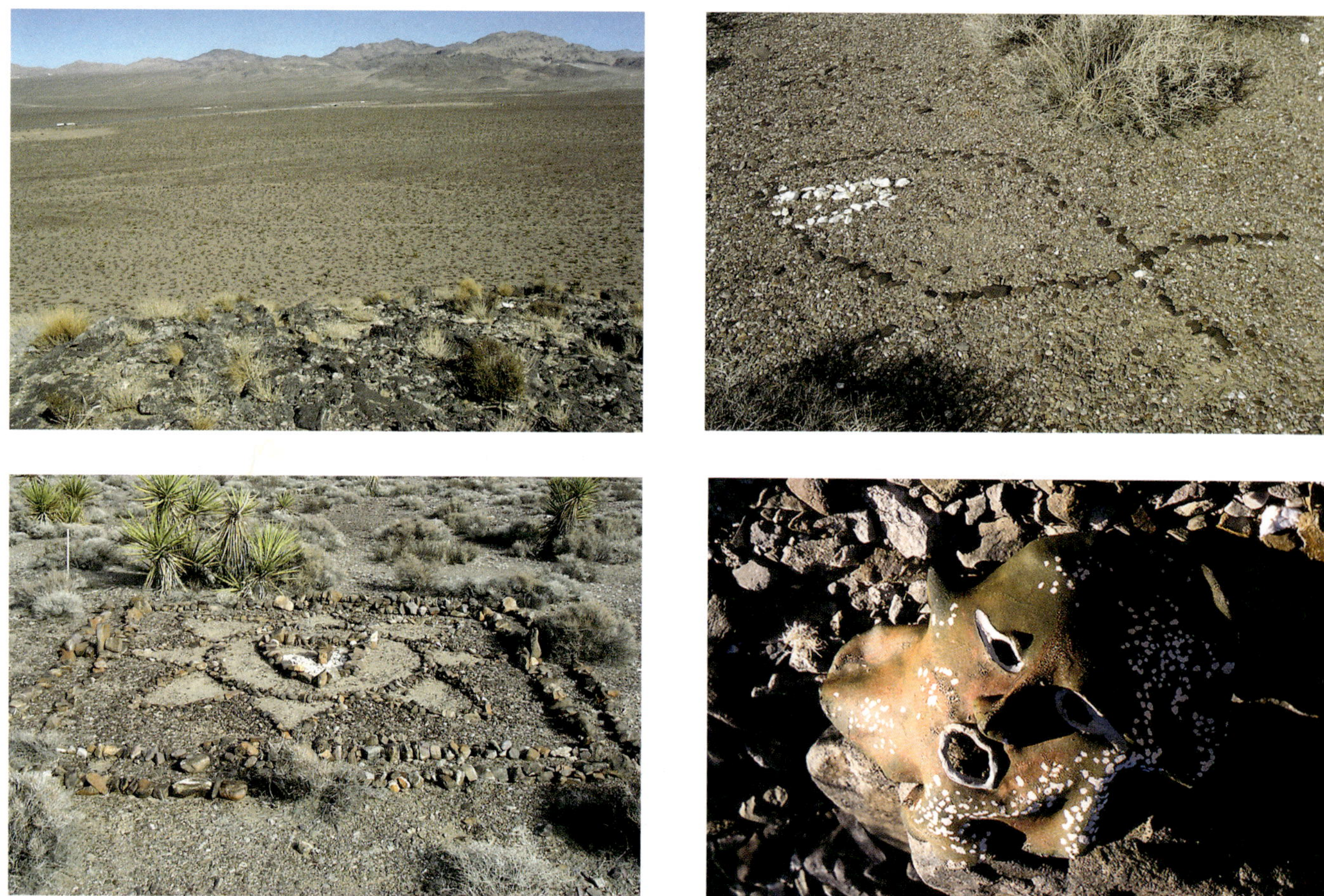

Nevada Peace Camp, outside of the Nevada Test Site that was used for live nuclear weapons tests until the 1990s. *Top: Left* – A general view of the site of the peace camp looking northeast from pagoda hill. Highway 95 cuts across this picture, separating the peace camp from the test site (© Desert Research Institute). *Top: Right* – Christian fish symbol (© Desert Research Institute). *Bottom: Left* – A desert garden comprising rocks lain in the form of a flower © Desert Research Institute. *Bottom: Right* – One of four masks each placed within stone circles (© W D Cocroft)

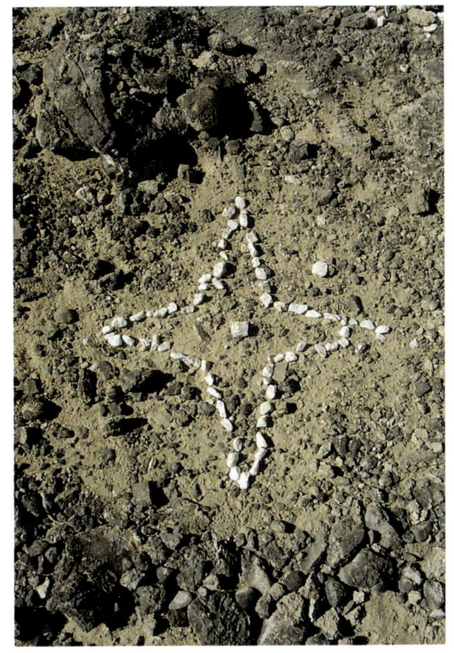

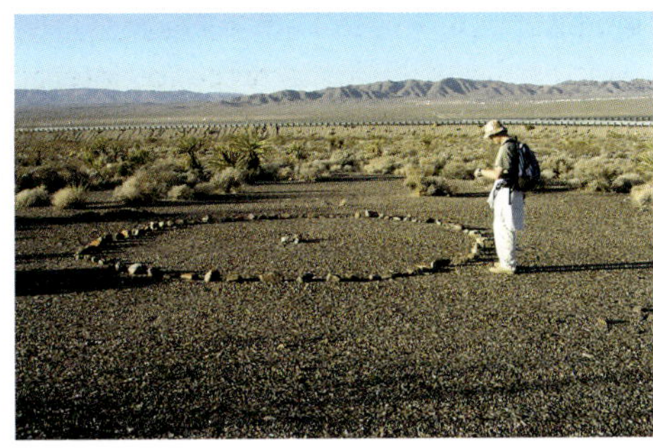

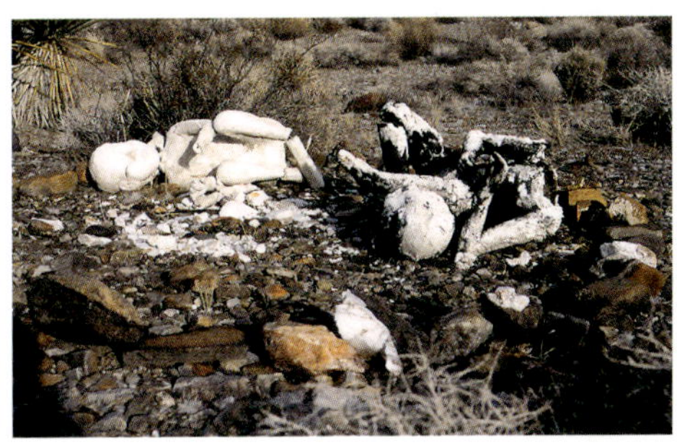

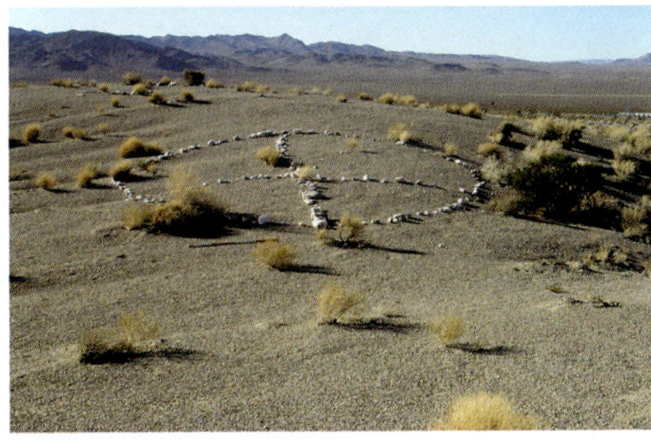

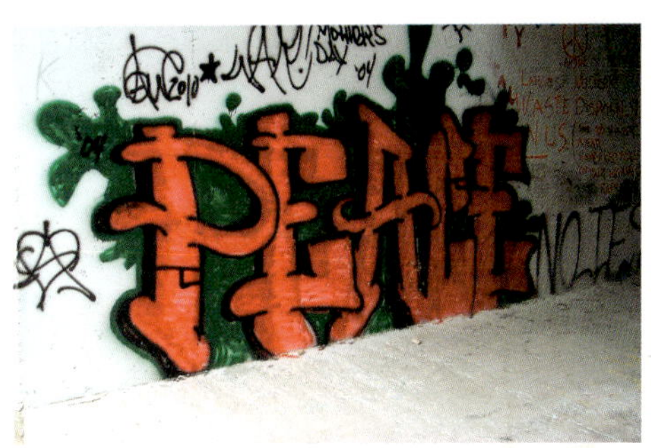

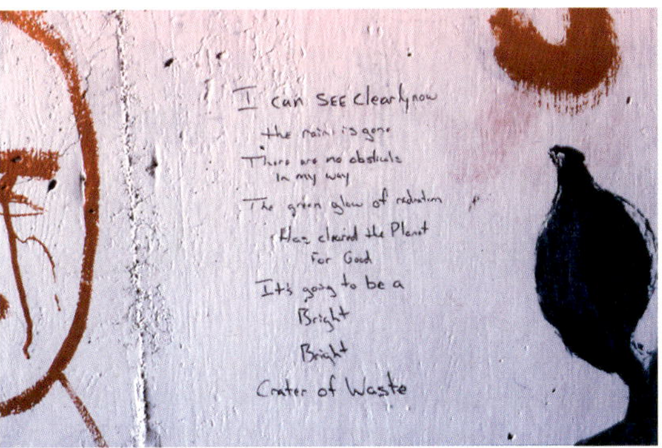

Nevada Peace Camp.
Top: Left – Pagoda Hill compass
(© Desert Research Institute).
Bottom: Left – Large peace symbol laid out in
stone of the side of a hill
(© Desert Research Institute).
Right: From top – Large stone circle
(© Desert Research Institute).
Shadow children (© W D Cocroft).
Peace graffiti in a highway underpass beneath
Highway 95, this tunnel gave access from the
peace camp to the perimeter of the test site
(© Desert Research Institute).
Tunnel graffiti The Final War
(© John Schofield)

complex are the stone arrangements at Peace Camp, Nevada, representing in clear and obvious terms the diverse groups that contributed to this protest community. In a remote desert environment, over 700 stone features were created, their symbolism and form marking their origin within Christian, Buddhist, Jewish, New Age and native American Western Shoshone traditions: stone circles for example, Christian 'fish' symbols, Franciscan crosses, stars of David, and the incorporation of tortoise shells into stone arrangements, the tortoise being sacred to the Western Shoshone. Arrangements, statuary and sculpture also reflect the presence of Hiroshima veterans at Peace Camp in the form of two 'shadow children', life-size plaster casts of children placed within a stone circle. Here the art is interpreted both as reflective of a diverse community working together towards a common and strongly-held objective, and as a response to the hostile environment in which the protestors lived, often for months at a time. Protest art is also present in the so-called Tunnel of Love – an underpass beneath the highway, linking Peace Camp to the Test Site. This was the only shade available, and the only wall surface for adorning. As a result the tunnels are highly decorated, with graffiti from the 1970s to the present.

Understanding the use of space has long been central in archaeological studies (see part II, spatial contexts section). By understanding how people use the spaces they occupy we learn about social structure, privilege and hierarchy, and the access different groups have both to space and information. For recent military sites there are documents that provide some of this information, and the sites' former occupants are sometimes available to interpret and explain. But even for this recent period it is often the physical space, and the clues within it that tells us most. Equally, from an archaeological viewpoint,

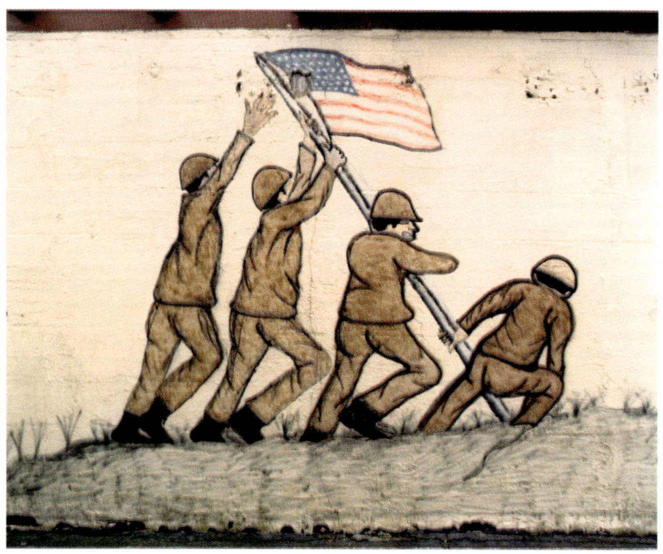 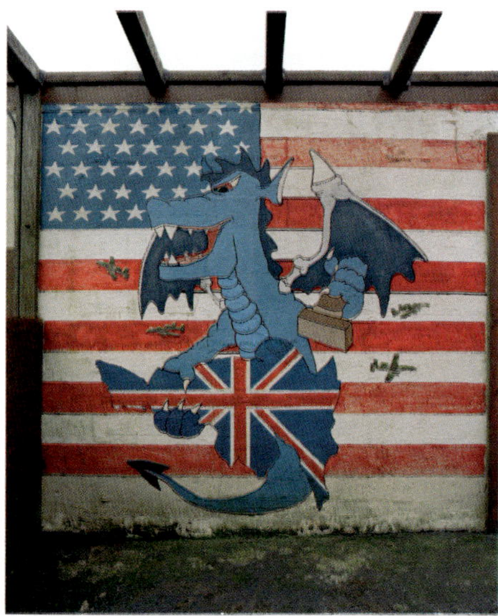

RAF Bentwaters, Suffolk, veranda of a hut for visiting aircrew
Left: **1980s a pastiche in aerosol of an iconic Second World War image by photographer Joe Rosenthal, United States marines raising the stars and stripes over Mount Suibachi, Iwo Jima, 23 February 1945. (AA021673)**
Right: **Mural incorporating the Gryphon emblem of the 81st Tactical Fighter Wing (AA021671)**
(© English Heritage)

attempts should be made to view the material culture separately, for an objective and independent perspective. In a similar way to the interpretation of prehistoric caves through the art that they contain, it is possible to interpret Cold War era buildings and the use of space within them through their art. The hardened avionics centre at Upper Heyford (Oxfordshire) is an example. Used to process and analyse electronic and photographic reconnaissance data, this is a semi-sunken two-storey structure containing large rooms filled with computers used to download and analyse data, and to prepare Electronic Counter Measures (ECM) equipment for the EF-111A Raven aircraft (Cocroft and Thomas 2003, 67). Within this building are numerous examples of war art, their location reflecting this functional allocation of space. This example is examined further on pp 123–8.

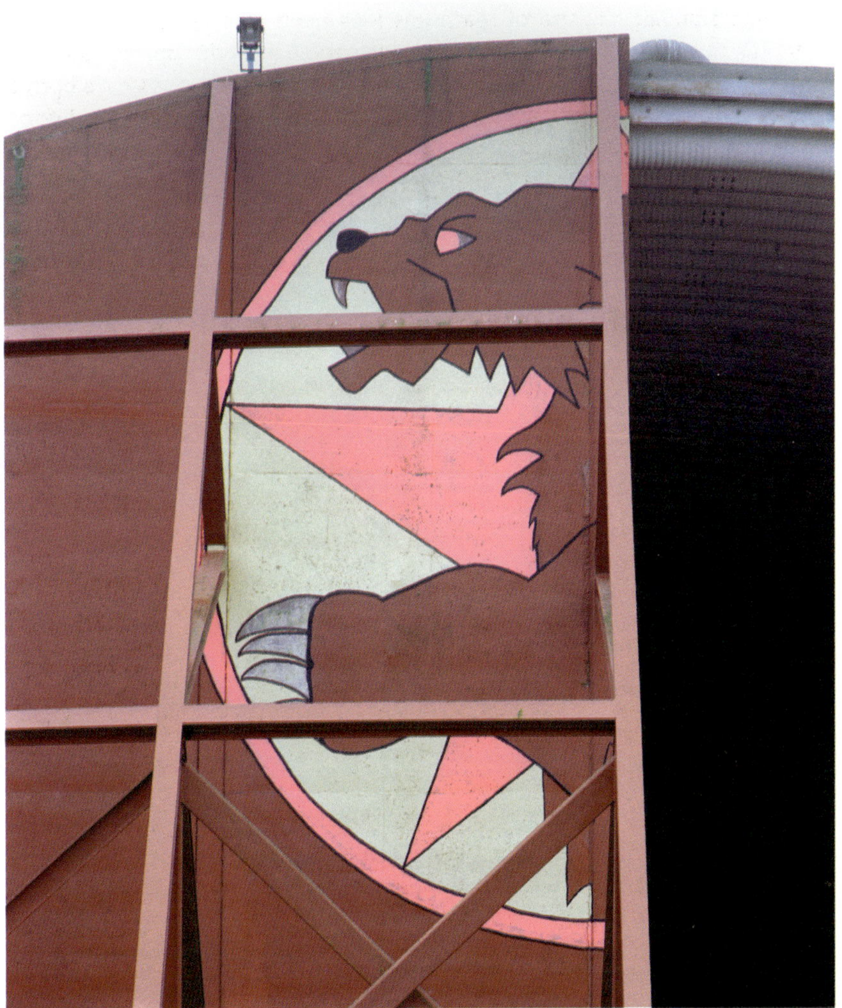

RAF Bentwaters, Suffolk, door of a hardened aircraft shelter used by 527th Aggressor Squadron who acted as a Soviet fighter unit to train United States aircrew. (AA021675 © English Heritage)

Put simply, war art breaks down into that which is corporate or communal (such as instruction drawings, or unit emblems) and that which is private. The latter might include doodling and graffiti, or pictures stuck to walls (pin-ups for example). Examples of the latter are more common where personnel are held against their wishes, such as prisoners of war for example, or where boredom or homesickness is experienced. At Brigg in Lincolnshire sketches can be seen on the walls of prisoner of war camp buildings – touches that give the sites an intimacy, a personal dimension, a degree of social significance alongside the interpretation and insights into camp life that they also provide.

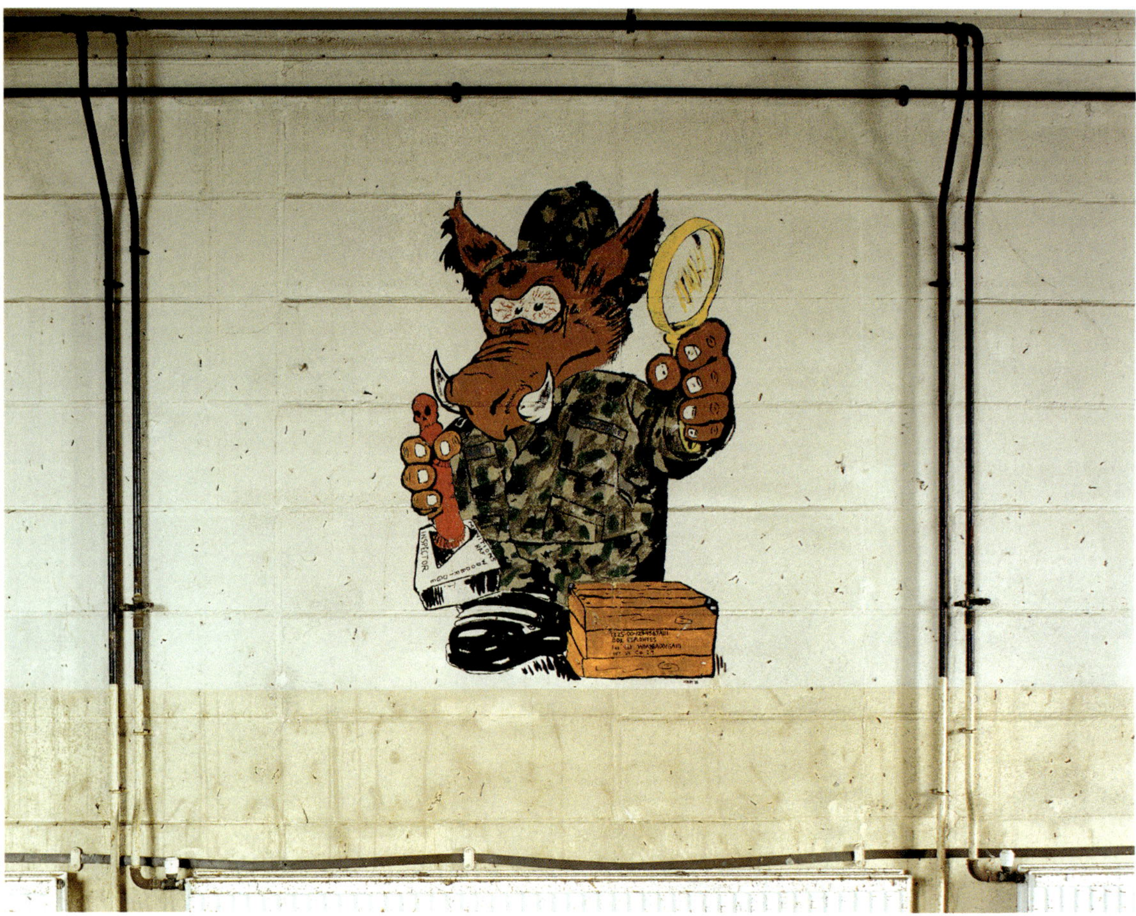

RAF Woodbridge, Suffolk, Ammunition Inspection Facility 255
Warthog 1988, name patch 'Death', painted by Wishy 1988 (AA054170 © English Heritage)

RAF Woodbridge, Suffolk, Special
Weapons Maintenance building 264
Left: From top – Building
entrance (AA054175)
Rear wall with boot and
foot prints (AA054174)
Metal grenade (AA054177)
Painted over Gerry
cartoon (AA054180)
Top: Right – Building
number (AA054176)
Middle: Right – 'Welcome to
Ammo Land' (AA054182)
Bottom: Right – Garfield and
Oddie cartoon (AA054181)
(© English Heritage)

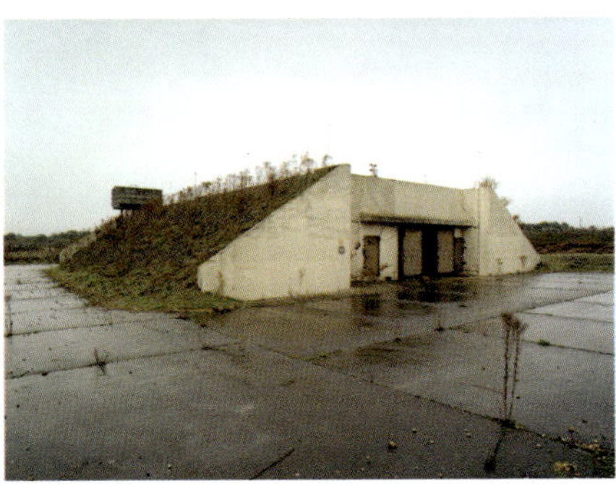

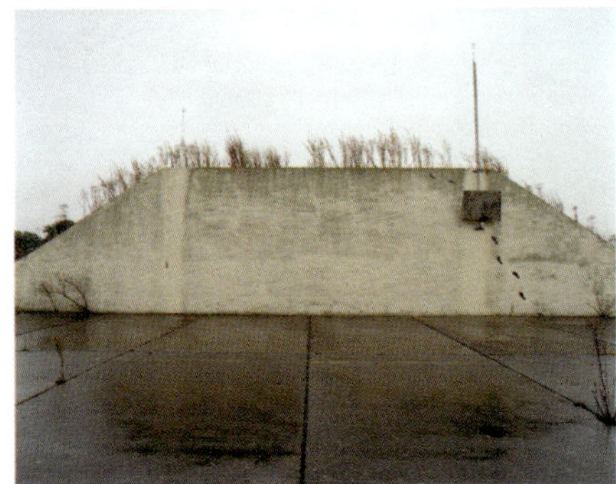

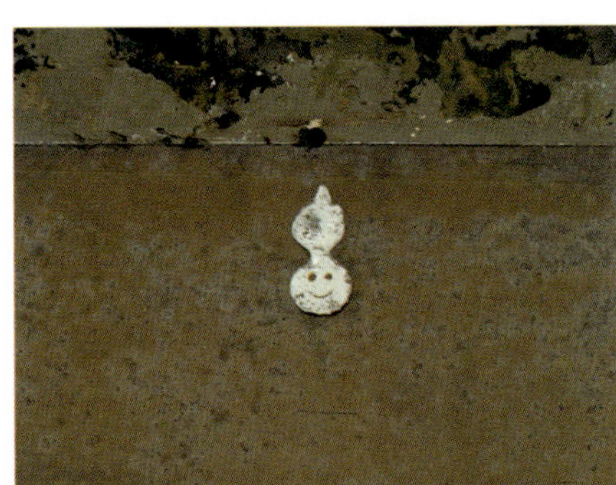

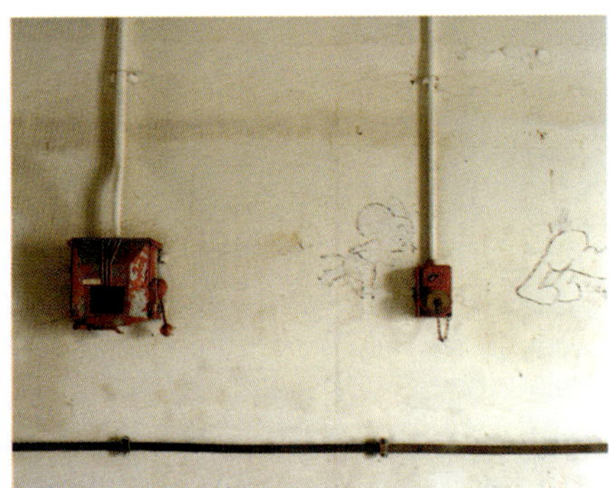

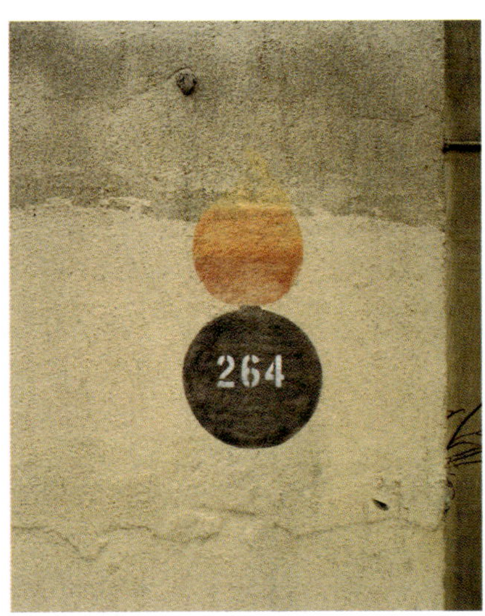

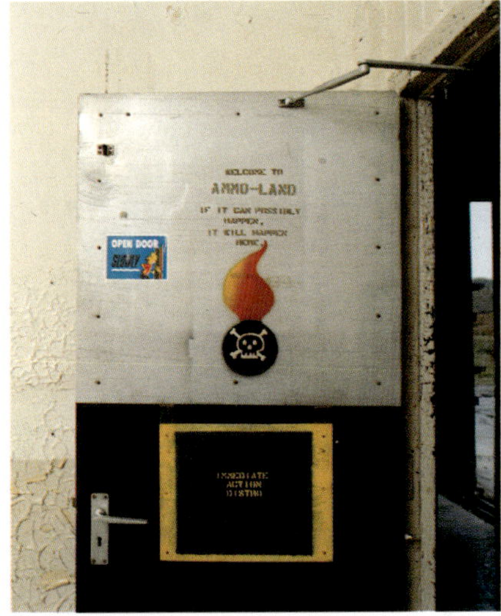

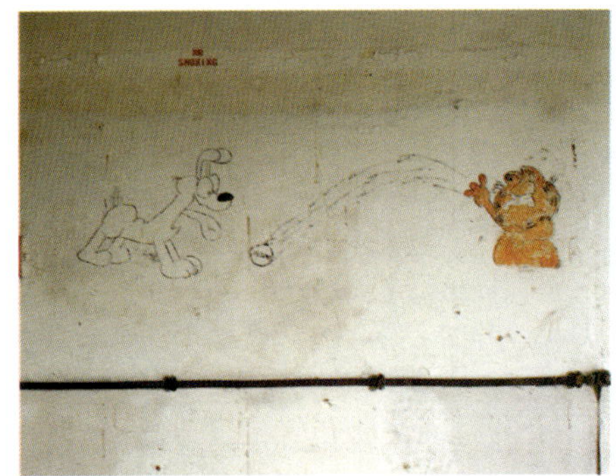

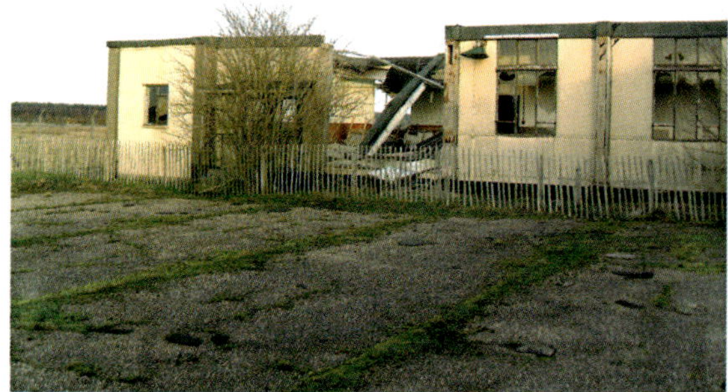
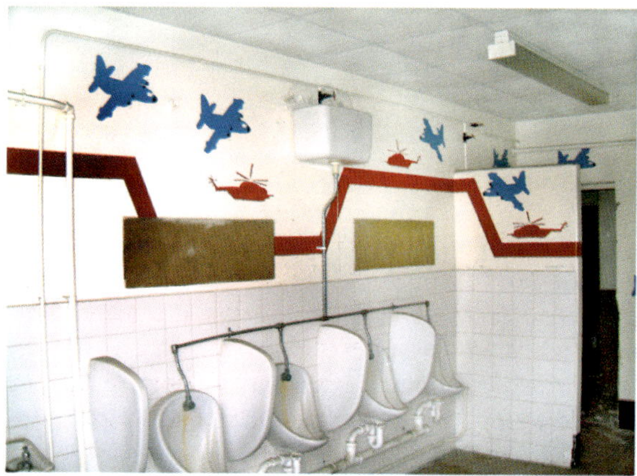
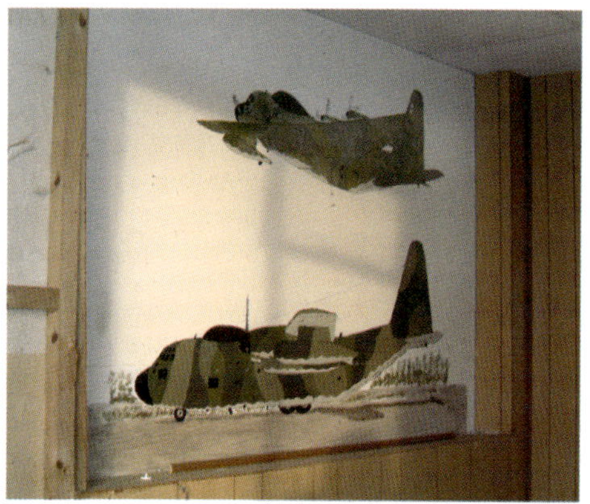
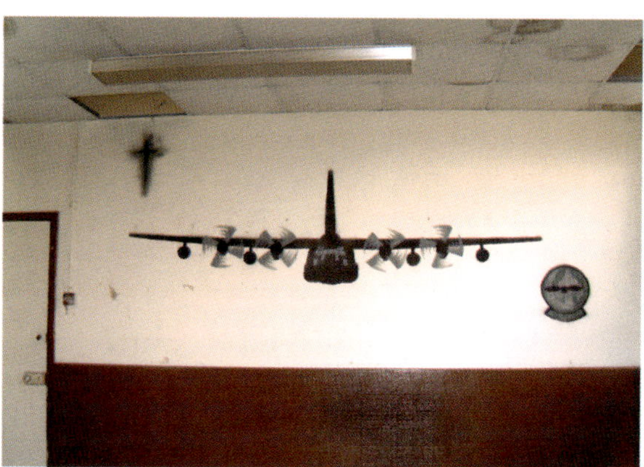

RAF Woodbridge, Suffolk, 39th Special Operations Wing Building, abandoned early 1990s
Top: Left – Exterior of rapidly deteriorating 'Seco' building
Top: Right – Latrine with stencils of Lockheed MC-130P Hercules and MH-53J Jolly Green Giant
(© R J C Thomas)
Bottom: Left – Lockheed MC-130P Hercules Combat Shadow (© R J C Thomas)
Bottom: Right – Lockheed MC-130P Hercules Combat Shadow flanked by blazing cross and unit patch
(© R J C Thomas)

CONTEMPORARY REPRESENTATIONS

It must be no coincidence that the Second World War and Cold War bases with which people most closely identify, and generally those with the best preserved or most impressive war art, are also those bases which have served as the inspiration for contemporary professional artists seeking to create their own record of a site and its influence. John Kippin's (2001) and the Wilson Twins' (Schjeldahl 1999) studies at Greenham Common are examples of this, as is Keith Watson's (2004) work, and Louise K Wilson's (2003) study of Spadeadam (Cumbria). Polly Feversham and Leo Schmidt described the value of contemporary representations of Cold War era monuments in their book *Berlin Wall Today* (1999). They noted how:

> Art possesses the power to promote a dialogue between past and future memories of a structure, helping to ensure its contemporary relevance and preventing it becoming moribund, static, a fly in amber. There is an argument that contemporary art has a vital, if largely unsung part to play in this respect, acting as an *agent provocateur* in re-energising spaces which by virtue of their very historicity are in danger of being sacrosanct. . . . Contemporary art – vital, provocative, of the moment – when forming a partnership with an historic building or place can act as a conduit to the interchange of time, memory and present history, challenging and de-naturalising complacent assumptions, establishing a building in the public consciousness and investing it with contemporary relevance. In short, making the historic fabric live. . . . In effect, creation is part of preservation (*ibid*, 166).

Perhaps this is why war art matters: because it represents that dialogue between the place and those that occupied it at some point in the recent past, the occupants 'making their mark', and investing the building, and the spaces it contains, with human relevance. The quality of the art is irrelevant, as is the difference between art that is officially sanctioned and that which is more subversive; and to some extent that which is contemporary and directly related to a site's primary military purpose, and that which is created after its abandonment. All of these examples create a narrative for the site, a comment on its function, status and people's attitude towards it. The question therefore isn't whether the art is 'good' or 'bad', but rather how it functions, as a therapeutic, morale-building or bonding activity, and the information it provides about the site and people's response to the spaces it contains. Archaeologists make sense of ancient sites by the artwork they contain, their symbolism and spatial configuration; this is now equally necessary for the contemporary past. The materials and images may be very different, but the principles are the same.

PART II

War art abroad

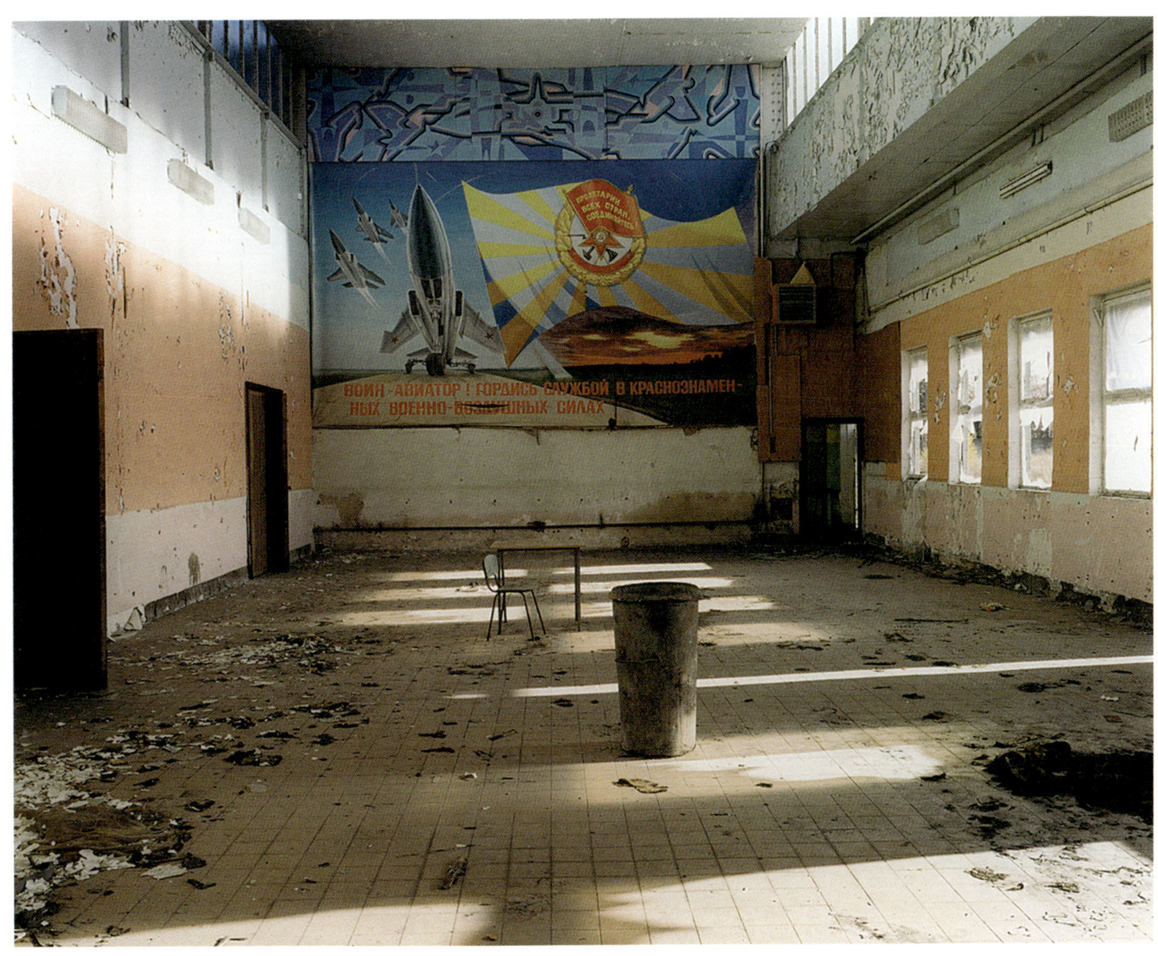

Recreation room, 'Warrior Airmen! Serve in your Red Army Airforce units with pride' Rangsdorf, Brandenburg (16.3.99 © Angus Boulton)

EUROPEAN EXAMPLES

STRAIT STREET, VALLETTA: MALTA – A COLONIAL LEGACY

Running through the heart of Valletta is Strait Street – a place that resonates with the sights and sounds of a turbulent past: the place where knights once duelled and, more recently, where sailors drank and danced and where musicians played, in the many bars and music halls that lined its sides. This was an urban experience similar to that in many other naval ports around the world, but it is different in two crucial respects: first, that Strait Street exists in a country that identifies strongly with the Catholic faith, making the presence of prostitution for example rather more difficult to accept; and second, that the area is largely undeveloped since it was finally abandoned from the 1960s. These photographs, from a larger collection, show how signage and graffiti have survived here, and provide the visual landmarks to a place that was effectively abandoned when the Navy withdrew after Malta's independence in 1964. The project, which continues, was funded by the British Academy.

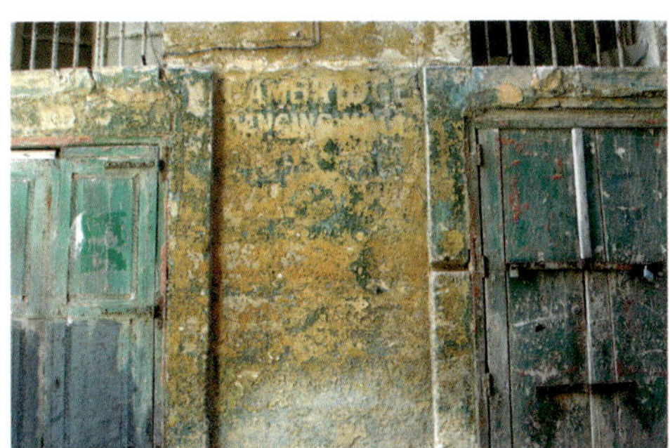

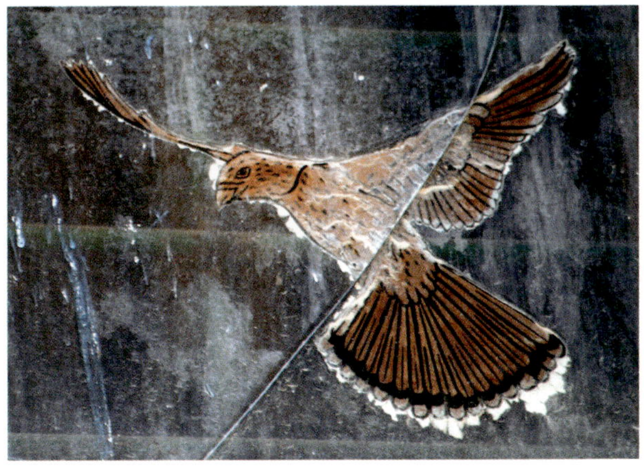

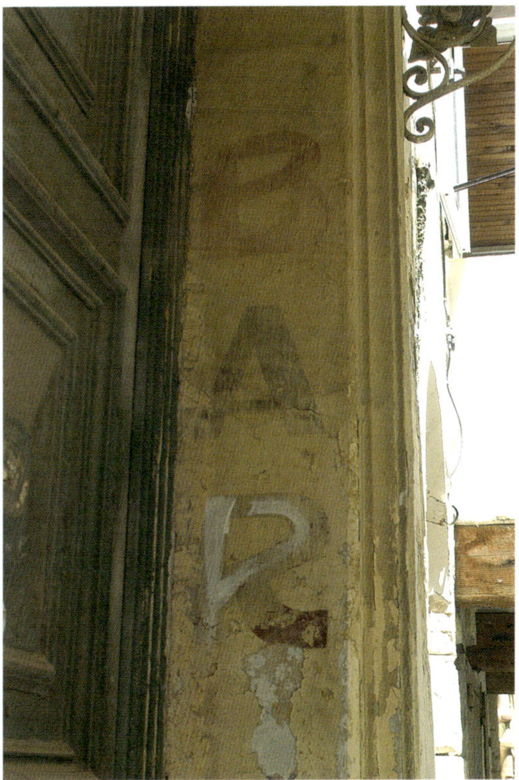

Images of Strait Street (© John Schofield and Emily Morrissey)

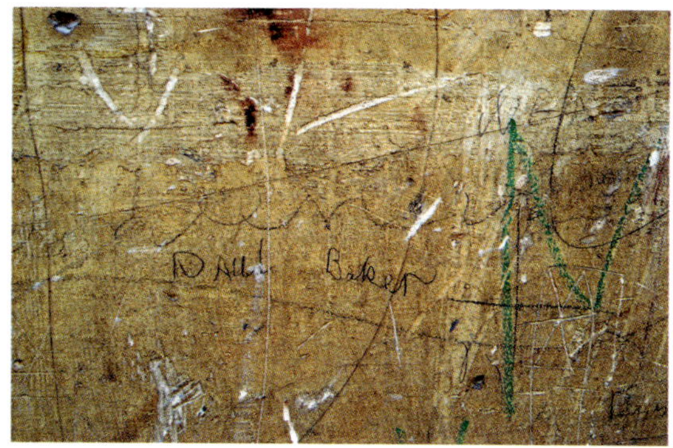
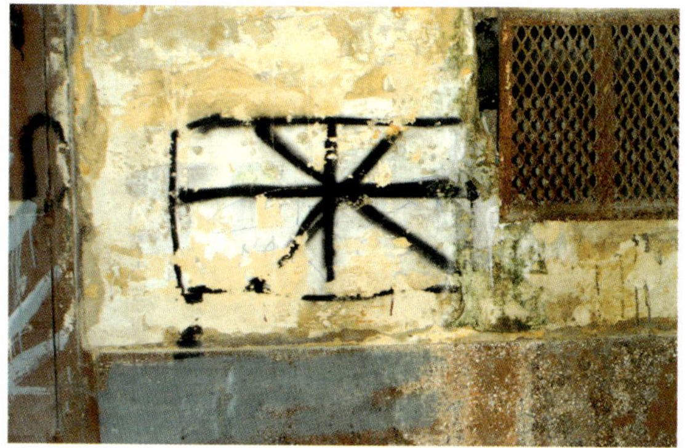
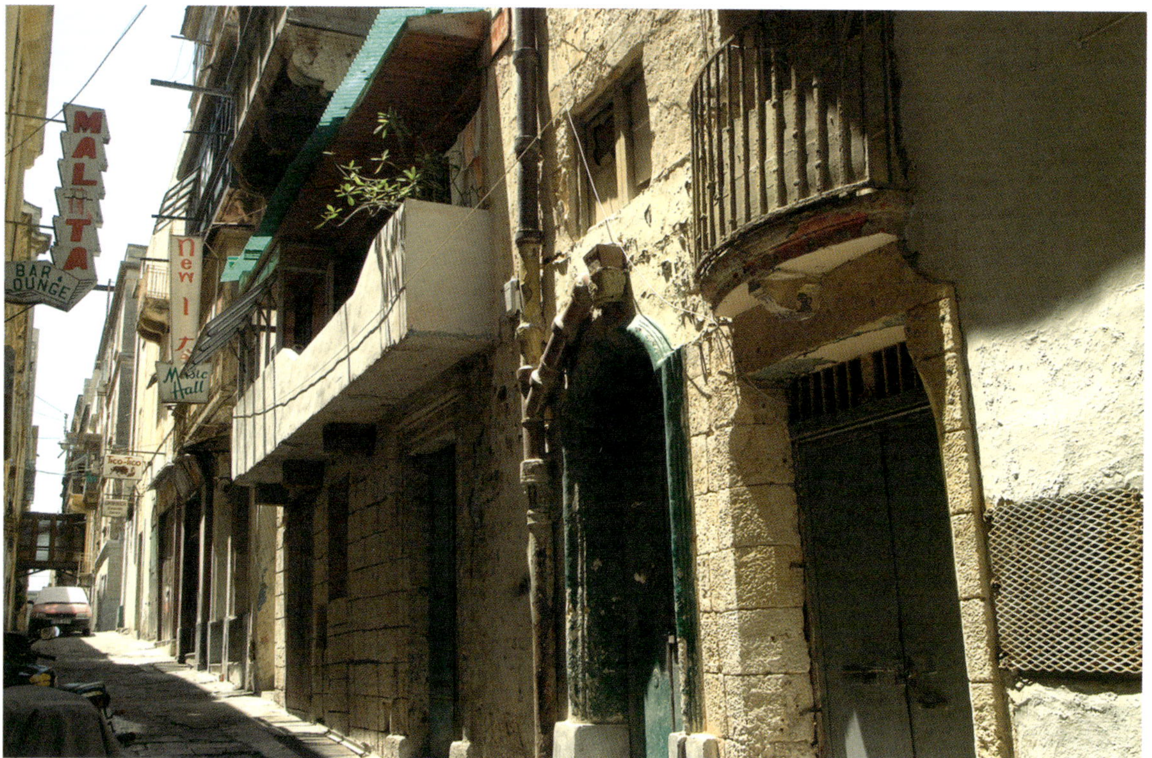

Images of Strait Street (© John Schofield and Emily Morrissey)

EASTERN EUROPE

In the Soviet Union, the use of Agitatsiia Propanganda, or Agit Prop, as a means of instilling political messages in the population may be traced back to the post-revolutionary period, after 1917. The use of posters and slogans painted on walls and military equipment was also commonly used during the Second World War to urge the armed forces on to victory. During the Cold War murals were a common feature of Soviet military bases, where they were used for political purposes, extolling the progressive nature of socialist society and the heritage of the Red Army. During this period, it may be viewed as an imperial army composed of many different nationalities for whom Russian was not always their first language. Murals were also frequently used for training purposes, examples including instructions on how to put on a chemical warfare suit, rifle stripping and the unit's role in the Great Patriotic, or Second World War. The majority of Soviet forces were

Nedlitz barracks, Potsdam, Soviet artillery division, 'Victory' parade ground mural (18.9.98 © Angus Boulton)

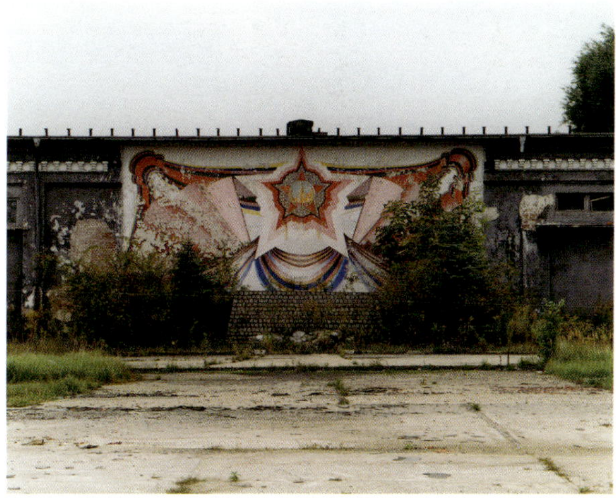

Jüterborg, Branden-burg, Altes Lager airfield, 'History of the unit', mural for the airforce fighter regiment, accom-modation block entrance (17.7.99 © Angus Boulton)

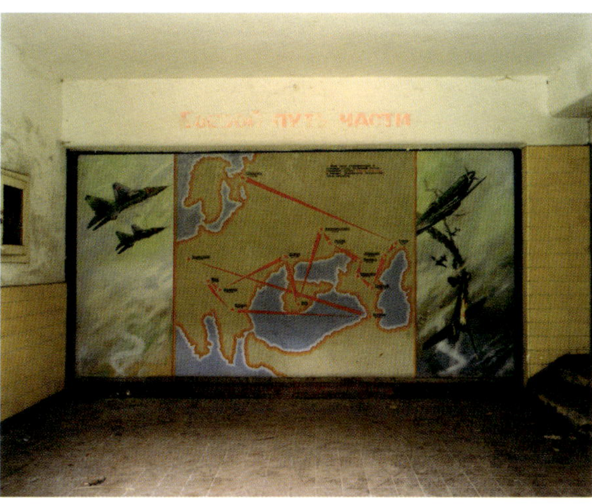

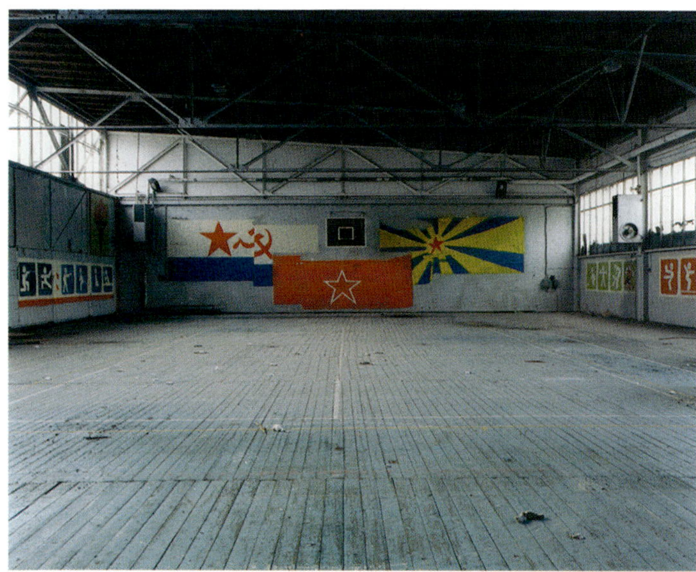

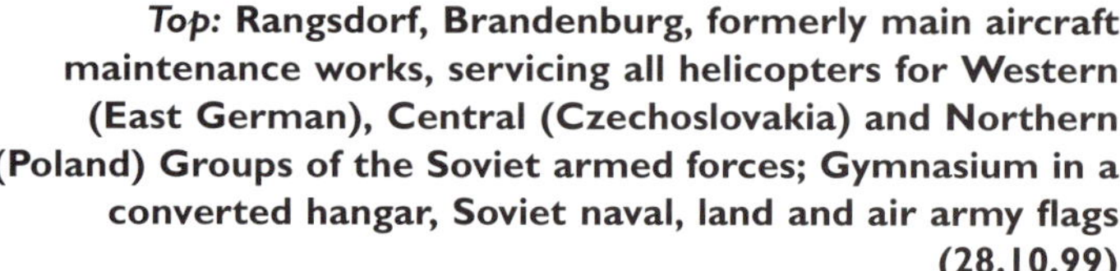

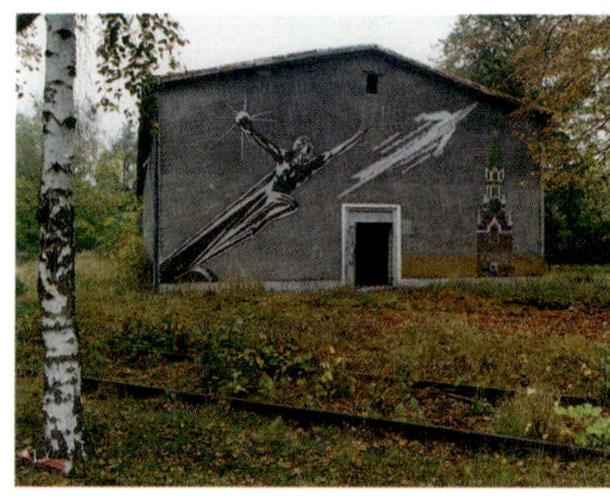

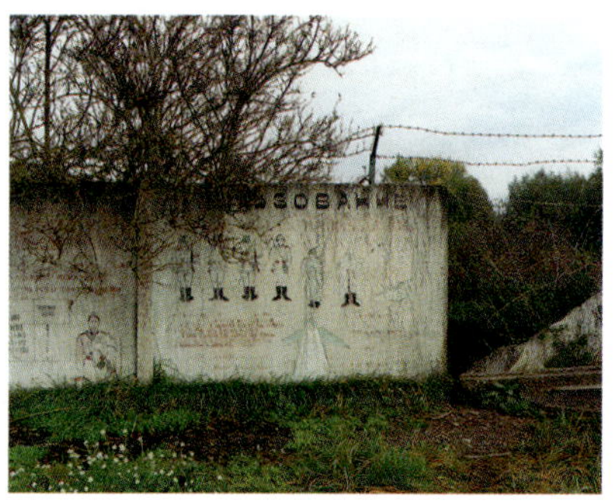

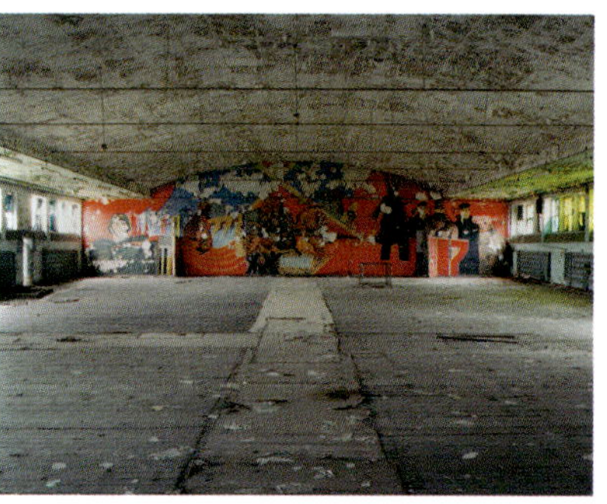

Top: Rangsdorf, Brandenburg, formerly main aircraft maintenance works, servicing all helicopters for Western (East German), Central (Czechoslovakia) and Northern (Poland) Groups of the Soviet armed forces; Gymnasium in a converted hangar, Soviet naval, land and air army flags (28.10.99)

Top Right: Jüterborg, Brandenburg, Altes Lager airfield; Artillery brigade munitions depot, gymnasium, exterior mosaic, broken bottle glass over paint (25.10.01) (© Angus Boulton); *Middle Right:* Krampnitz, Brandenburg; Surface to air missile regiment, perimeter wall, instructions against chemical attack (17.10.00)

Bottom Right: Krampnitz, Brandenburg; Motor rifle division, cinema mural (16.3.99) (© Angus Boulton)

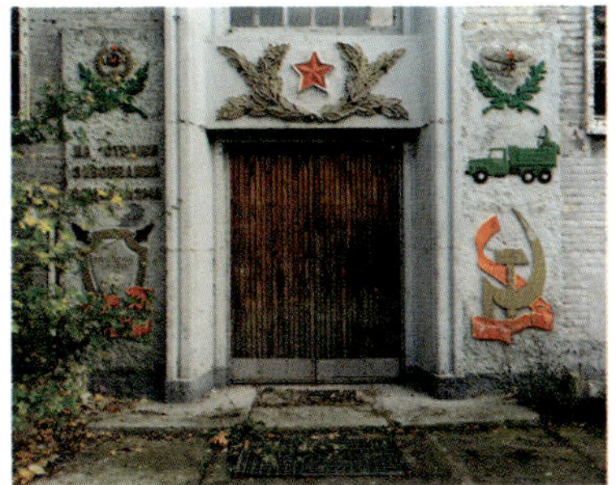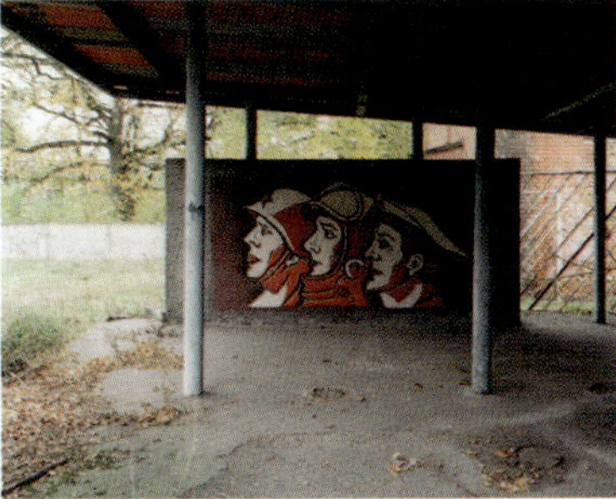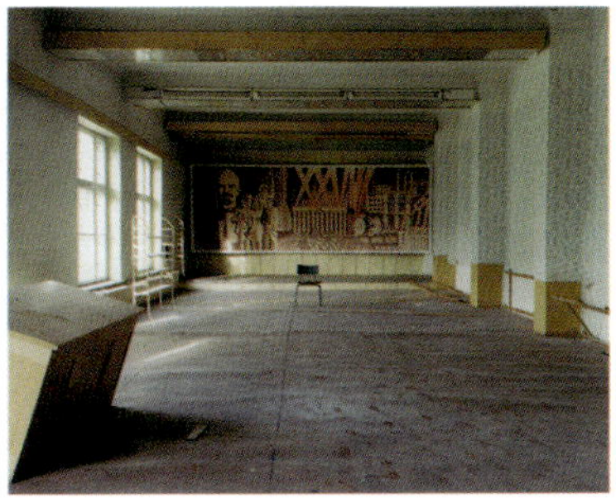

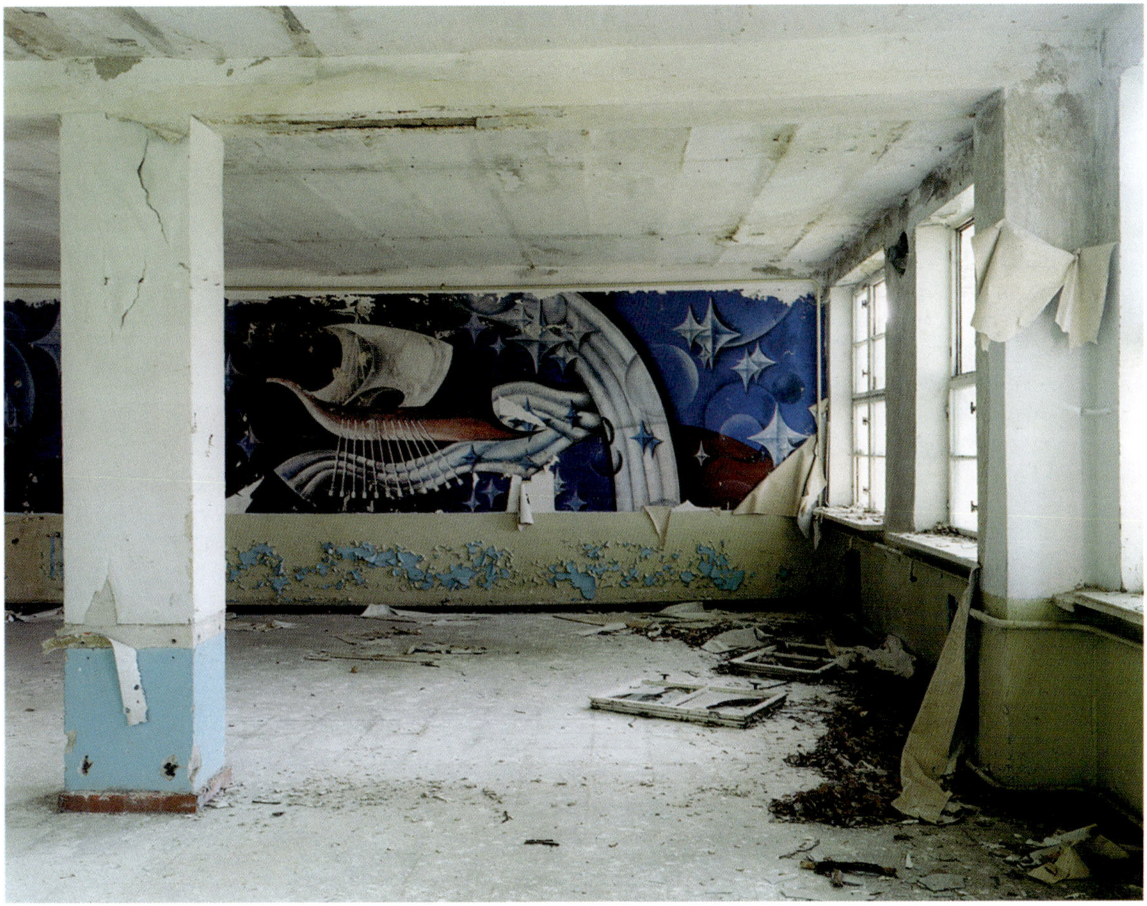

Top: Left – Krampnitz, Brandenburg; Relief sculpture around an entrance, replacing a Nazi relief on a former Wehrmacht cavalry school building (24.10.00) *Middle* – Neues Lager, Jüterborg, Brandenburg, soldier, airman and sailor relief sculpture (31.10.00) *Right* – Forst Zinna, Jüterborg, Brandenburg, engineer construction brigade, library (2.11.00) *Bottom:* Eberswalde, Brandenburg, maintenance brigade, recreation room (23.5.02) (© Angus Boulton)

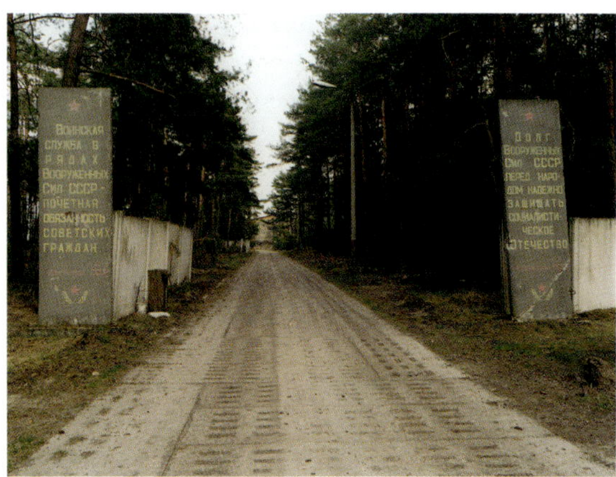

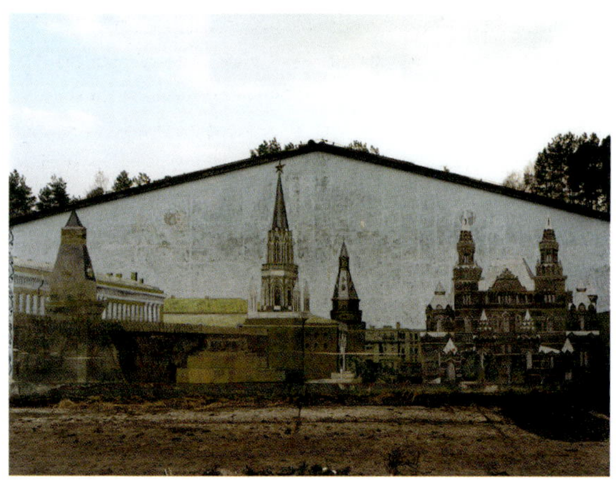

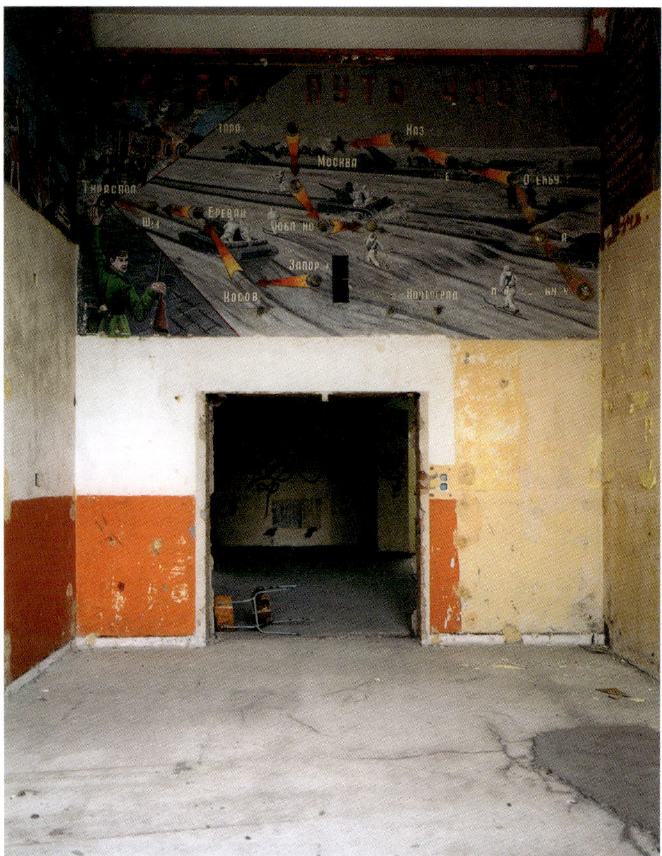

Top: Left – Stolzenhain, Brandenburg, was one of the two facilities guarded by KGB troops where nuclear warheads were stored, which in time of war would have been issued to East German army units; Communist slogans on inner perimeter wall (11.4.03)
Right – Cultural centre, Kremlin mural (11.4.03)
Bottom: Left – Halle, Sachen Anhalt, Guards motor rifle division, 'History of the unit' mural (8.5.03)
(© Angus Boulton)

restricted to their bases and cultural centres and this isolation played an important role in the life of these communities. The bases were decorated with patriotic scenes, but in some dining areas romantic landscape scenes are also found ranging from desert islands to central European castles near tree-lined lakes. Most of the artwork found in more communal areas of the bases is of a high technical quality. Within the barrack areas less well-executed murals are found, but the theme is often still military hardware. Only in very rare instances are frivolous murals found. One example is deep in the bunker complex at Falkenhagen, Brandenburg, where there are 1992 Christmas greetings and cartoon figures, one of which appears to be a copy of the Disney character Pluto. This late example was, however, drawn when the bunker was being dismantled and Soviet forces were beginning their withdrawal from Germany. It is also at Falkenhagen, where many of the bathrooms in the apartments built for Soviet officers in the early 1990s are decorated by paintings of fish. These were probably painted by the officers' wives.

PROTEST, SECTARIANISM AND CONFLICT

NORTHERN IRELAND MURALS

The archaeological landscape of Northern Ireland contains much evidence for the Troubles that have occurred there. Perhaps its most potent images are the murals that remain throughout the urban landscape. These were often placed on the end gables of terraced houses, a prominent position ideal for emphasising the message or propaganda that organisations wanted to put across to their supporters and enemies. The murals are often large and hard to ignore. In Northern Ireland para-military murals are integral to everyday life; they served to reinforce the notions of their artists and create identity and divisions between areas of the urban landscape. They were also places where artwork was constantly being repainted; art was not a stable factor and as a representation of the Troubles it was adapted accordingly.

Para-military wall art in mural form began around 1908 in Northern Ireland. The first murals painted by loyalists in Belfast and Derry depicted the Battle of the Boyne and William III's victory. Other visual celebrations before this included marches, flags, banners and bunting. The first mural in Derry was painted in 1920 and still exists (Rolston 1992; 1995).

It was not until after the 1981 hunger strikes that nationalist murals became more common. Before this phase of the Troubles, any nationalist attempts to create visual displays were rare, severely punished or banned. In 1980 a republican youth was shot dead for painting a slogan on the wall; the policeman concerned said he had mistaken the paintbrush for a gun (Jarman 1998, 1). The most longstanding

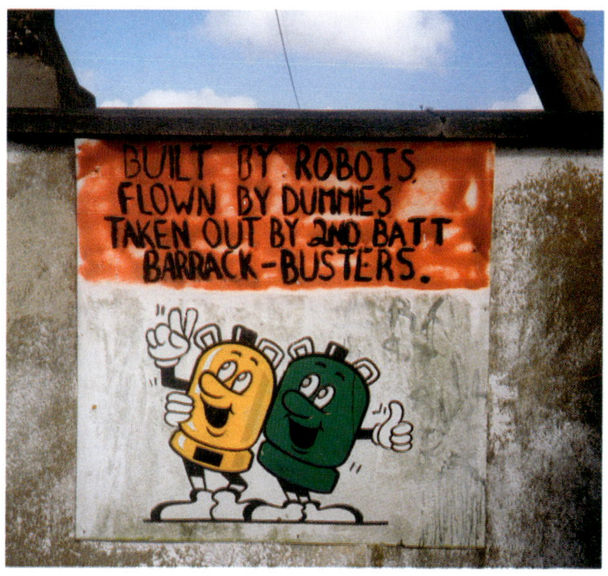

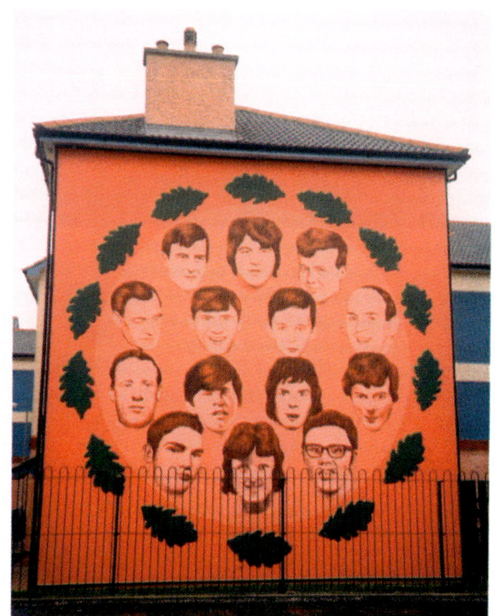

***Left:* Barrack-buster, Crossmaglen, County Armagh**
***Right:* Bloody Sunday, Derry (© Jonathan McCormick)**

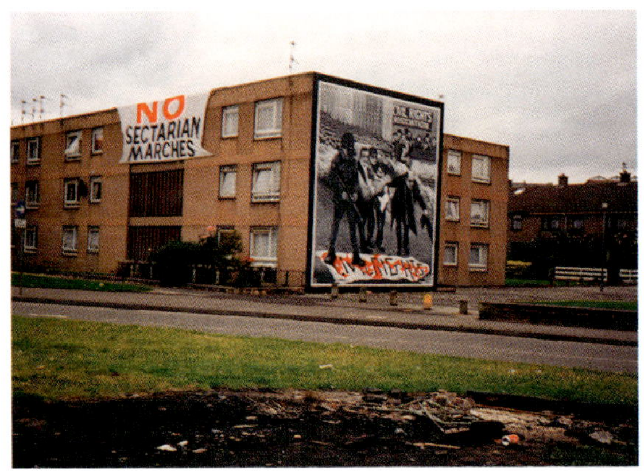

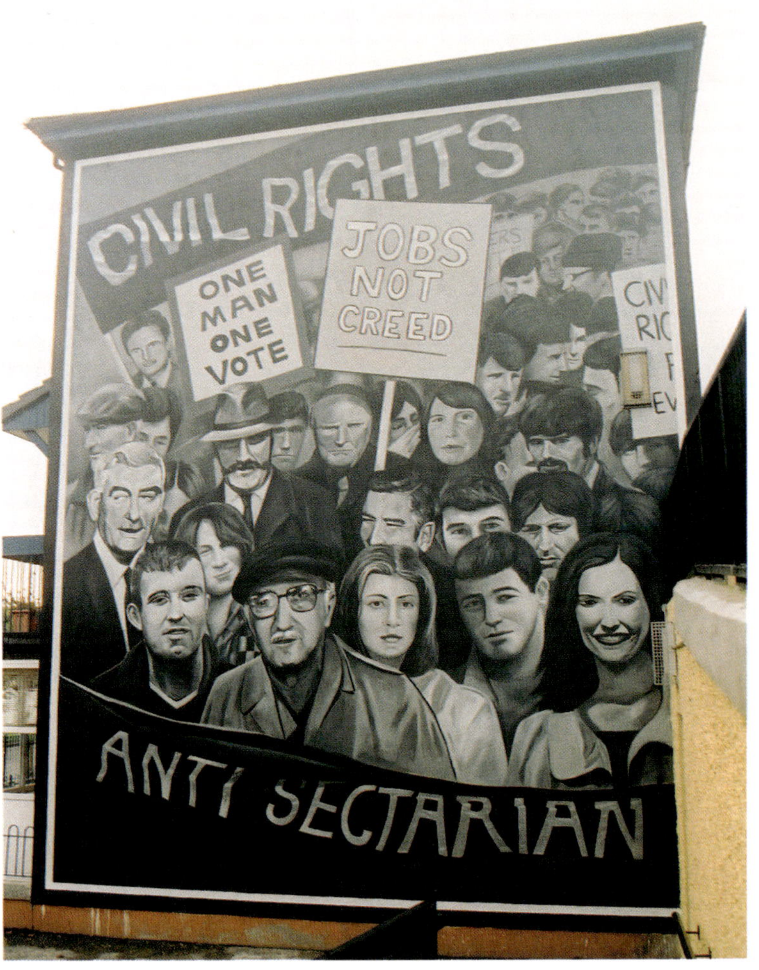

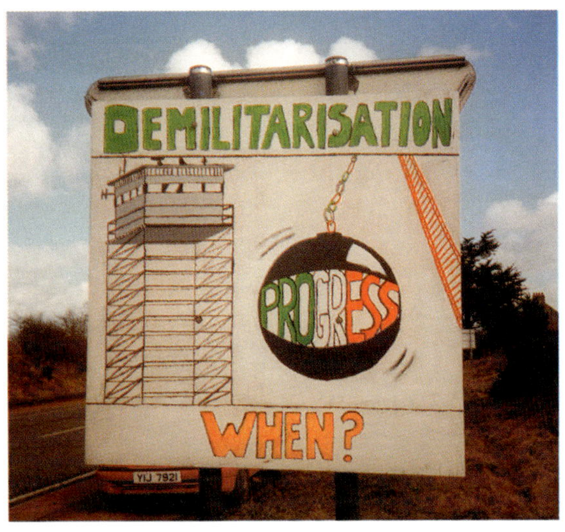

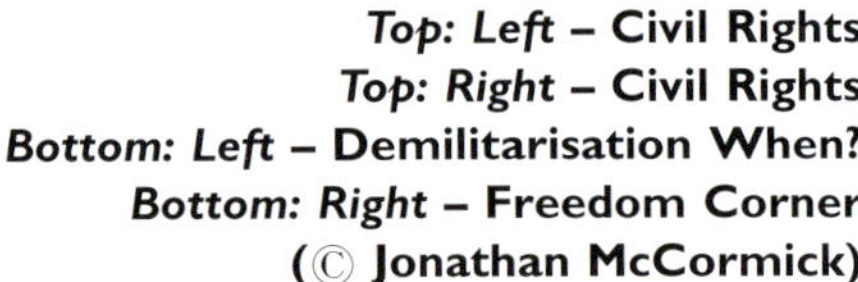

Top: Left – Civil Rights
Top: Right – Civil Rights
Bottom: Left – Demilitarisation When?
Bottom: Right – Freedom Corner
(© Jonathan McCormick)

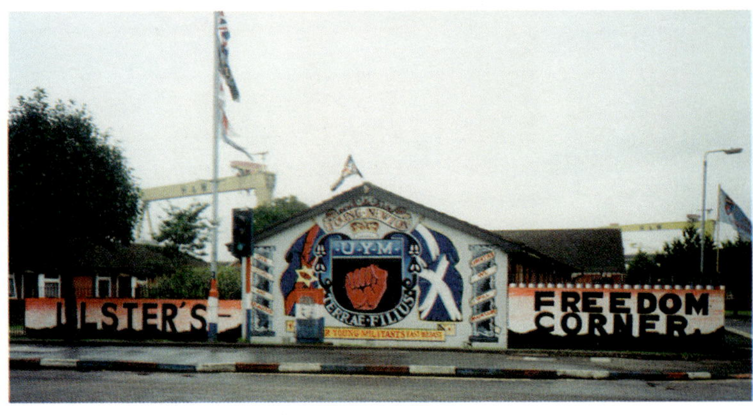

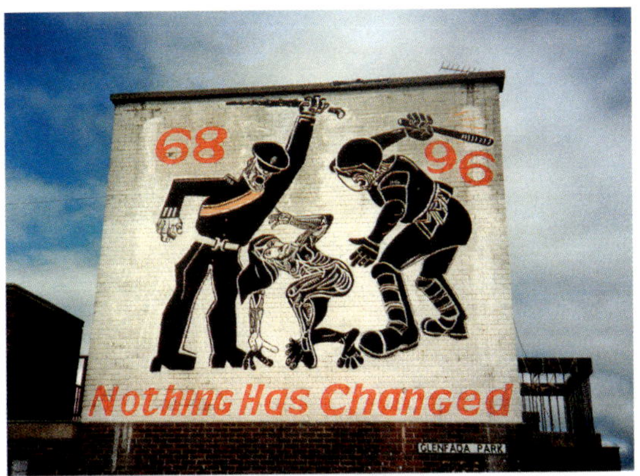

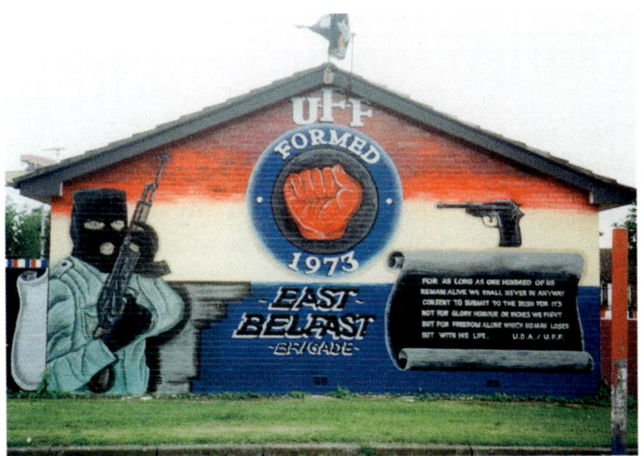

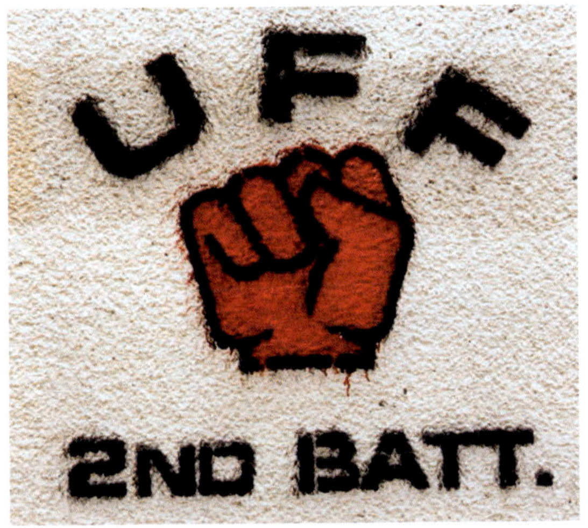

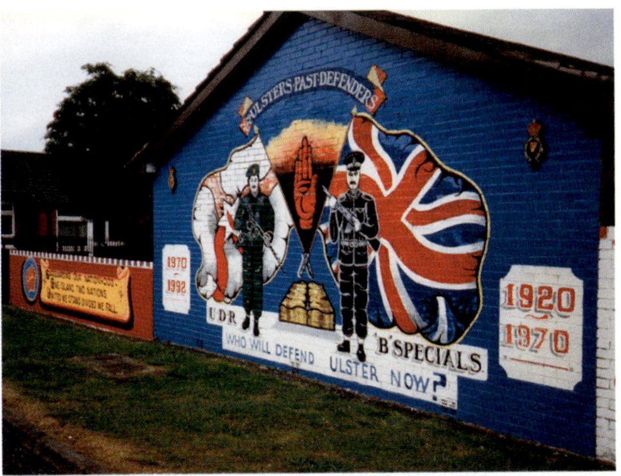

Top: Left – **Nothing has changed;** *Top: Right* – **Ulster Freedom Fighters;** *Bottom: Left* – **Ulster Freedom Fighters, stencil;** *Bottom: Right* – **Ulster's Past Defenders (© Jonathan McCormick)**

nationalist mural exists on a gable wall in the Bogside (Derry). It has been there since 1969, and proclaims, 'You Are Now Entering Free Derry' (Jarman 1998, 5). This mural emerged during a time when barricades were being erected to divide and protect the two communities from each other. Now the wall is on an isolated stretch of dual carriageway. Yet, although it is no longer part of a housing estate it is still regularly maintained and a place where people gather to commemorate Bloody Sunday (Jarman 1998, 5).

In common with Northern Ireland, much of the commemorative street art in Israel and Palestine is commissioned by the various armed factions. Many political slogans were clear incitements to violence and were regularly white-washed over if the Palestinian leadership wished to signal that it was trying to curb the actions of militants. During the 1990s murals became a feature of the struggle between the Israelis and the Palestinians. These include images of those killed while mounting raids against Israel, or killed by Israeli attacks. These images take the form of portraits or complex calligraphy.

PROTEST AND THE SUBVERSION OF MILITARY STRUCTURES

In many abandoned military establishments, graffiti, and more rarely well-executed murals, are a common accompaniment to the vandalism that hastens their dereliction and destruction. Most is produced by transient groups. The act of gaining access to disused defence sites may involve some physical or legal risk. It may be seen as a test for the group members. The resulting graffiti may be applied as a marker to the achievement of entry into a forbidden place and claiming the space, perhaps just for a short time span, as well as an act of rebellion by defacing property. Elsewhere, other groups, some involved in black magic, as in the former radar bunker at RAF Bempton (East Riding of Yorkshire), have laid claim to these abandoned places with their own distinctive murals. The underground building at Bempton has been decorated with sexually explicit murals on many of the walls (Dearing 2002). One view is to consider this vandalism, damaging the character of wartime buildings; another is to recognise a separate phase of reuse, something archaeologists are used to dealing with for earlier periods. There is a difference between graffiti which is damaging and can compromise a site's historic character, and that which adds to it. There is often a fine line between them, but graffiti subsequent to a site's abandonment, or even during its use, can sometimes be a positive contribution to documenting the history of a site.

More rarely where peace protestors have broken into military establishments they too may mark buildings or machines. The feminist symbols painted on a wall in the former cruise missile shelter compound at RAF Greenham Common (West Berkshire), probably post-date the withdrawal of the missiles, but represent a symbolic invasion of military space nevertheless.

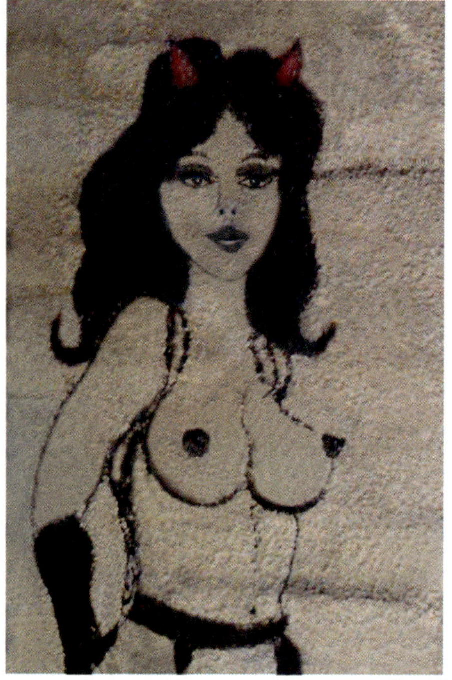

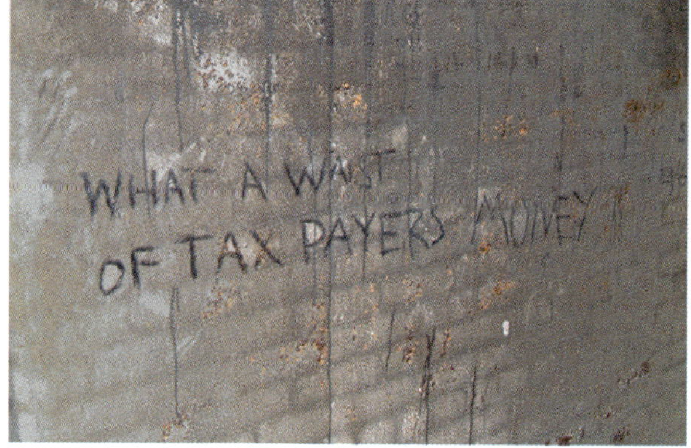

RAF Bempton, North Yorkshire, abandoned early 1950s radar bunker
Left: **Detail of one of a number of explicit 1960s images painted on the bunker walls after abandonment, secondary additions are probably associated with devil worship**
Right: **'What a waist of tax payers money'**
(© R J C Thomas)

The Verne, Dorset, High Angle Battery
Late 1960s/early 1970s
Dylan from the Magic Roundabout (© R J C Thomas)

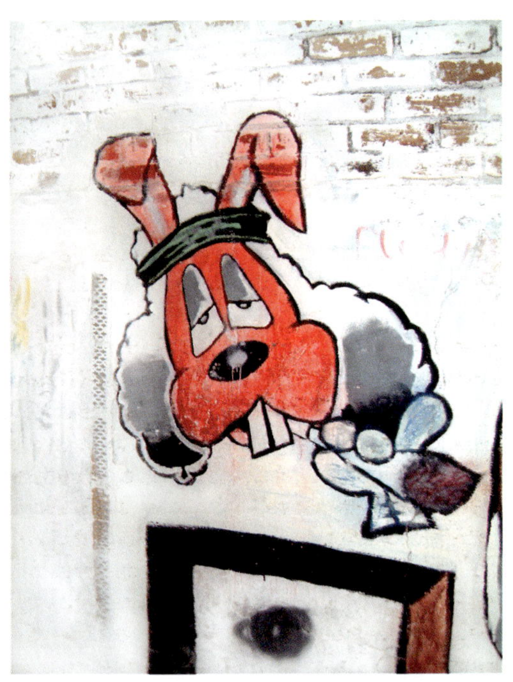

Southrop Airfield, Wiltshire, artwork probably applied during the late 1960s or early 1970s
Sick quarters (© Alan Strickland)

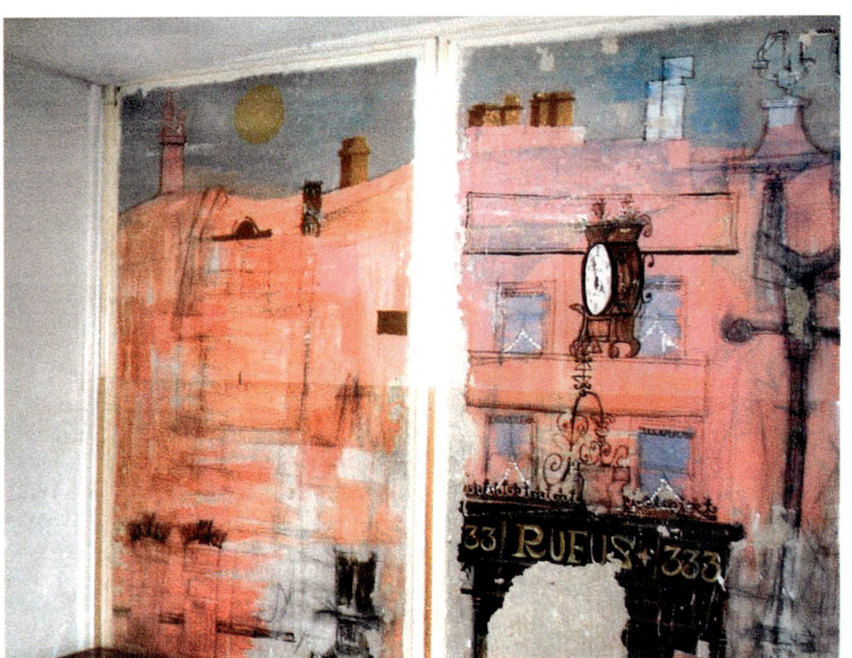

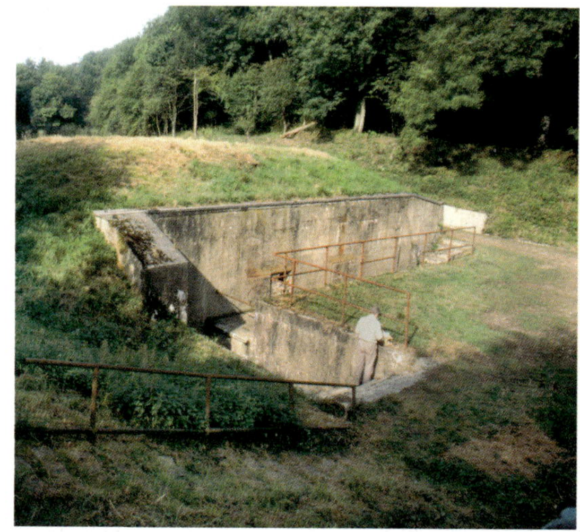

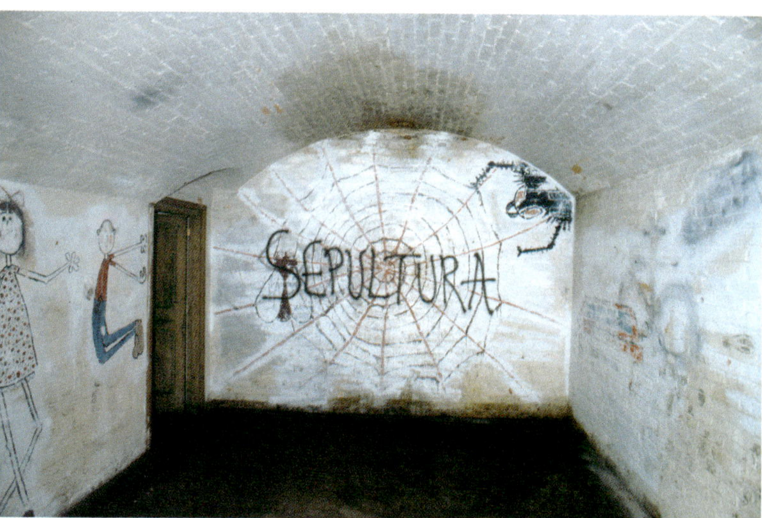

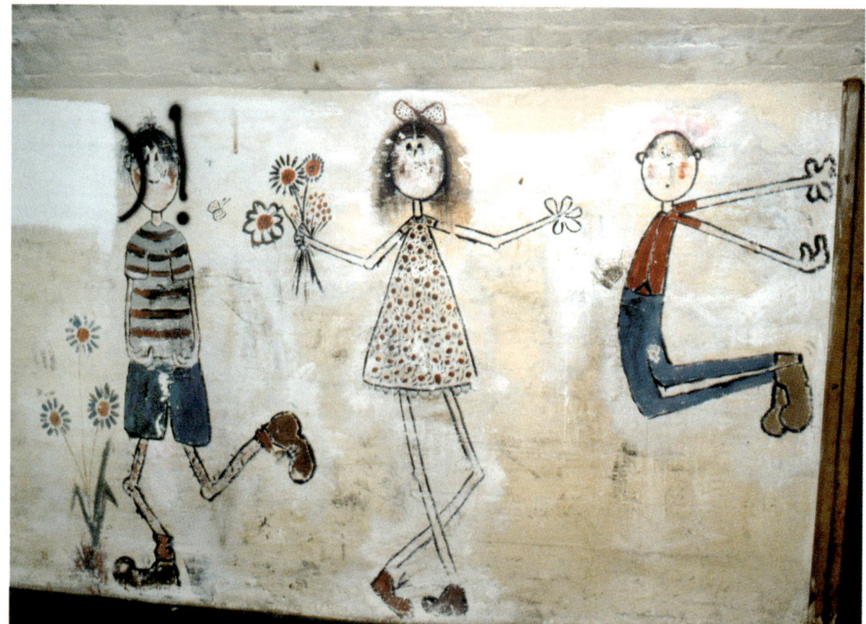

Betchworth 19th-century Mobilisation Centre, Surrey
Top: Left – General view
Top: Right – Sepultura
Bottom: Figures
(© R J C Thomas)

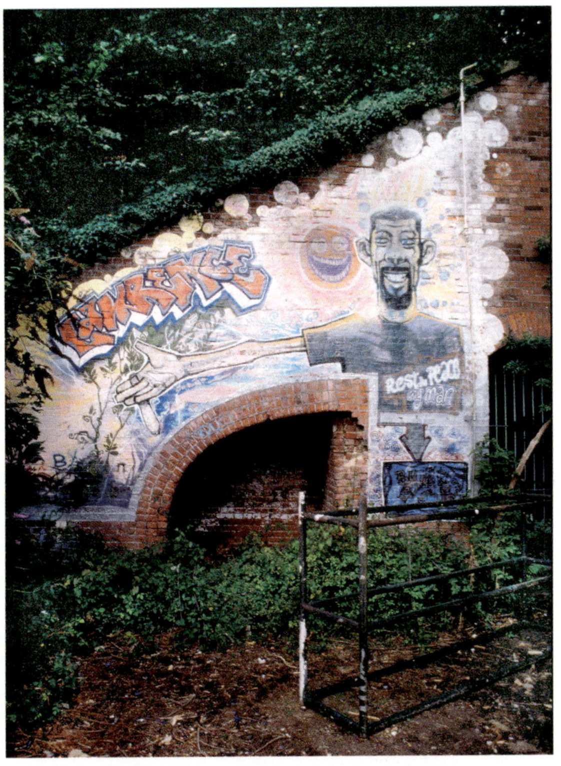

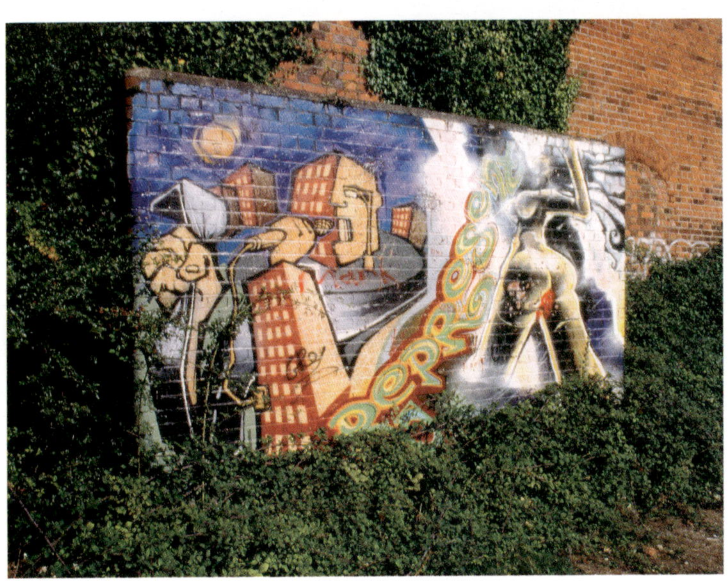

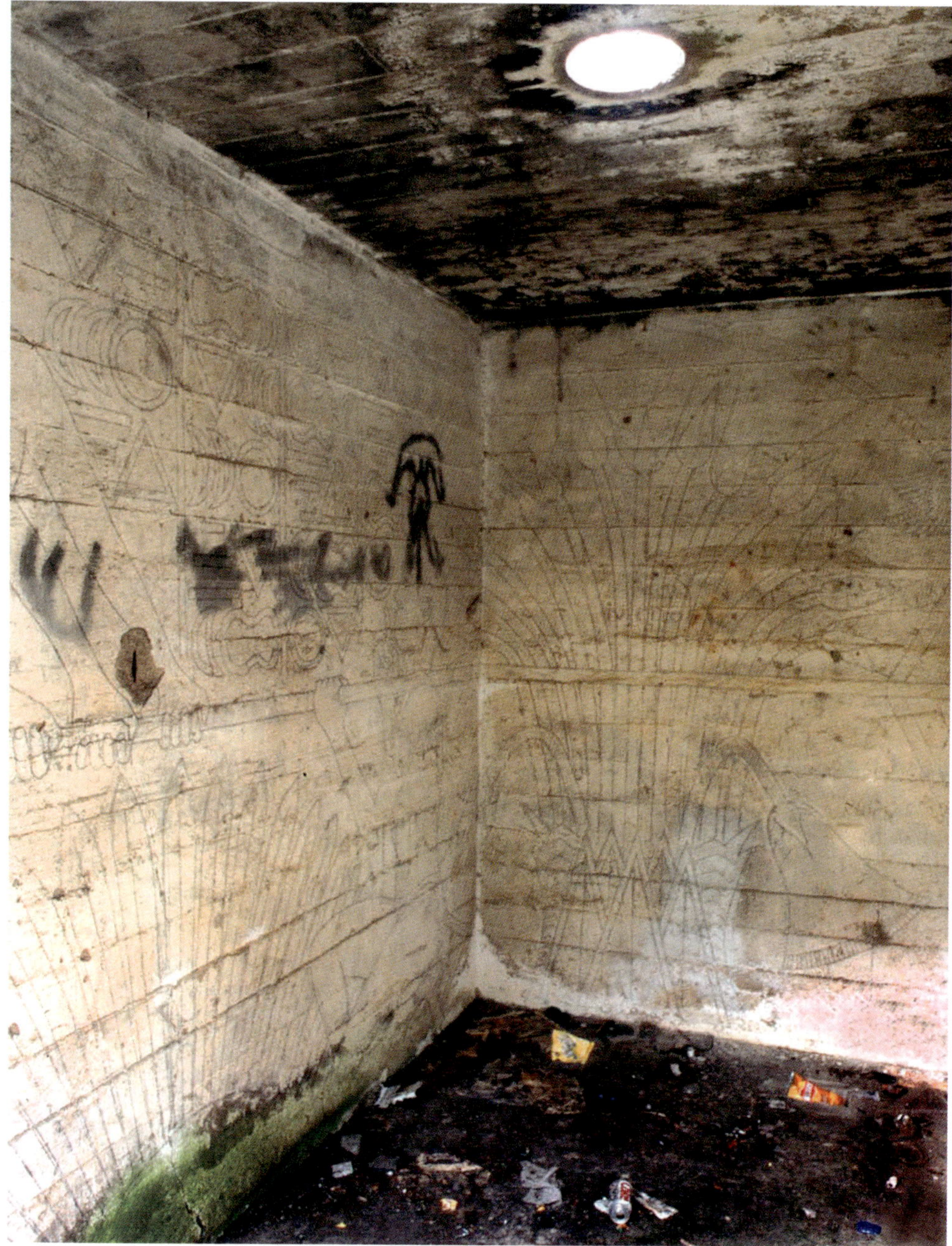

**Lavernock Point, Glamorgan, Heavy Anti Aircraft battery
Egyptian design (© R J C Thomas)**

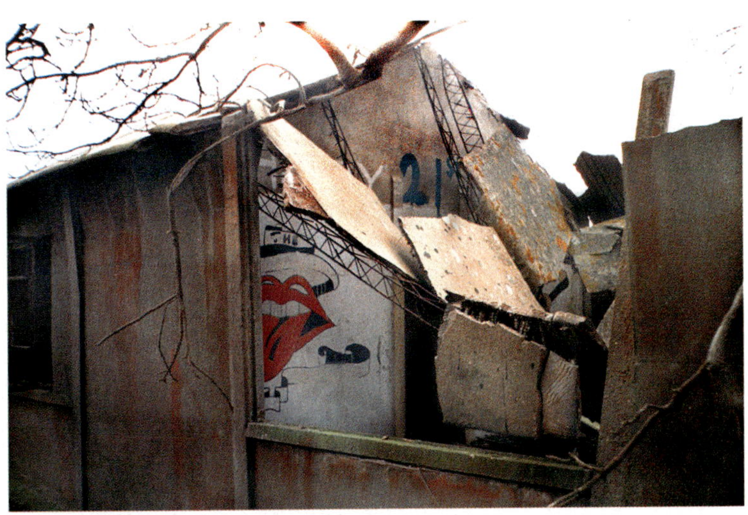

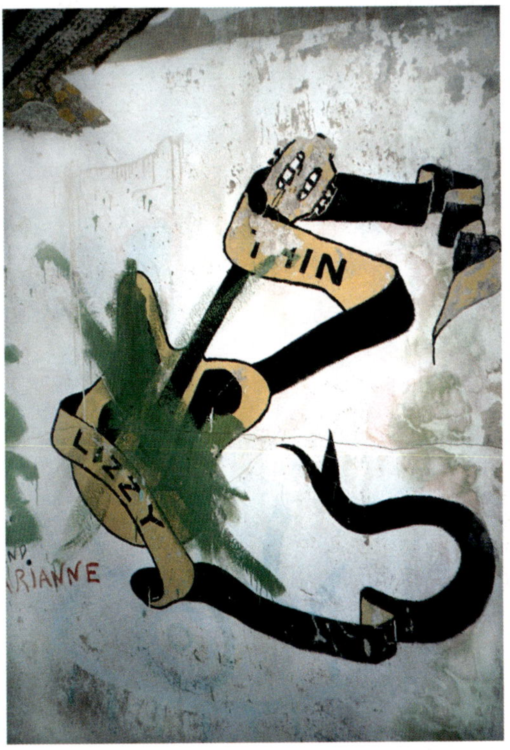

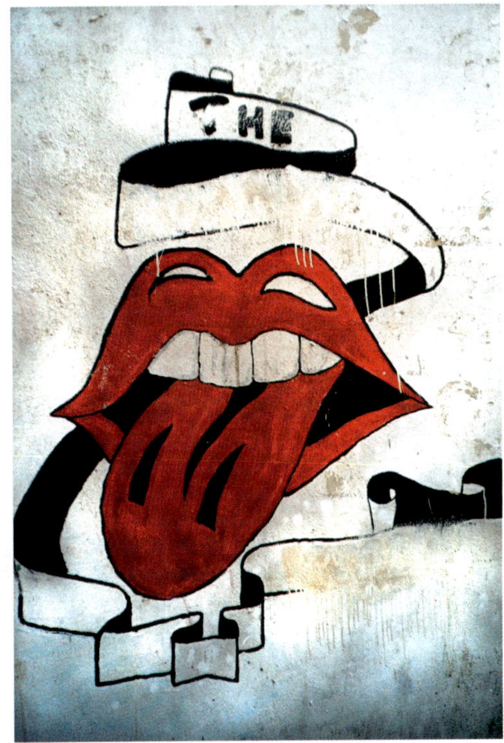

RAF Woodbridge, Suffolk
Top: **Collapsed building**
Bottom: Left – **Thin Lizzy**
Bottom: Right – **Rolling Stones**
Paintings probably date from the late 1970s
(© R J C Thomas)

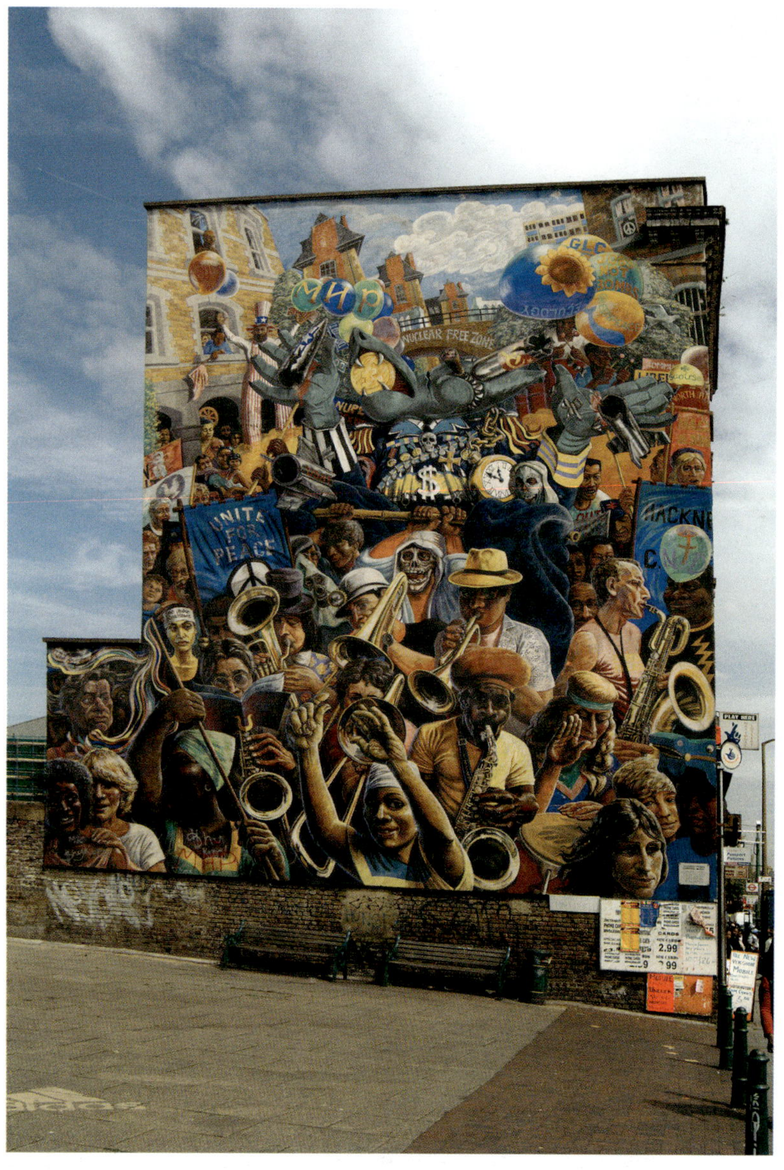

Dalston Lane, Hackney, Greater London
Left: The mural was inspired by the 1983
Hackney Peace Carnival. It was designed by
Ray Walker (1945–84) painted by Mike Jones
and Anna Walker, and opened by Tony Banks
MP, then Chairman of the Greater London
Council
(© English Heritage DSC0085)
Right: Dedication
(© English Heritage DSC0097)

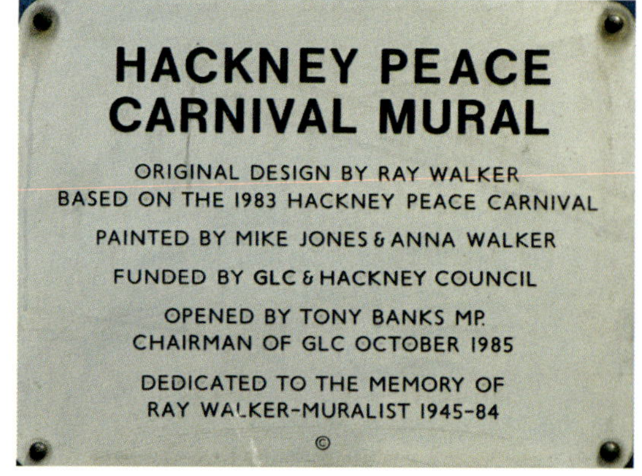

Dalston Lane, Hackney, Greater London
Top: **Nuclear Free Zone (DSC0096)**
Bottom: **Uncle Sam (DSC0094)**
(© English Heritage)

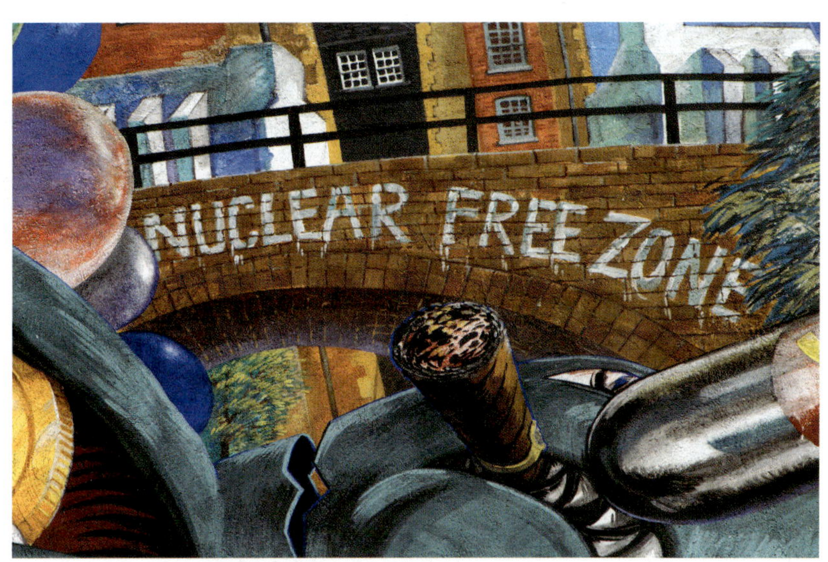

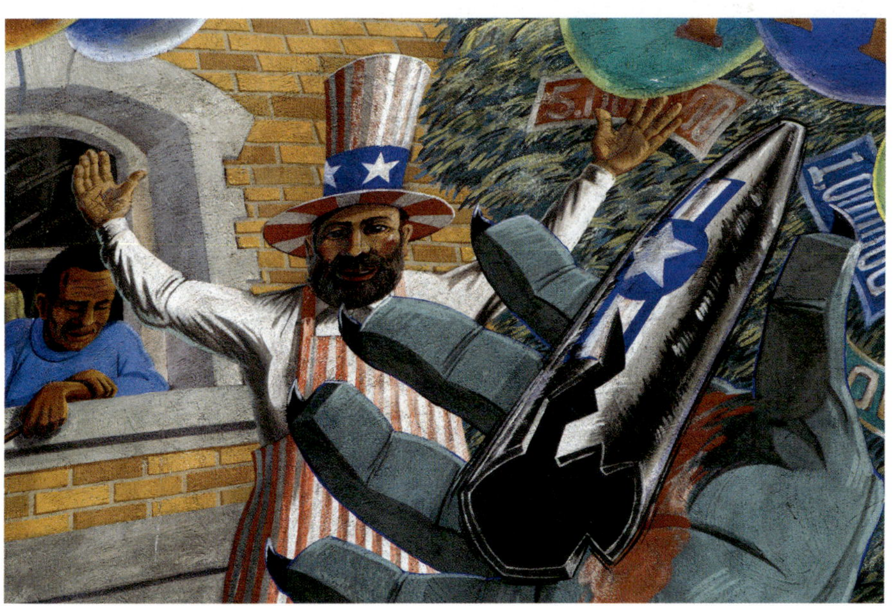

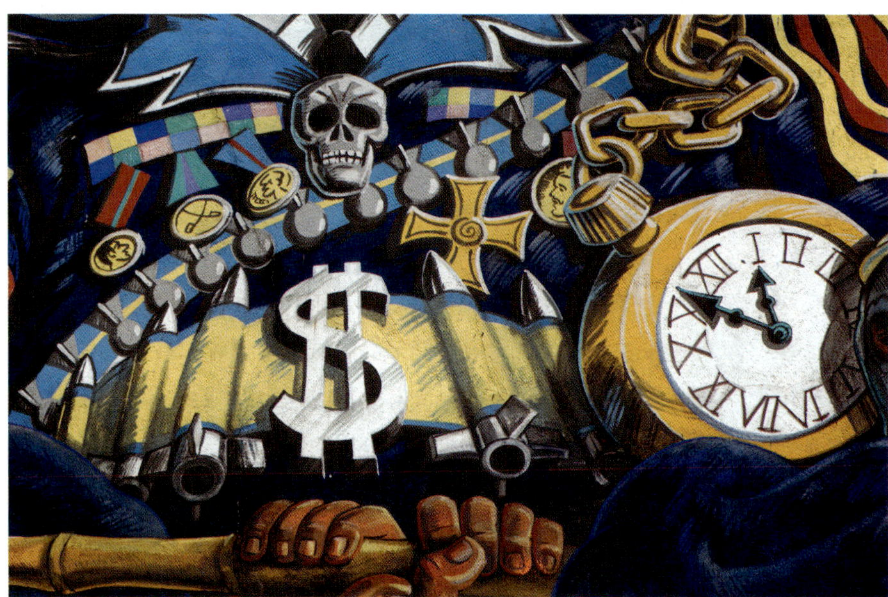

Dalston Lane, Hackney, Greater London Dollar (© English Heritage DSC0095)

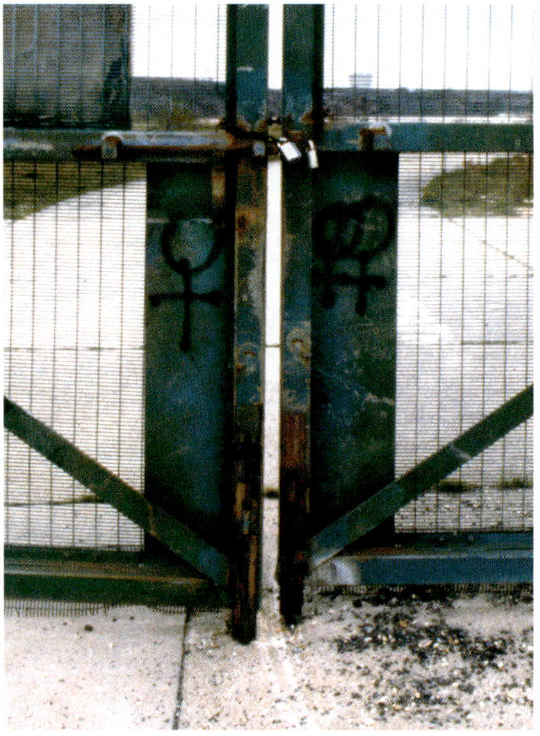

RAF Greenham, Berkshire Gate to entrapment area, feminist graffiti (© R J C Thomas)

THE BERLIN WALL

The most famous military structure to be decorated by graffiti was the Berlin Wall. By the late 1960s there was a thriving counter culture scene in West Berlin and graffiti became almost as endemic as in New York, with few surfaces escaping decoration. During this period, and into the 1970s, most graffiti on the wall was restricted to words or slogans, or to people simply writing their name on a structure that some regarded as the 'eighth wonder of the world' (Baker 1993, 720). It was not until the late 1970s, partly facilitated by the East Germans replacing the earlier wall with smooth prefabricated panels, that the larger murals

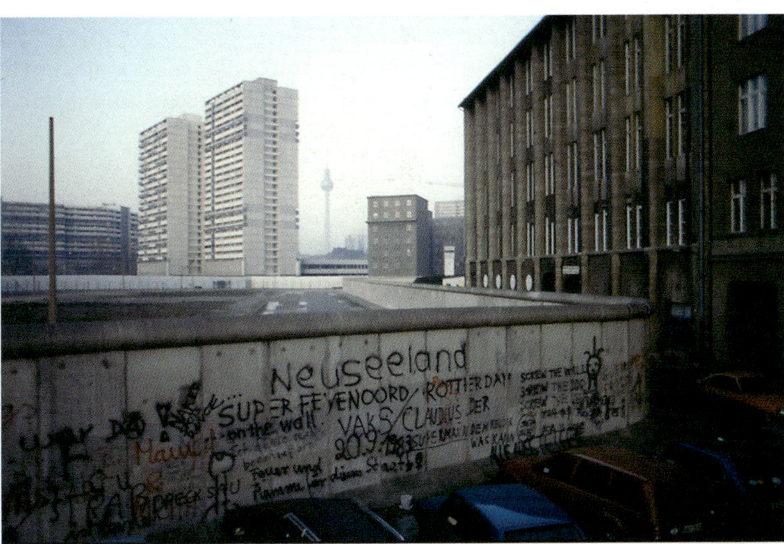

The Berlin Wall, junction of Zimmer Strasse and Axel Springer Strasse, during the early 1980s graffiti was largely restricted to words (© W D Cocroft)

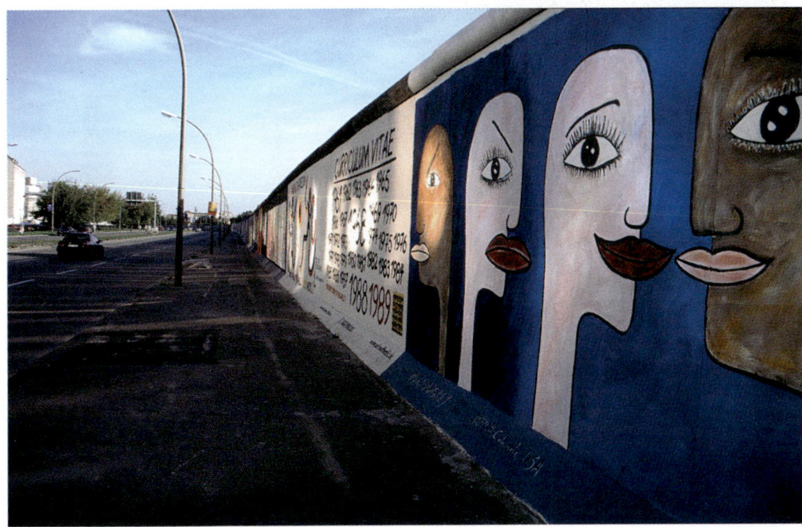

East Side Gallery, Mühlenstrasse, Berlin. Tolerance by Mary Mackey of Denver, Colorado, photographed in September 2000 shortly after the image was repainted by the artist (© W D Cocroft)

began to appear. One of the most famous was a 100m mural of inter-linked human figures painted by the New York graffiti artist Keith Haring (Baker 1993, 721; Feversham and Schmidt 1999, 62). Throughout this period the Wall remained a deadly and active military structure. A reminder of its grim function was provided by a group of expelled East German dissidents, who in 1986 painted an eye-level white line along a section of the Wall, symbolically cancelling the commodification of the Wall as a tourist attraction and restating its true meaning. The East German border guards regularly whitewashed the western face of the wall in a losing battle to reassert their control and influence the outsider's first impression of the German Democratic Republic. In early 1990, following the opening of the Wall, the still functioning East German government invited a group of 118 artists from 21 countries to emulate the western graffiti tradition by decorating a section of the pristine rear, or hinterland wall, along Mühlen Strasse. It's now known as *The Eastside Gallery* and is the longest surviving section of the wall. For many of the eastern artists the symbol of fear, oppression and separation now provided a medium to express their repressed feelings and emotions (Feversham and Schmidt 1999, 148–56).

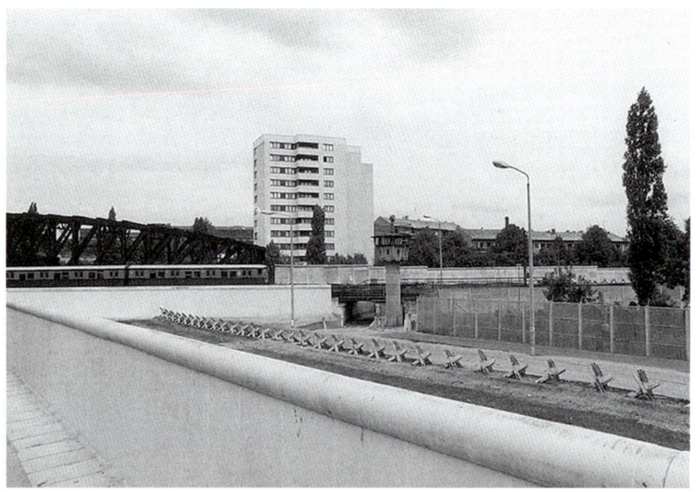

Border guard photograph showing the area to the north of Nordbahn-hof railway station near Hedwig cemetery

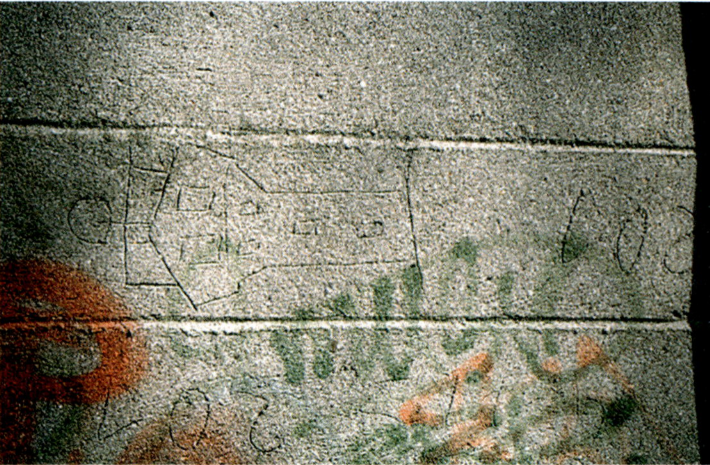

Watch tower graffiti on the hinterland wall in Hedwig cemetery, it is located to the right of the watch tower in the previous photograph (© Leo Schmidt)

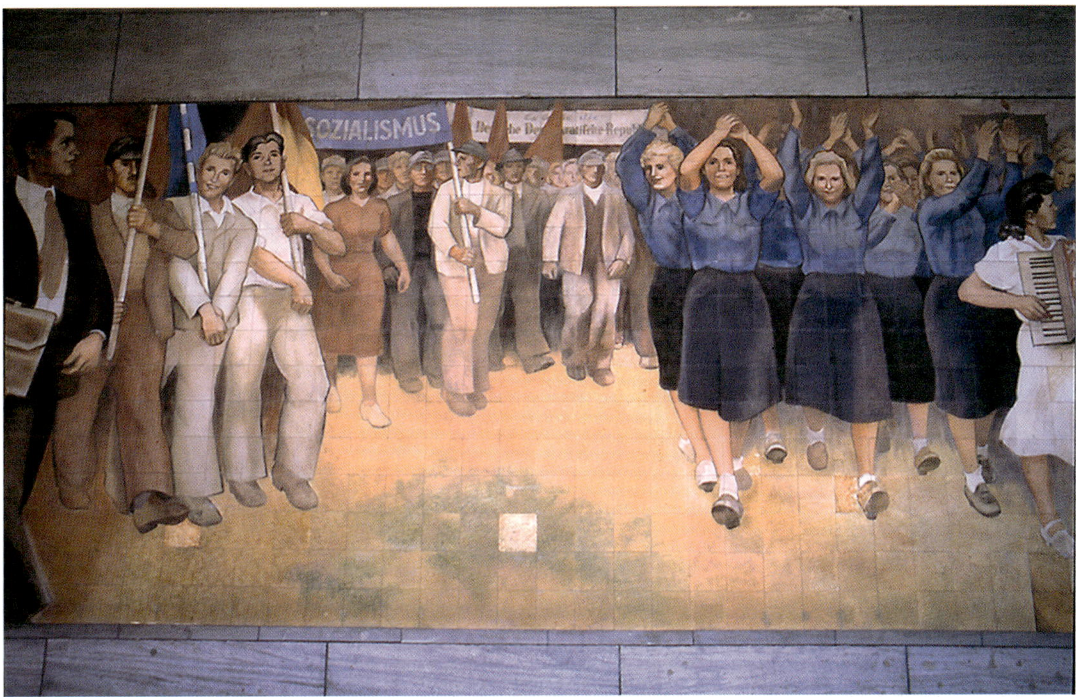

Berlin, Federal Ministry of Finance, built in 1933–35 as the German Aviation Ministry and subsequently used by a number of East German ministries until 1990. The 1950 Meissen tile mural by Max Lingner celebrates the founding of the German Democratic Republic on 1 October 1949 claiming the building for the new socialist government, the mural representing a triumph of socialist technology forged by artist and workers
(© **W D Cocroft**)

MILITARY BUILDINGS AND AIRCRAFT

CAMOUFLAGE

Camouflage was another type of painted official adornment that became synonymous with military buildings during the twentieth century. During the First World War examples are rare: at Chilwell (Nottinghamshire), a munitions factory, a contemporary photograph shows a dapple-patterned building, designed to obscure its form from the air (Cocroft 2000, 187). During the Second World War camouflage was routinely applied to military structures and armaments factories. This usually took the form of alternating blocks of colour to break up the shapes of buildings. On larger structures, such as aircraft hangars, street scenes and woodland landscapes were painted to disguise their function. Smaller structures, such as pillboxes, were painted to blend into the local street or beach scene.

The principle of many of the camouflage schemes of this period was derived or influenced by the experiences of hunters and zoologists like Abbott H Thayer, Sir John Graham-Kerr and Hugh Cott; however, for the design of camouflage the military turned to the art community for assistance. During the First World War artists such as Solomon J Solomon, were recruited to design camouflage schemes for the army. At sea, Lieutenant Commander Norman Wilkinson, a marine

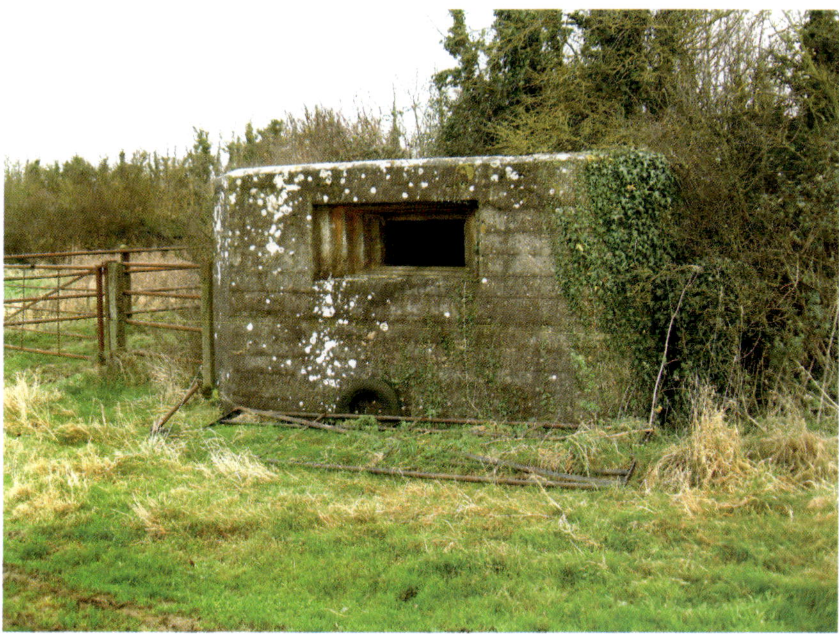

**Pawlett Hill,
Somerset
Pillbox
(© R J C Thomas)**

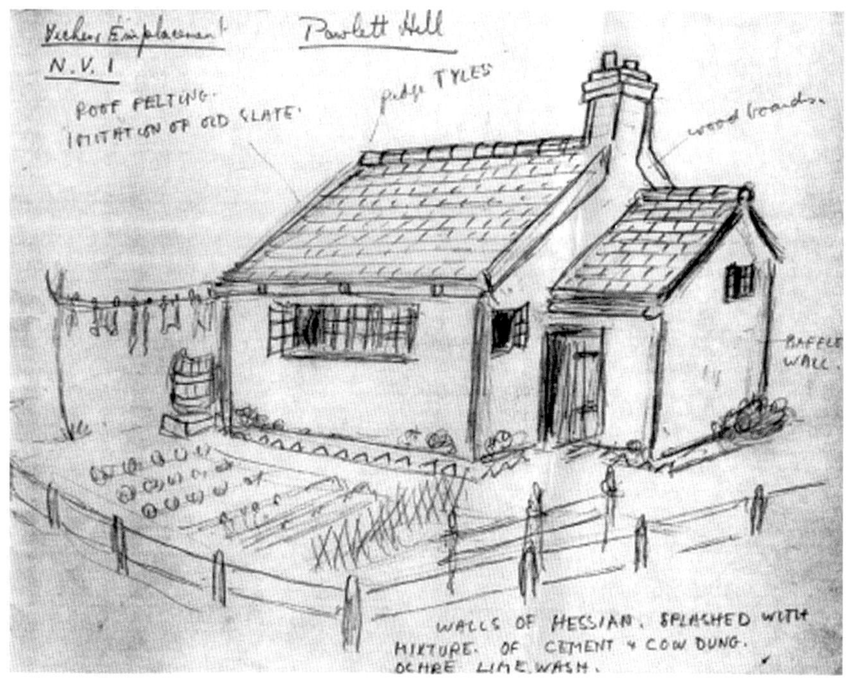

Pawlett Hill, Somerset Contemporary view of the camouflage scheme designed for the pillbox shown on the previous page (© Henry Wills Collection – English Heritage NMRC Swindon)

artist, suggested painting ships with dazzle patterns to break up their outlines. To support this work a dazzle section was set up at the Royal Academy of Arts in London, where women artists were employed to design individual patterns for ships (Newark et al 1996, 15–19). The imperial German air force used a similar principle with its lozenge patterned aircraft. Later in the century camouflage was widely applied to military uniforms, and ironically what was designed to conceal may now be used to distinguish different forces.

NOSE ART

There is a close link between examples of mural art and nose art that appeared on wartime aircraft. The decoration of aircraft was practised by all countries in both world wars, although nose art is regarded by some as a distinctive American art form (Ethell and Simonsen 1991, 7). Many of the images were inspired by popular contemporary culture. In most instances the artists who painted the images were drawn from the units they served with and are generally unknown. Gifted artists were highly prized by their units and would be paid in money or gifts to execute designs on aircraft and clothing. One artist was Nilian Jones who was attached to the 352nd Fighter Group based at Bodney (Norfolk). In addition to painting designs on the Group's Mustang fighters, he also decorated

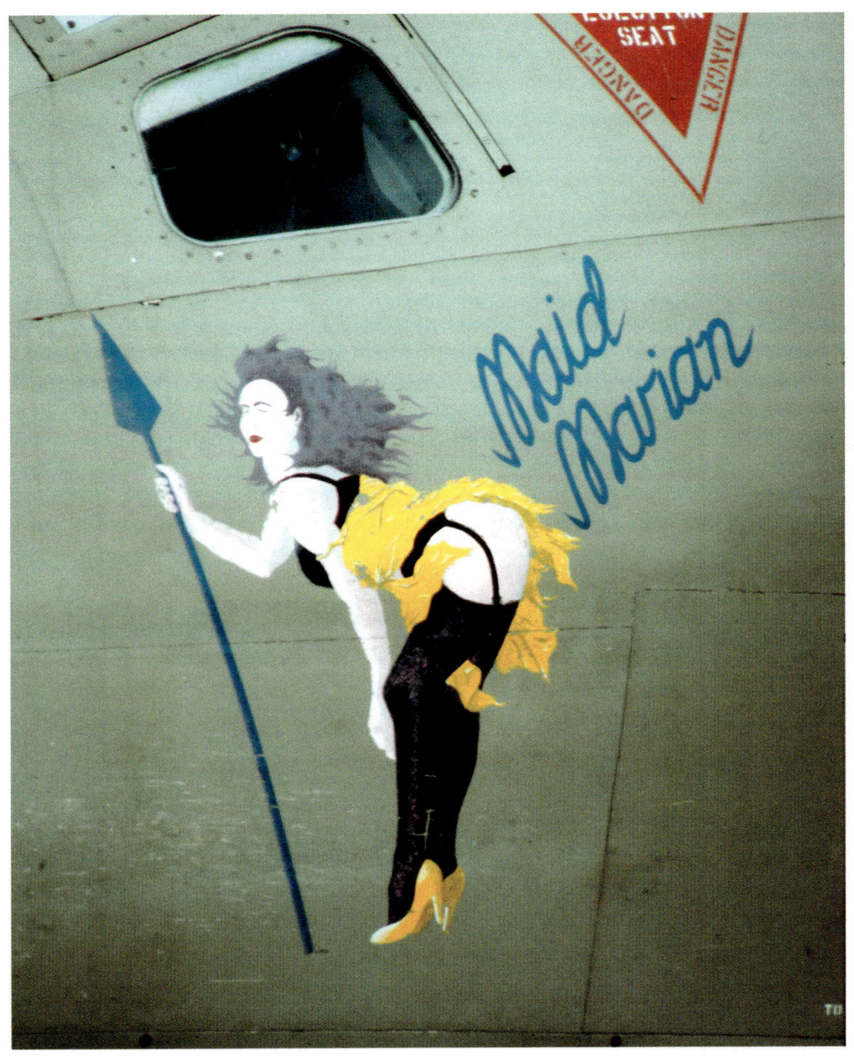

'Maid Marian' Modern RAF nose art applied by Corporal Andy Price to the nose of a Victor K2 refuelling tanker during the 1991 Gulf War *Operation Granby* (© R J C Thomas)

the Group's buildings with scantily clad female figures. Another talented artist was Arthur De Costa. Originally assigned as cook in the officers' mess, this self-taught artist was appointed as the 355th Fighter Group's official artist. His work included the application of nose art, as well as painting female angels in the officers' mess. At Great Ashfield (Suffolk) home of the 385th Bomb Group, the artist was a British civilian Anne Jospehine Hayward, who decorated both aircraft and recreational buildings (Ethell and Simonsen 1991, 60, 94, 120).

SUBTERRANEAN ART

At Spring Quarry, Corsham (Wiltshire), a vast underground complex was created in the Bath stone quarries to provide accommodation for munitions storage and for the manufacture of aircraft engines and gun barrels. Engine production was the responsibility of the Bristol Aeroplane Company under the management of the Oxford educated Reginald Verdon Smith, a great nephew of the firm's founder. He not only insisted that the workshop areas should be painted white, against the Ministry of Aircraft production's suggestion of dull red, but also commissioned Olga Lehmann (1912–2001) to paint murals on the canteen and other walls to brighten the workers' subterranean lives (McCamley 1998, 198–9). She was a classically trained artist at the Slade School of Fine Art, and had a distinguished career encompassing set dressing for film and television, portraiture, mural painting and costume design. Indeed the perspective of many of the images is suggestive of contemporary theatre or film set design.

Nearly 50 of these remarkable murals survive within the tunnels at Corsham. Many of the scenes show quintessentially English scenes, optimistically showing a better future after the war.

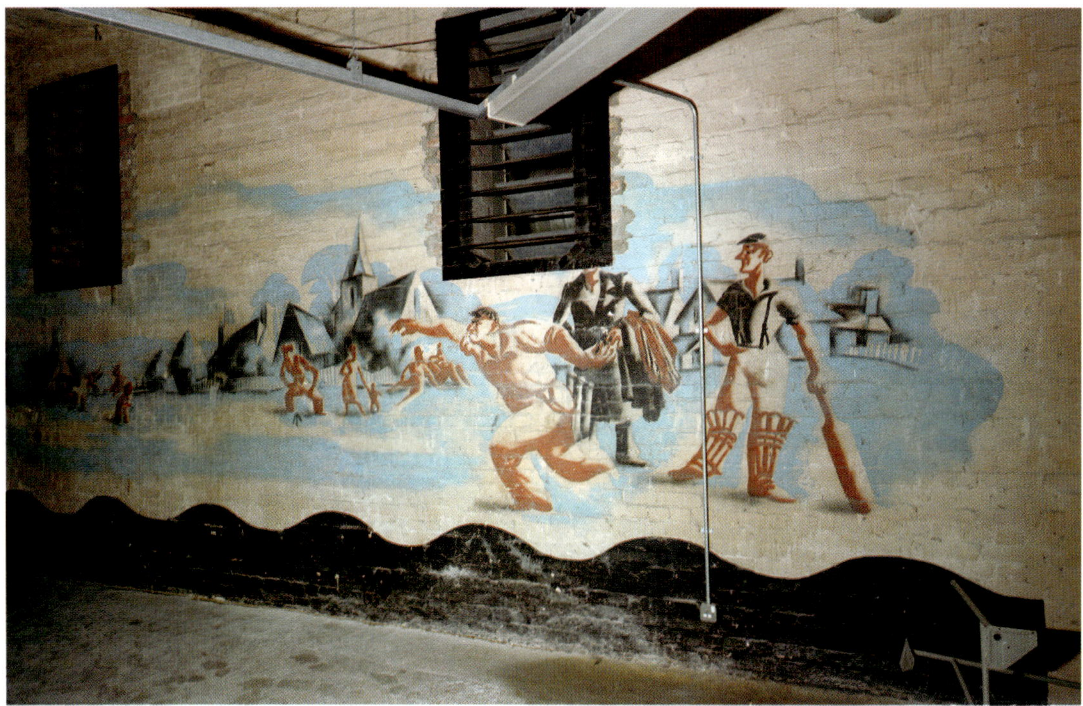

Corsham, Wiltshire, underground munitions store Cricket (AA26518 © English Heritage)

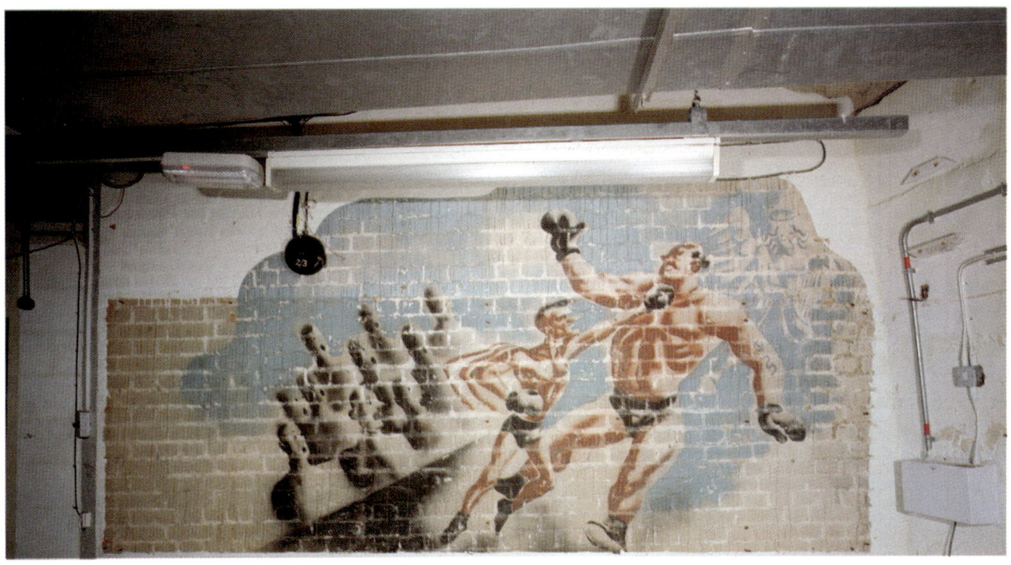

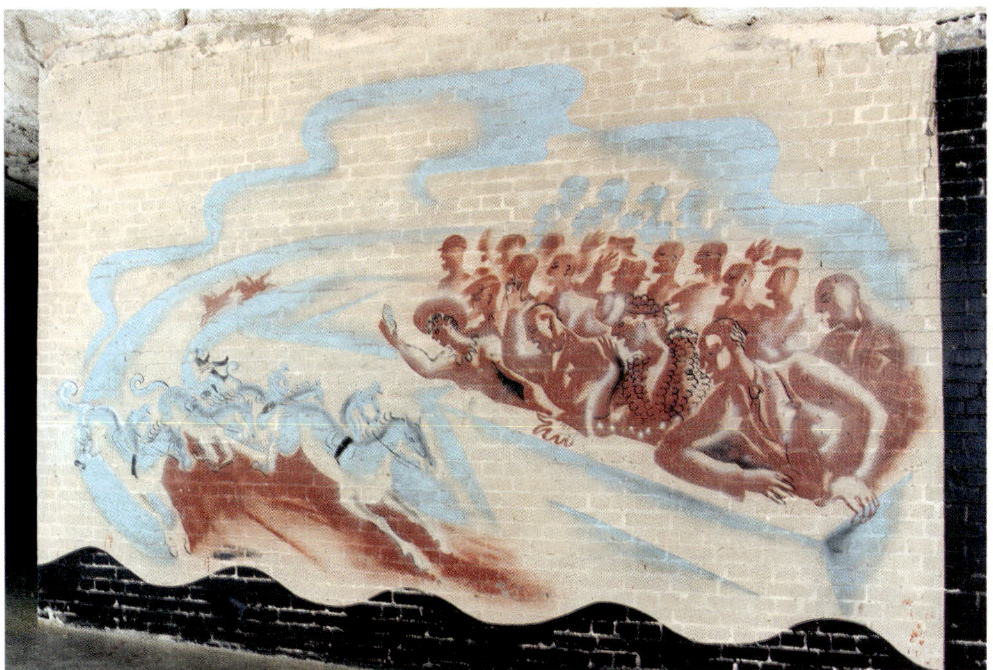

Corsham, Wiltshire, underground munitions store *Top:* **Boxing (AA26516)** *Bottom:* **Horse racing (AA26513) (© English Heritage)**

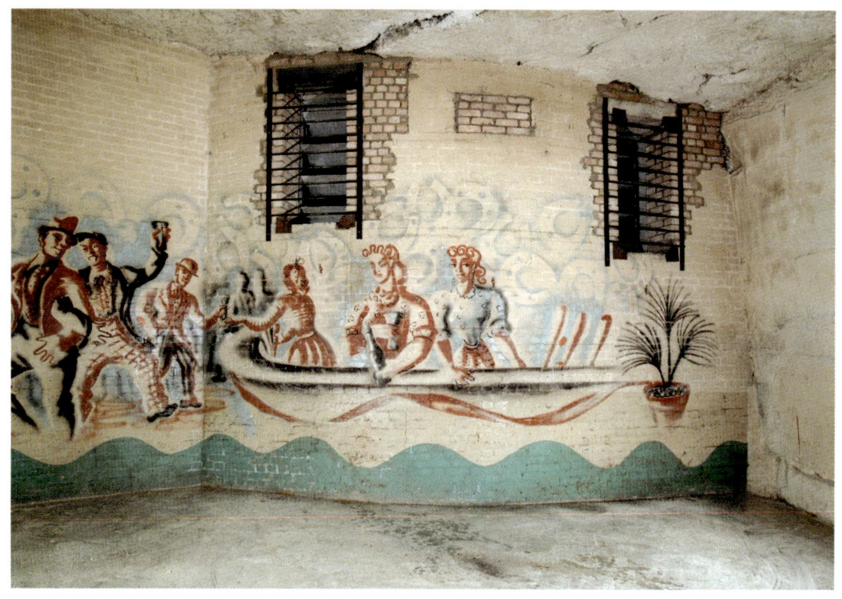

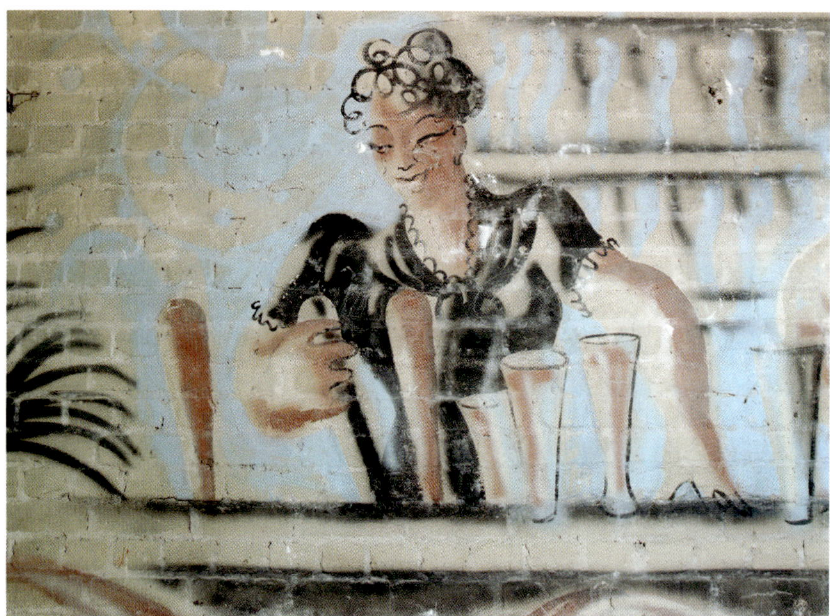

Corsham, Wiltshire, underground munitions store *Top:* **Bar (AA26509)** *Bottom:* **Barmaid (AA26506) (© English Heritage)**

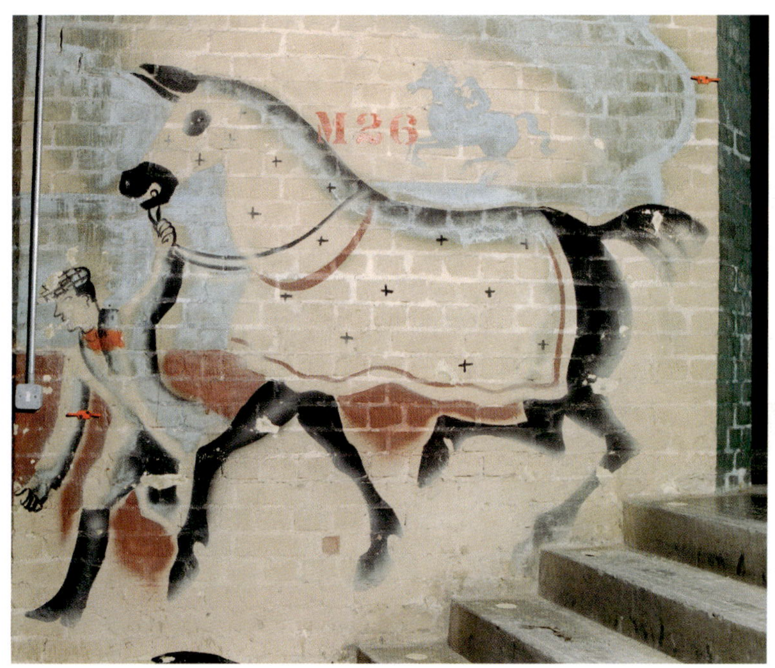

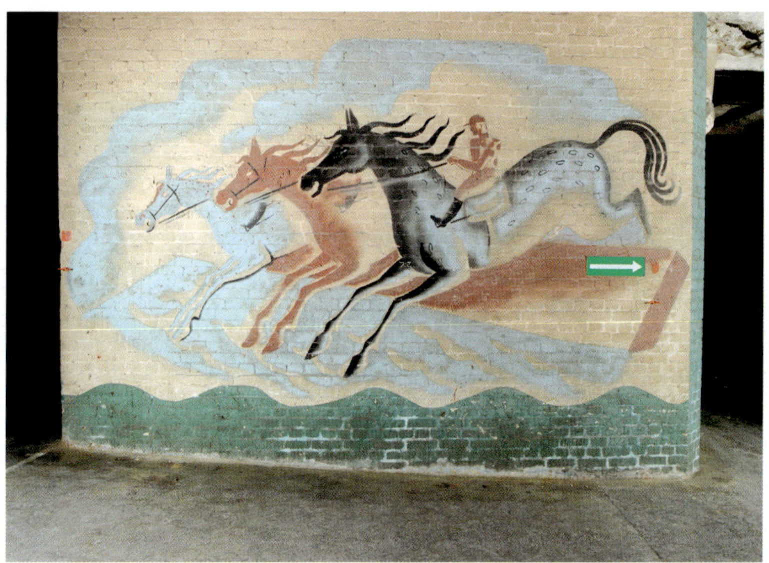

Corsham, Wiltshire, underground munitions store *Top:* **Horse and steps (AA26536)**
Bottom: **Horse racing (AA26534) (© English Heritage)**

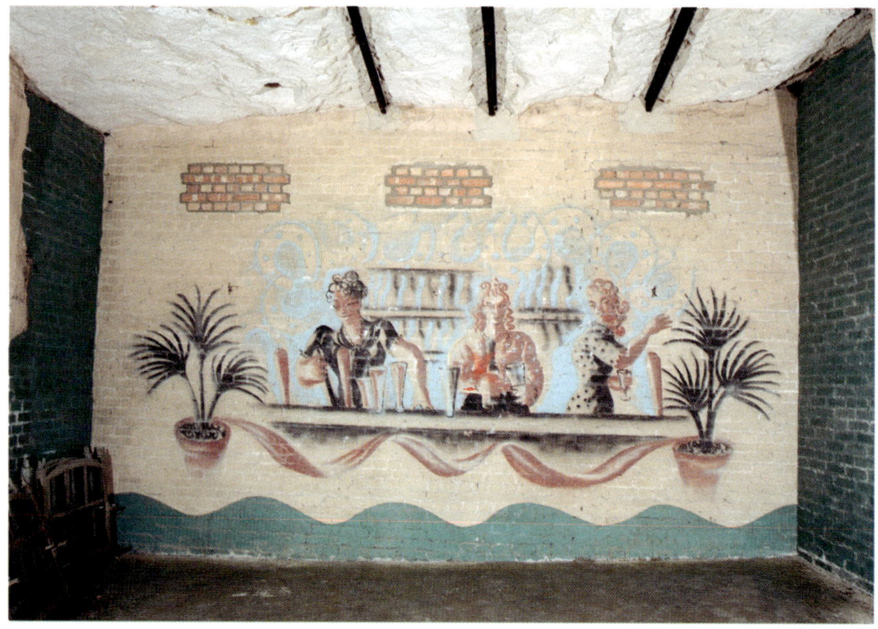

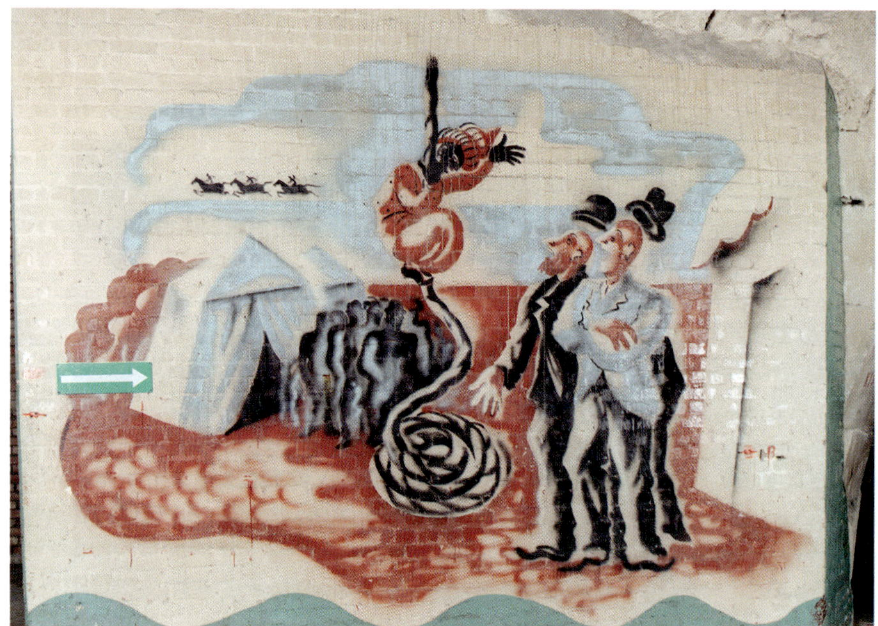

Corsham, Wiltshire, underground munitions store *Top:* **Bar (AA26532)** *Bottom:* **Rope trick (AA26528) (© English Heritage)**

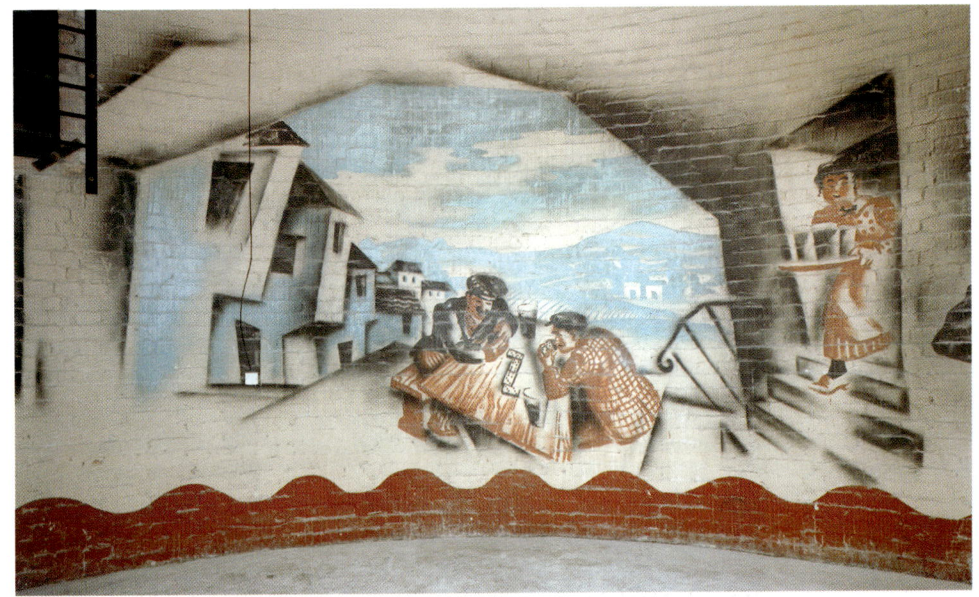

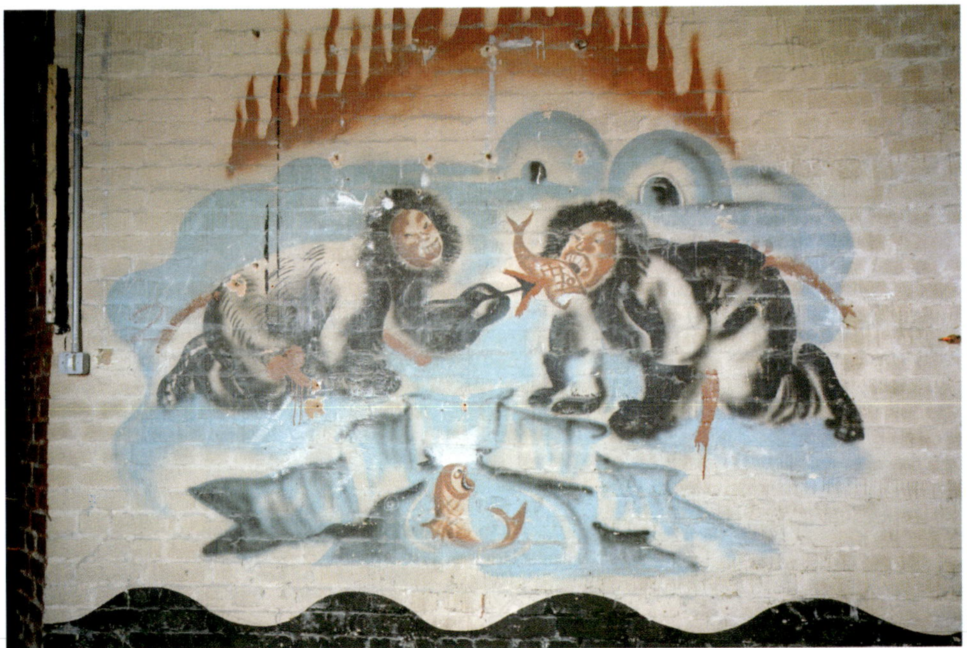

Corsham, Wiltshire, underground munitions store *Top:* **Dominos scene (AA27628)**
Bottom: **Eskimos (AA27620) (© English Heritage)**

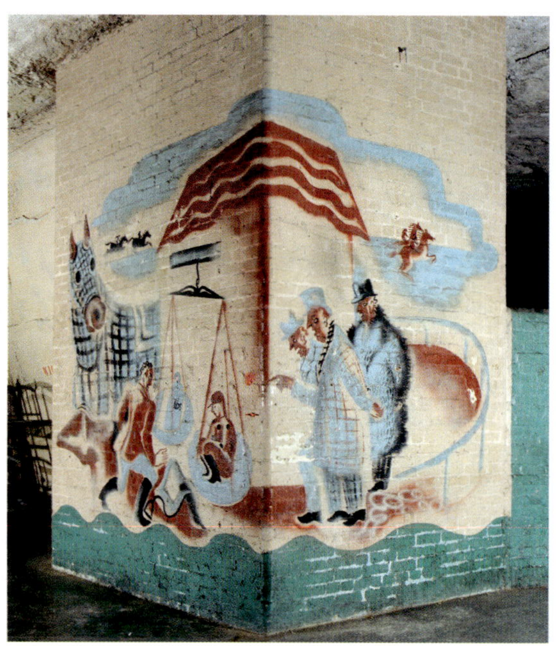

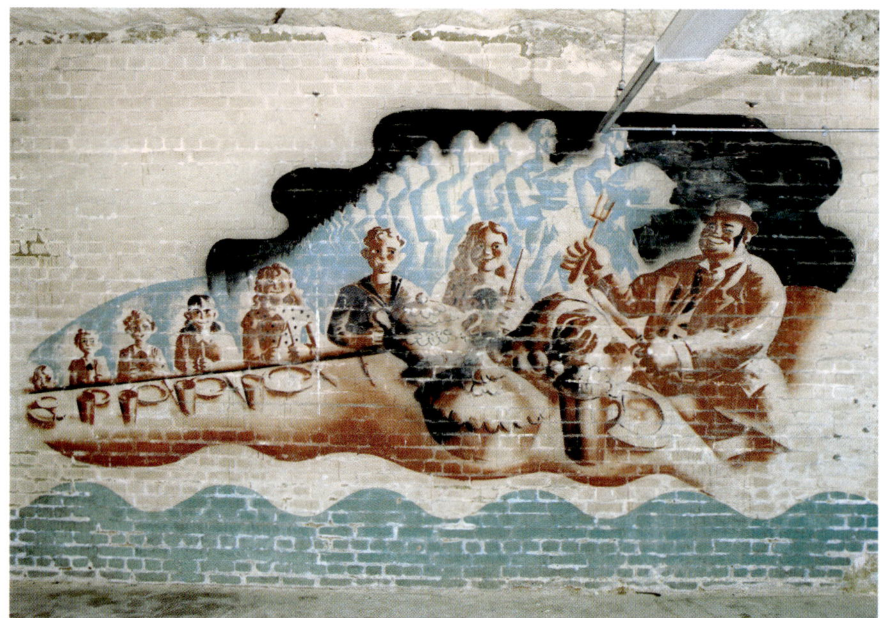

Corsham, Wiltshire, underground munitions store *Top:* **Weighing jockeys (AA27617)**
Bottom: **John Bull (AA27648) (© English Heritage)**

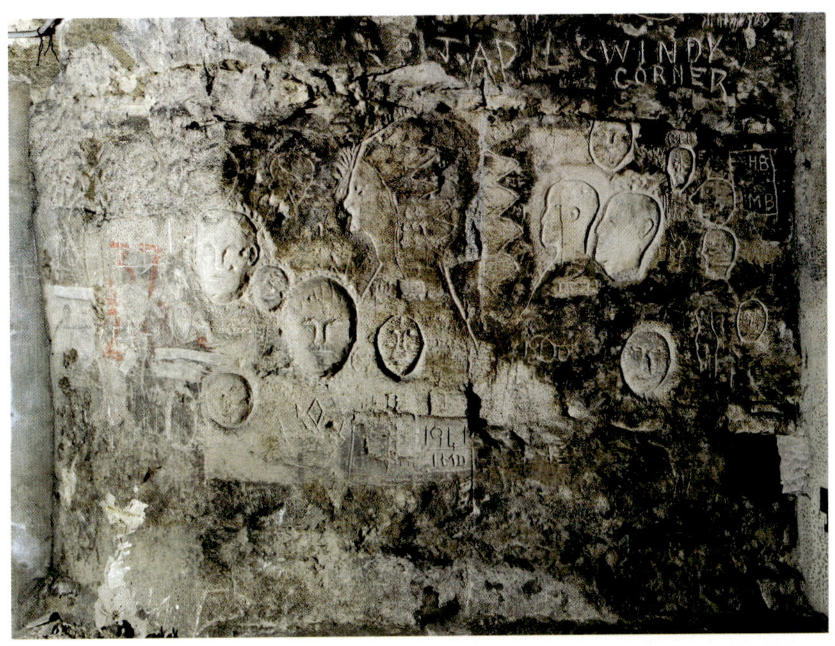

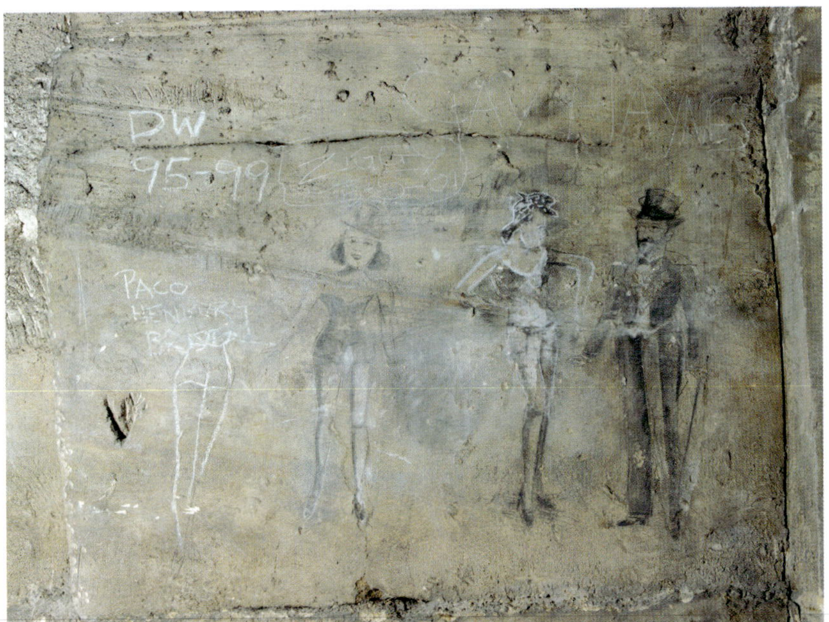

Corsham, Wiltshire, underground munitions store *Top:* **Windy Corner (AA27644)** *Bottom:* **Pencil drawing (AA27641) (© English Heritage)**

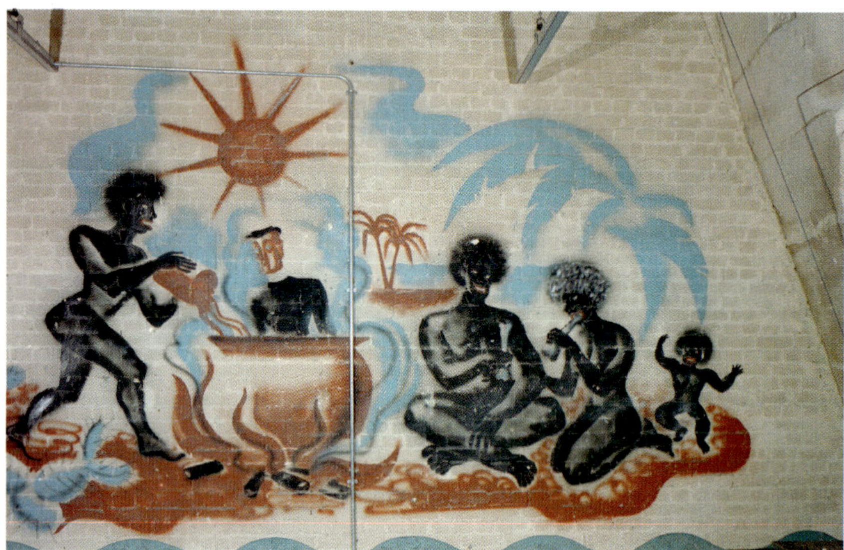

Corsham, Wiltshire, underground munitions store Cannibals (AA27640 © English Heritage)

The dominant theme is of horse racing, perhaps with an associated country fair. Other images are of a village cricket match and John Bull carving a joint of beef, surrounded by large pies and a mug of foaming ale. Other murals show drunken carousing, although in one scene the drunkards are confronted by a Salvation Army band, their leader brandishing a copy of the War Cry. The characters in the paintings are all treated with sympathetic good humour, but the inspiration for a scene of Eskimos feeding one another fish and a missionary being boiled alive by cannibals are totally baffling.

The use of art to brighten the lives of other subterranean dwellers was not only restricted to England. In the forts of the 1930s French Maginot Line, examples include works by well-known graphics artists of the day who had been mobilised into the army; at Bois de Bousse is work by Daniel Derveaux and at Village de Coume a mural entitled the Le triomphe de la medicine by Robert Humblot (1907–1962) (Wahl Nd, 162, 248). In the later German fortifications along the Atlantic coast are numerous examples of wall paintings. In the heavily fortified submarine pens at La Pallice is a crudely painted image of a U-boat sinking a ship, while its crew escape in two life boats (Brothé 1995, 49). In the fortifications of Hitler's Atlantic Wall are officially sanctioned patriotic slogans, usually in gothic script, along with art work executed to make their interiors more attractive.

SPATIAL CONTEXTS

As we have seen, the location of war art varies from small confined areas used only for storage, where art is intended for restricted view, to more communal spaces such as squadron bars where military personnel socialised. In the smaller more confined spaces images demonstrated the isolation of the artists' work. At Upper Heyford, for example, the so-called 'flashomatic' image is located in a small room once used for storage, which led off a much larger room in which more people worked. There is another image in the same room which can be seen through the doorway, but the 'flashomatic' mural can only be seen once inside the storeroom.

Wall art displayed in a larger space is in the squadron bar of Building 98 at RAF Alconbury (Cambridgeshire). Here a large warthog is prominently sited, in a space integral to the interaction of those on the base. Associated with this is a panel of graffiti, in which members of the base have written their nicknames on the wall. Access to these images is for all.

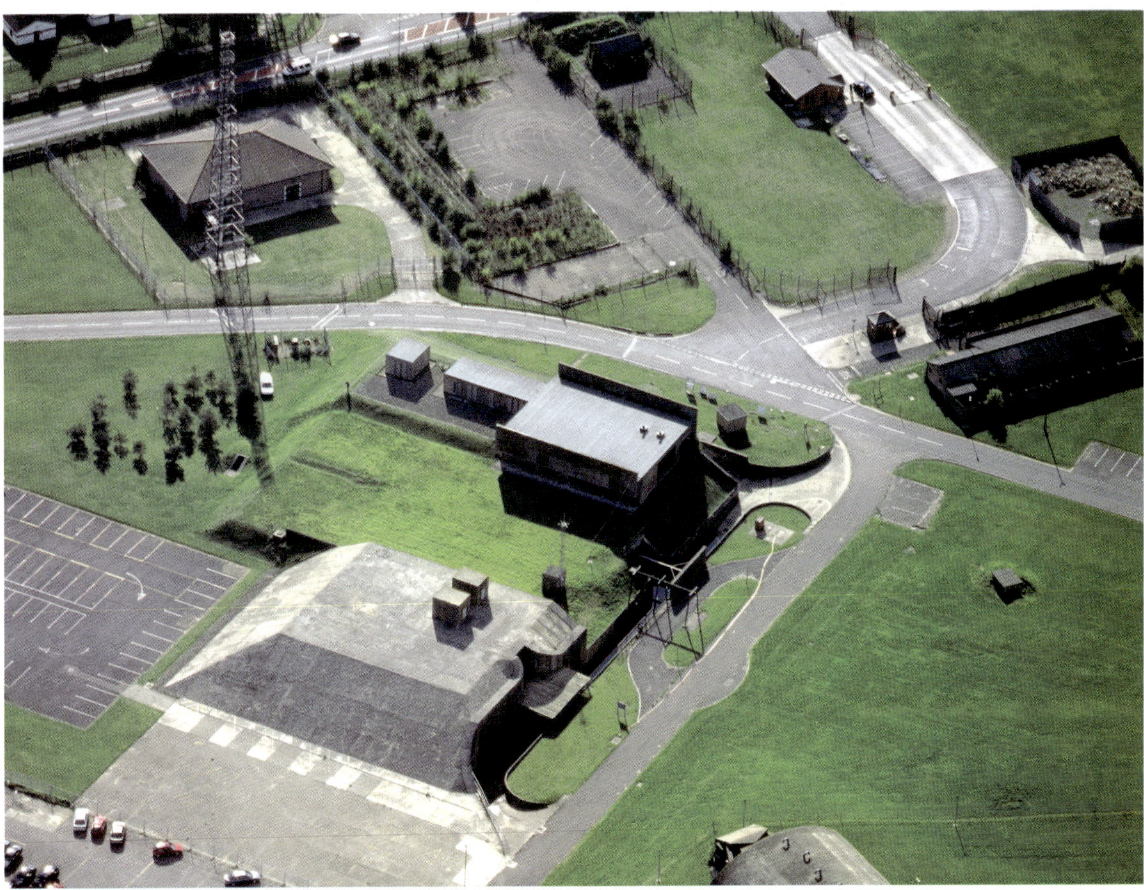

RAF Upper Heyford, Oxfordshire, the Avionics Centre, Building 299 (© NMR 18518/20)

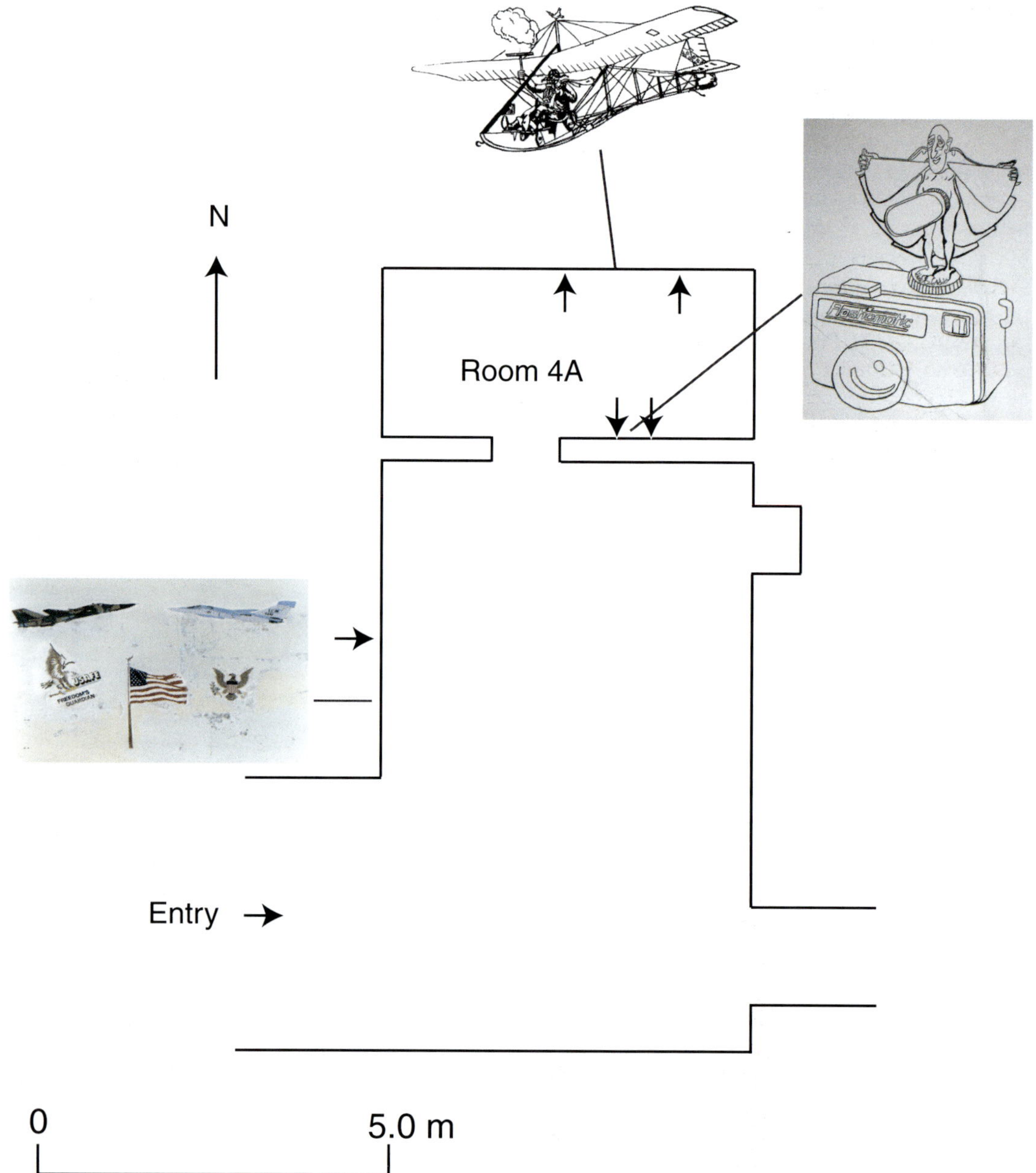

Diagram showing the relative positions of murals around the store room in the **Avionics Centre, Upper Heyford**

RAF Upper Heyford,
Oxfordshire,
Avionics Building
(299),
Top: 20 CRS
Automatics and
F-111 (AA051450
© English Heritage)
Bottom: 20 TFW
EWS PODS (S)
HOP, door to room
11, raven sitting on
an AN/ALQ-131 (V)
Electronic Counter
Measures pod
(AA051451
© English Heritage)

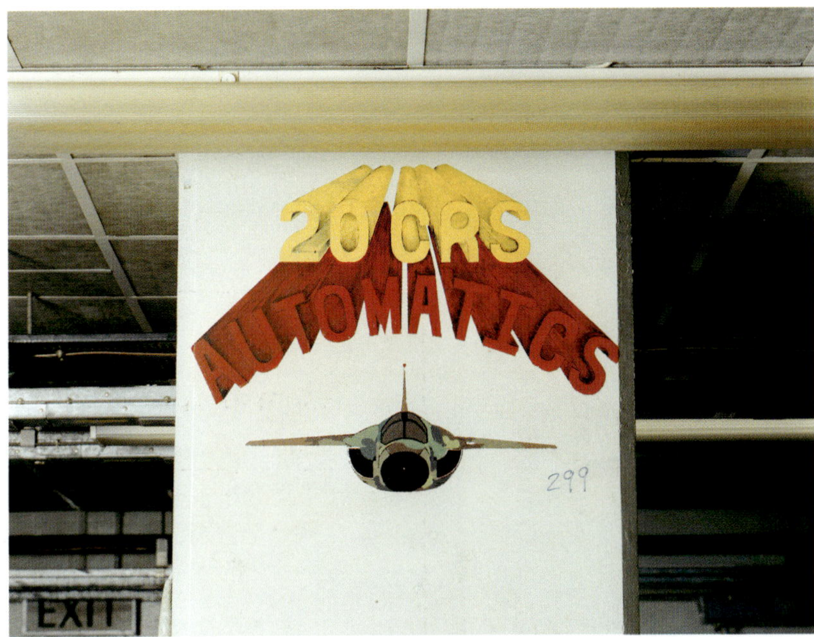

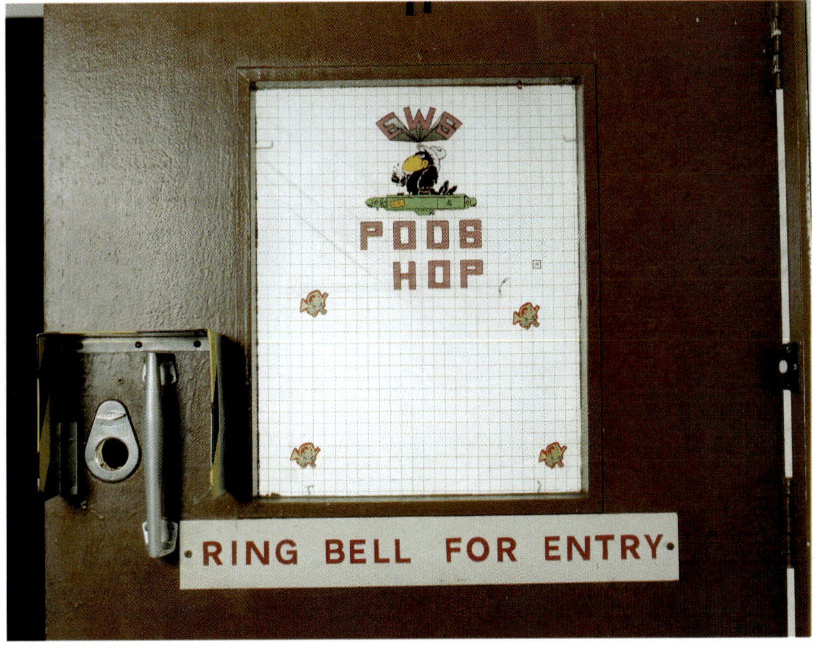

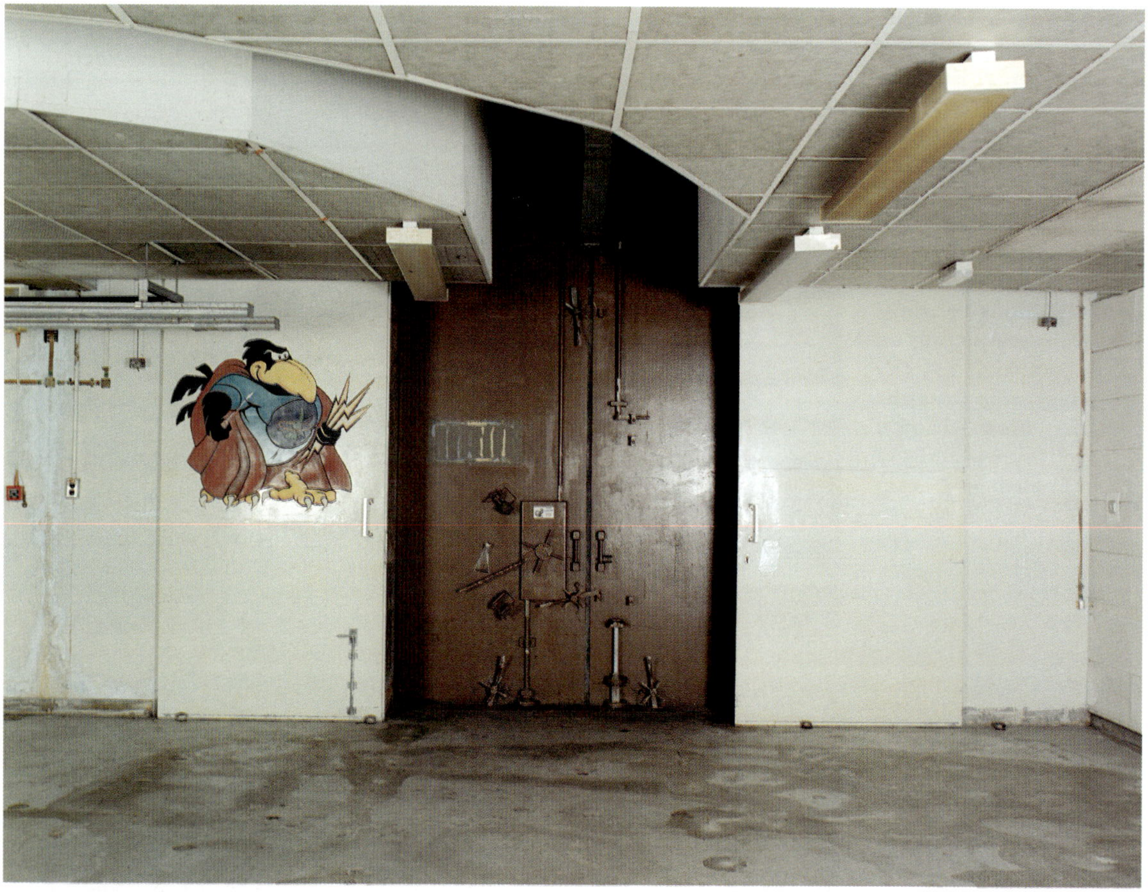

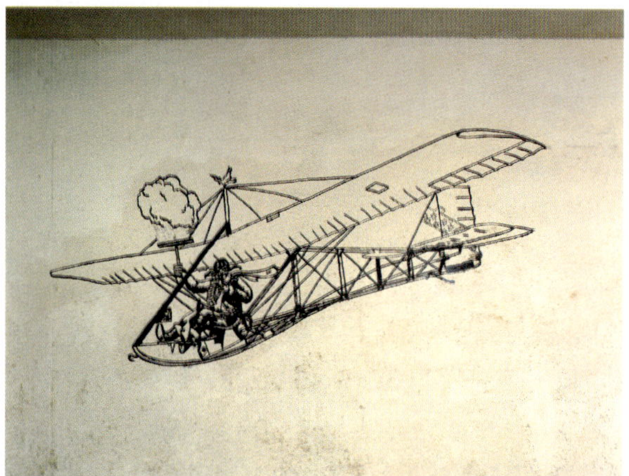

**RAF Upper Heyford, Oxfordshire, Avionics
Building (299),**
Top: **Entrance to F-111 pod servicing area
F-111 mural (AA051456) (see p 51 for
close up)**
Bottom: **Former store room, cartoon of
air photographer (AA051454)**
(© English Heritage)

**RAF Upper Heyford,
Oxfordshire, Avionics
Building (299),**
Top: **Former store room,
Flashomatic cartoon
(AA051455
© English Heritage)**
Bottom: **F-111 Mural
(AA051453
© English Heritage)**

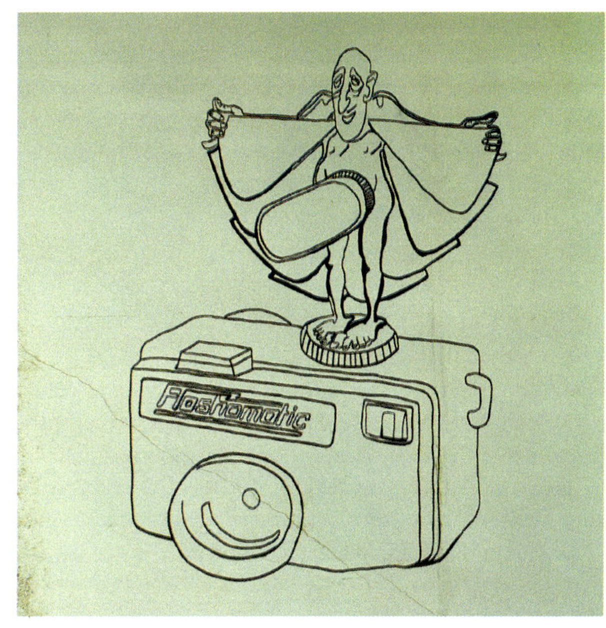

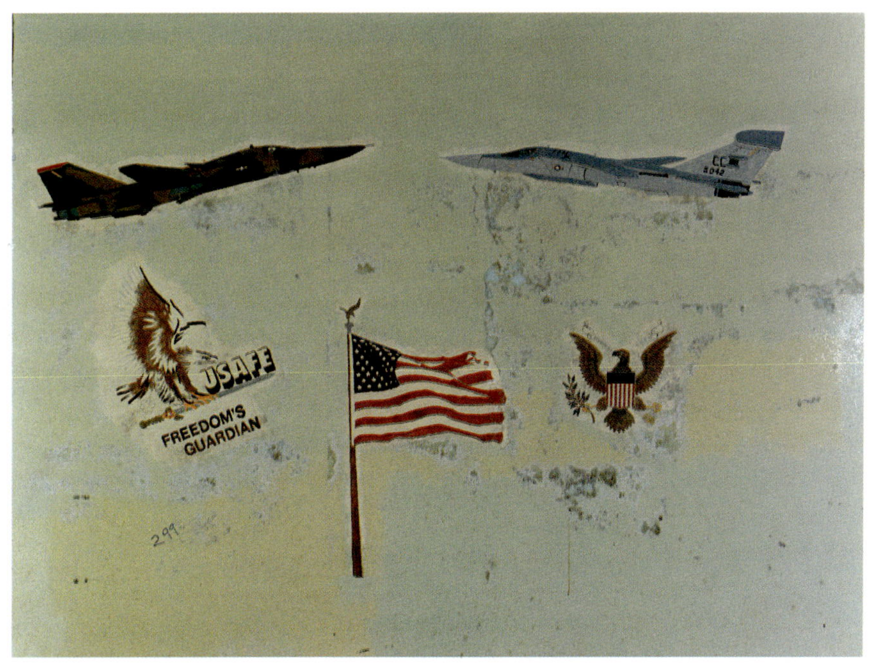

Also communal are the large murals painted on the outside of hangars. These murals command a different kind of space within the military site; it is an interactive part of the base, and something that can be seen from distance, dominating the visual landscape. Contrast this with large paintings of Jaguar aircraft flying over the Iraqi desert painted on the inside of the hangar doors at RAF Coltishall (Norfolk). While just as big, these can only be appreciated by the ground crews of the particular squadron operating within the hangar.

THE DEATH STAR CORRIDOR

The connection between contemporary art and war art can be clearly seen in *Traces of Conflict: The Falklands Revisited 1982–2002* (Ashcroft 2002). Here a collaboration is described between the then Commander of British Forces on the Falkland Islands, and four artists, all of whom remembered the Falklands War from childhood. The Commander sought to improve a mile-long corridor at the Mount Pleasant base that connected living accommodation with other facilities. Officially known as the Millennium Mile, its military occupants knew it as Death Star Corridor. The aim was to improve the signage and brighten the environment by inviting artists to create murals and exhibitions. An example is the work of Elaine Shemilt.

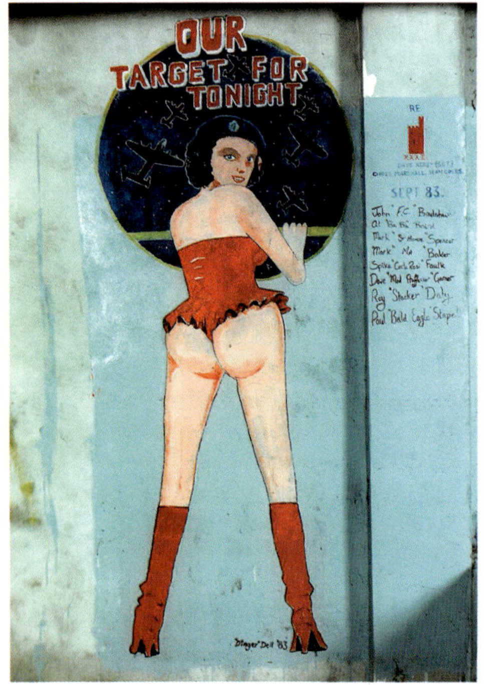

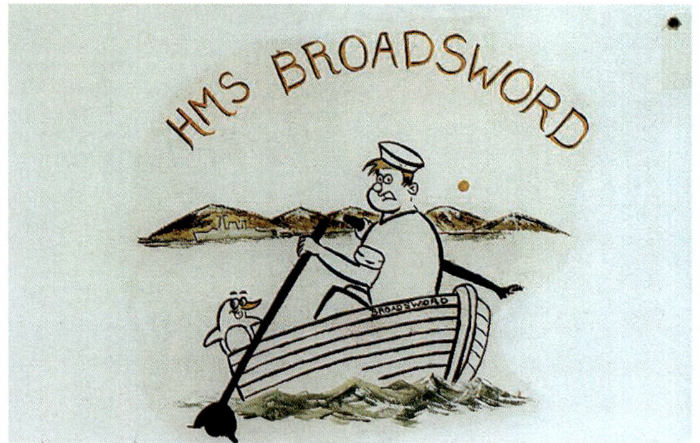

Ajax Bay, Falkland Islands
Left: **Our target for tonight, painted 1983**
Right: **Type 22 Frigate HMS Broadsword F88**
(© Keith Angus)

Ajax Bay, Falkland Islands
Top: '**Where R+R became a myth**'
Bottom: **Snoopy**
(© **Keith Angus**)

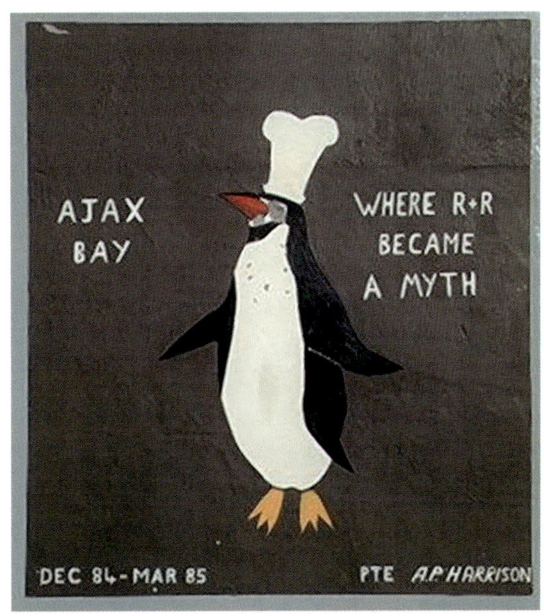

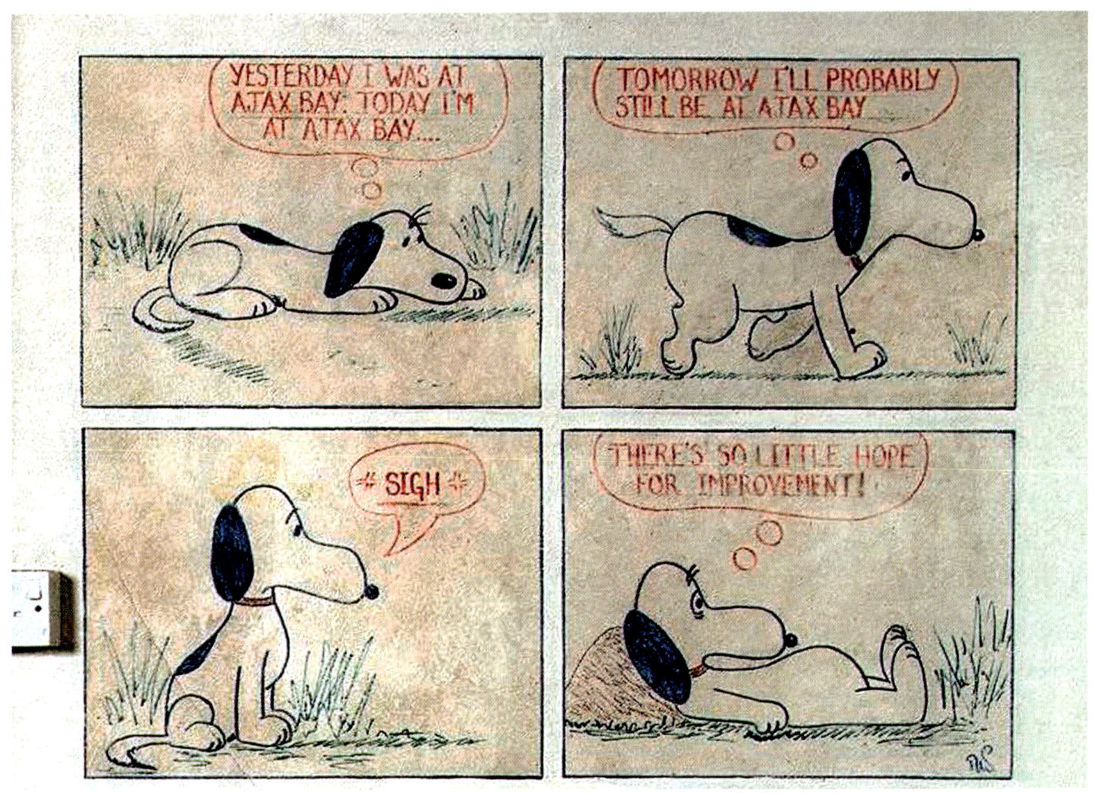

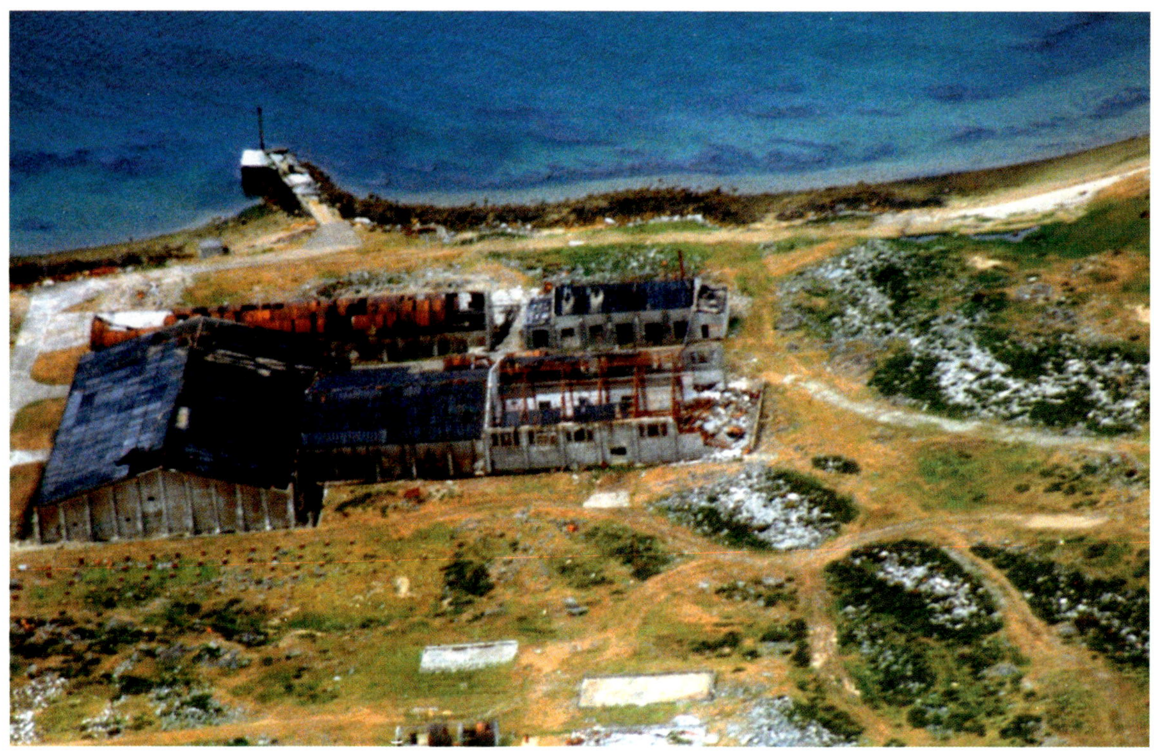

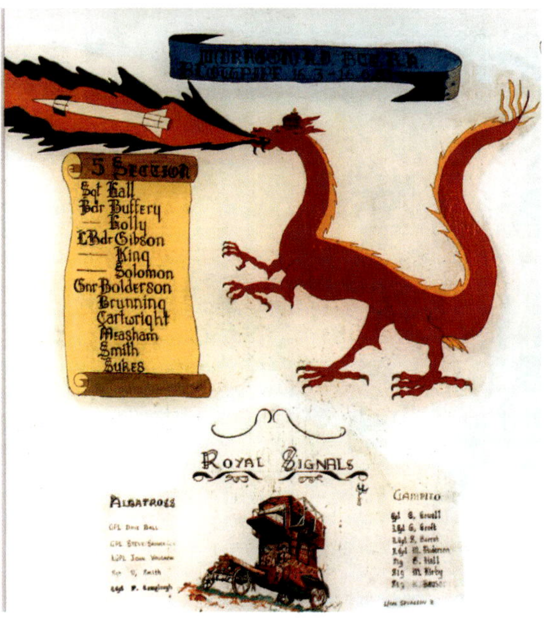

Ajax Bay, Falkland Islands
Top: **Buildings used as a field hospital by British troops**
Bottom: **Dragon (© Keith Angus)**

Ajax Bay, Falkland Islands
Is this the face of concern?
(© Keith Angus)

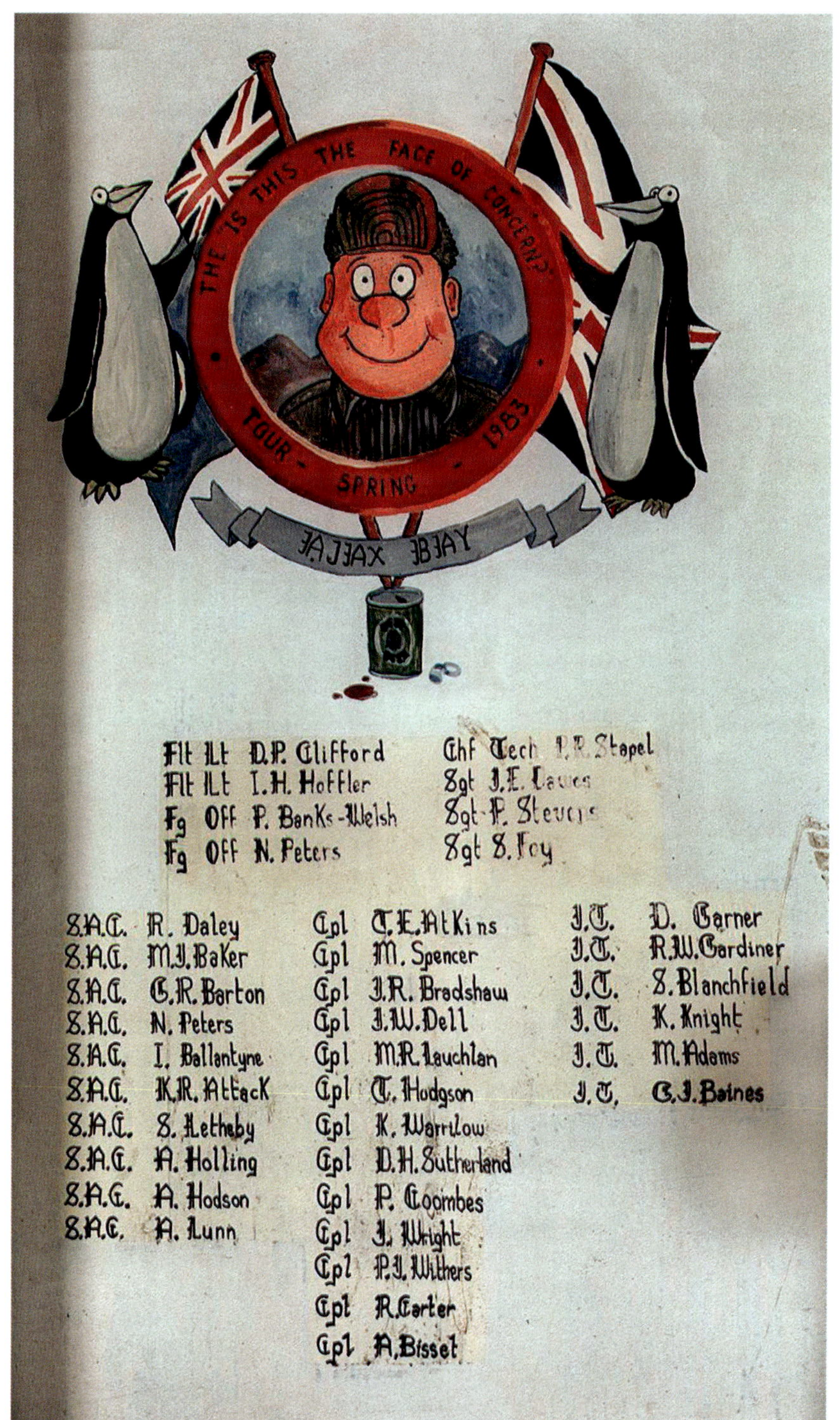

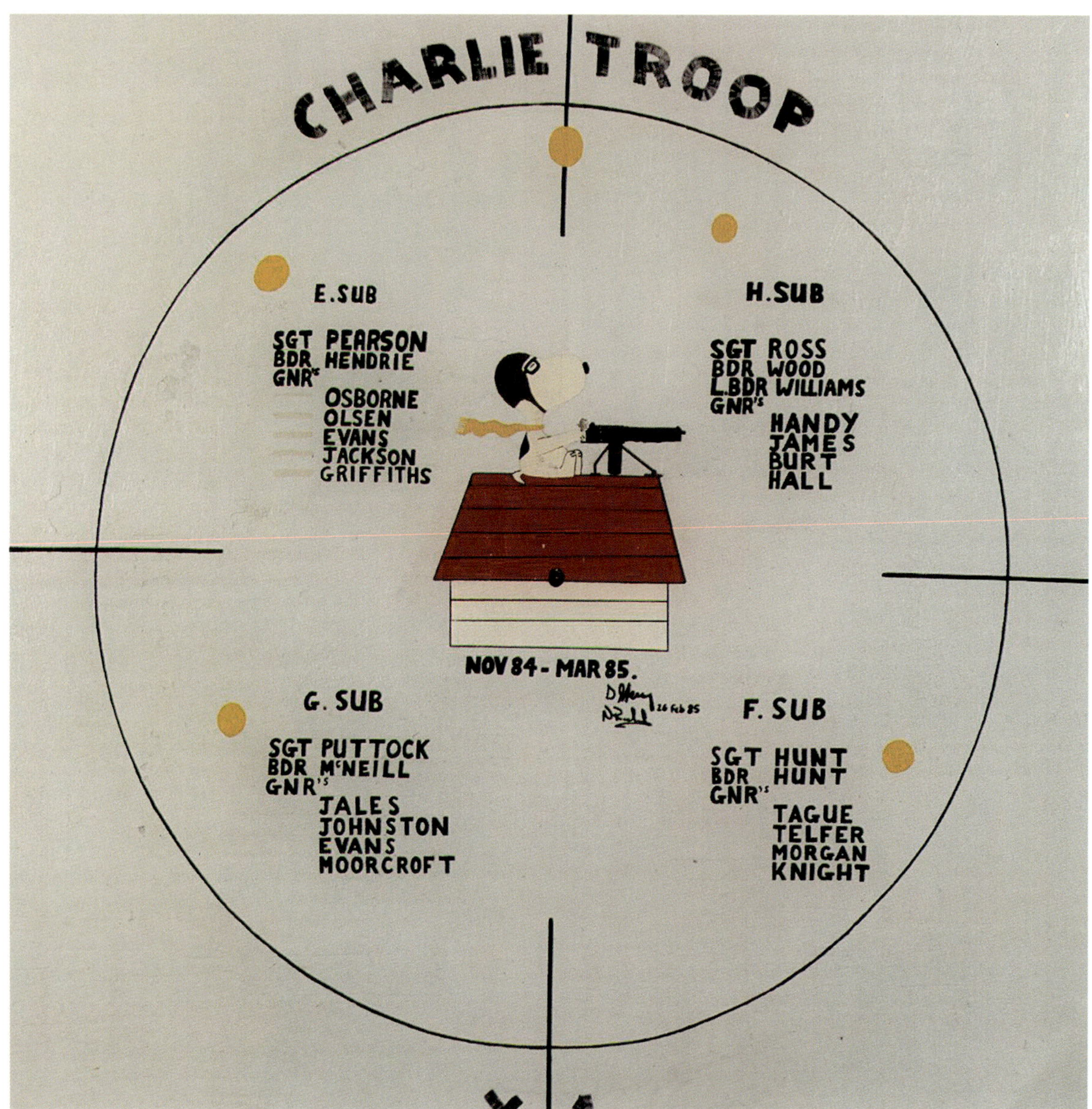

Ajax Bay, Falkland Islands
Charlie Troop (© Keith Angus)

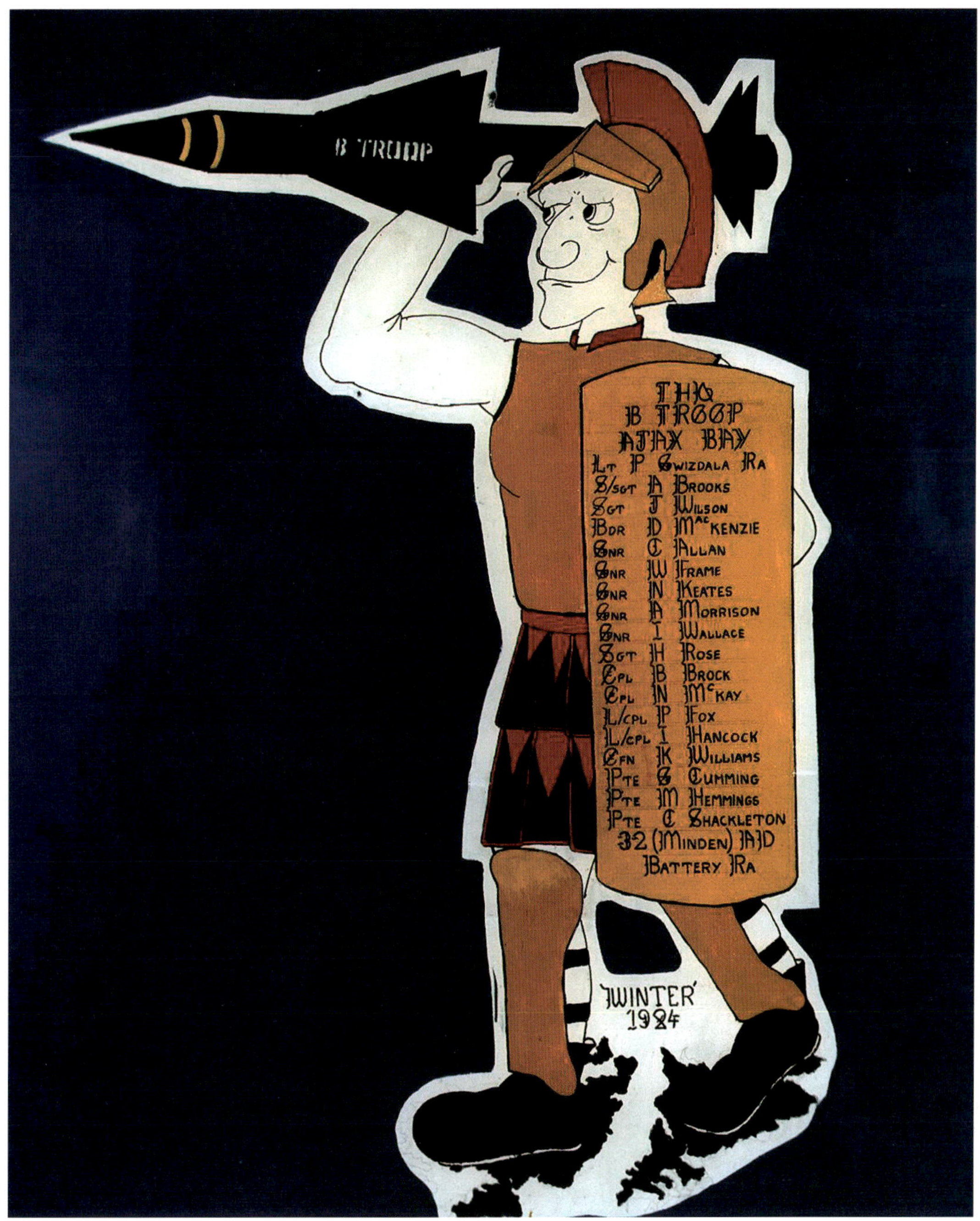

Ajax Bay, Falkland Islands
Roman soldier (© Keith Angus)

In 1982, 3 Commando Brigade Royal Marines landed at Ajax Bay and established a logistics depot in an abandoned meat refrigeration plant. This later became a Field Hospital, and the one at which Surgeon Rick Jolly famously declared that his mission was to save lives, British or Argentinean. The windowless dark shed was derelict at the time and its thick insulated walls were found to be covered in soldiers' graffiti, inside and out. Those on the inside walls were often carefully executed drawings and poems that demonstrated a range of emotions from aggression and fear to loneliness. These graffiti are now permanently displayed in Death Star Corridor where today's soldiers can see them. Elaine Shemilt's own ghostly presence within the ruins forms the essence of her own work 'Fragments', which formed her contribution to the commissioned exhibition by artists at the Imperial War Museum, and which features in the accompanying book (Ashcroft et al 2002).

REFERENCES

Ashcroft, R, *et al* 2002 *Traces of conflict: The Falklands Revisited 1982–2002*. Imperial War Museum with University of Dundee
Baker, F, 1993 The Berlin Wall: production, preservation and consumption of a 20th-century monument, *Antiquity* **67**, 709–33
Bojorquez, C, 2004 Los Angeles 'CHOLO' style graffiti art. *www.hip-hop-network.com*
Brothé, E, 1995 La Base Sous-Marine de la Pallice, *39–45 Magazine* 109–110, 43–49
Cantwell, J D, 1989 *Images of War British Posters 1939–45*. London: Public Record Office
Cambridge Evening News 1993 Adding gloss to the past, *Cambridge Evening News* 8 April, 1
Coad, J G, 1989 *The Royal Dockyards 1690–1850: Architecture and Engineering Works of the Sailing Navy*. Aldershot: Scolar Press
Cocroft, W D, 2000 *Dangerous energy – the archaeology of gunpowder and military explosives manufacture*. Swindon: English Heritage
Cocroft, W D, and Thomas, R J C, 2003 *Cold War: Building for nuclear confrontation, 1946–89*. Swindon: English Heritage
Cunliffe, B, and Garratt, B, 1994 *Excavations at Portchester Castle Volume V: Post Medieval 1609–1819*. London: The Society of Antiquaries
Dearing, M, 2002 Welcome to paradise: the erotic drawings of Bempton, *Illegal Media* **6**, 3–7.
Douet, J, 1998 *British Barracks 1600–1914: Their Architecture and Role in Society*. London: HMSO
English Heritage, 2004 *Military Wall Art: Guidelines on its Significance, Conservation and Management*. London: English Heritage.
Ethell, J L, and Simonsen C, 1991 *The history of aircraft nose art: WWI to today*. Sparkford: Haynes
Feversham, P, and Schmidt, L, 1999 *The Berlin Wall Today*. Berlin: Verlag Bauwesen
Ganz, N, 2004 *Street Art from Five Continents Graffiti World*. London: Thames & Hudson
Glines, C V, 1993 The jacket that lives forever, *Air Force Magazine*, **76** no 9, 60–5
Hartcup, G, 1979 *Camouflage – A history of Concealment and Deception in War*. Newton Abbot/London: David & Charles.
Jarman, N, 1998 Painting landscapes: the place of murals in the symbolic construction of urban space, in A Buckley (ed) *Symbols in Northern Ireland*. Belfast: The Institute of Irish Studies. Taken from CAIN website: *http://cain.ulst.ac.uk/bibdbs/murals/jarman.htm*
Kenyon, J, 1990 *Medieval Fortifications*. London: Leicester University Press
Kimball, J A, 2004 *Trench Art: an illustrated history*. USA: Silverpenny Press
Kippin, J 2001 *Cold War Pastoral: Greenham Common*. London: Black Dog Publishing Ltd
Lewis-Williams, D J, 1995. Some aspects of rock art research in the politics of present-day South Africa, in K Helskog and B Olsen (eds) *Perceiving Rock Art: Social and Political Perspectives*. Oslo: Instituttet for Sammenlingnende Kulturforskning, 317–37
McCamley, N, 1998 *Secret Underground Cities: an account of some of Britain's subterranean defence, factory and storage sites in the Second World War*. Barnsley: Leo Cooper
Newark, T, Newark Q, and Bosarello, J F, 1996 *Brassey's book of camouflage*. Brassey's: London
Rolston, B, 1992 *Drawing Support: Murals in the North of Ireland*. Belfast: Beyond the Pale Publications. Taken from the CAIN Website: *http://cain.ulst.ac.uk/bibdbs/murals/rolston1.htm*
Rolston, B, 1995 *Drawing Support 2: Murals of War and Peace*. Belfast: Beyond the Pale Publications. Taken from the CAIN Website: *http://cain.ulst.ac.uk/bibdbs/murals/rolston2.htm*
Saunders N J, 2002a The ironic 'culture of shells' in the Great War and beyond, in J Schofield, W G Johnson, and C Beck (eds) *Materiel Culture. The archaeology of twentieth century conflict*. London: Routledge, 22–40
Saunders, N J, 2002b *Trench Art*. Princes Risborough: Shire Publications Ltd
Schjeldahl, P, 1999 *Jane and Louise Wilson*. London: Serpentine Gallery
Wahl, J B, nd *I'll était unefois: la Ligne Maginot, Nord-Lorraine-Alsace*. France: Jerome
Ward, T H G, 1951 The psychological relationship between man and aircraft, *British Journal of Medical Psychology* **31**, 283–90
Watson, F, 2004 *The Hush House: Cold War sites in England*. Hush House Publications.
Wilson, L K, 2003 *Spadeadam*. (Film, privately distributed)

FURTHER READING

Anon 1992 Picture This…, *Country Life*, December 10th
Anon 2003 Iraq War Nose Art, *Aviation News*, June 2003, 442
Baber G, Scarffe M, and Hall R, 1991 Grandma's War, *RAF Yearbook Special – Air War in the Gulf*, 19–21
Baker, F, 2002 The Red Army graffiti in the Reichstag, Berlin, in G Nash, & C Chippindale (eds), *European Landscapes of Rock-Art*. London: Routledge 20–38
Black, I, 1992 *Desert Air Force*. London: Osprey Aerospace
Bowman, M W, 2003 *Wild Blue Yonder*. London: Cassell
Dowson, T A, 1994 Reading Art, Writing History: Rock Art and Social Change in Southern Africa, *World Archaeology* **25**, 332–42
Dube, S, 1994 Prince backs bid to save PoW's chapel, *The Western Mail*, 8th February, 1994
Gotts, S, 1980 Artwork of the Eight, *After the Battle* **30**, 47–53

Higgs, D, 1993 Haunting Images, *Aeroplane Monthly*, May 1993

Hildebrandt, R, 1988 *The Wall Speaks*. Berlin: Verlag Haus am Checkpoint Charlie.

B Lowry, B, ed,1995 *20th Century Defences in Britain*. York: Council for British Archaeology

Milsom, J, and Zaloga, S, 1977 *Russian Tanks of World War 2*. Cambridge: Patrick Stephens Ltd

March, P R, 1992 *Desert Warpaint*. London: Osprey Aerospace

Mouland, B, 2000 The War Paint Warriors, *Daily Mail*. 7th September, 24–25

Ramsey, W G, 1994, Eighth Wall Art Conservation Society, *After the Battle* **86**, 24–31

Simonsen, C, 2001 *RAF & RCAF Aircraft Nose Art in World War II*. Ottringham: Hikoki Publications Ltd.

Slater, R, 2002 The Writing is on the Wall, *Sanctuary* **31**, 58–59

Valiant, G M, 1987, 2001 *Vintage Aircraft Nose Art*. St Paul, MN: MBI Publishing Company

Index

Page numbers in italics refer to illustrations and/or their captions.